The Cameroon–Nigeria Border Dispute:
Management and Resolution, 1981-2011

Hilary V. Lukong

Langaa Research & Publishing CIG
Mankon, Bamenda

Publisher
Langaa RPCIG
Langaa Research & Publishing Common Initiative Group
P.O. Box 902 Mankon
Bamenda
North West Region
Cameroon
Langaagrp@gmail.com
www.langaa-rpcig.net

Distributed in and outside N. America by African Books Collective
orders@africanbookscollective.com
www.africanbookcollective.com

ISBN: 9956-717-59-2

Cover Photo:
Presidents Biya, Obasanjo
and UN Secretary General, Annan
in Geneva, January 2004.
Courtesy of *Cameroon Tribune.*

To Jacky

Table of Contents

Illustrations

Map

Plate

Tables

Table

Foreword

Cameroon and Nigeria entered the 21st century with optimism as the two countries waited impatiently for the International Court of Justice (ICJ) to schedule the public hearing of their border dispute Cameroon deposited at The Hague in March 1994.It was only until February/March 2002 that the ICJ heard the case and passed its verdict in October of the same year, followed by its implementation. Prior to the ICJ adjudication, Cameroon and Nigeria had extraordinarily managed the numerous border skirmishes that cropped up between them preventing them from degenerating into full scale wars.

The book, *The Cameroon–Nigeria Border Dispute: Management and Resolution, 1981–2011* provides an incisive analysis of the causes, dynamics and denouement of the dispute, 30 years after its escalation in 1981. It was equally 30 years ago that I revised the penultimate draft of my *Philosophiae Doctor* (PhD) on "Trans-Frontier Relations and Resistance to Cameroun-Nigeria Colonial Boundaries, 1916-1945." My study unveiled how intra-ethnic relations, intra-regional economic relations, the missionary penetration and political gimmicks favoured trans-frontier movements which made the enforcement of frontier regulations difficult.

Hilary V. Lukong has carefully threaded how these socio-economic factors and other historico-diplomatic and geostrategic considerations contributed to the persistent border skirmishes between Cameroon and Nigeria. The primary merit of this book lies in the presentation of the different levels of the conflict from the causes through their management, to settlement and resolution. This in-depth study makes for a compelling and compulsive reading. His authoritative analysis on the Cameroon-Nigeria border dispute is proof to the fact that he has a wealth of information on the subject. The book is welcomed as it could serve as a guide for conflict transformation in a globalised world.

As the new wave of cooperation and partnership defines the globe, effective conflict resolution between Cameroon and Nigeria must not only be limited to resolving the issues that sparked off the conflict, but must contain the means for handling future incidents and a gem of confidence building. Therefore, the appropriate mantra to sustainable peace between the two countries should be couched on the following. First, the effective implementation of the June 2006 Greentree Accord which instituted a five-year special regime (2008-2013) to Nigerian nationals in Cameroon's Bakassi Peninsula and at the same time committing Cameroon to develop the area; second, the physical demarcation of the entire boundary; third, the enforcement of border regulations to respond to frontier exigencies; fourth, the implementation of bilateral agreements reached since independence and finally; charting out new areas of cooperation between the two brotherly countries.

V.G. Fanso
Yaounde,
July 2011

Acknowledgements

I am deeply grateful to a number of people who helped me in one way or the other towards the realization of this book. I owe an immense debt of gratitude to Dr Zacharie Saha who read the first outline of the book and suggested invaluable improvements. I also wish to thank my spouse, Jacky who willingly shouldered some of my responsibilities while I was out to gather material for the book; and her unfailing willingness to help with all phases of the work. This was a source of inspiration and comfort to me especially when my morale was at low ebb. I reserve special thanks to my brother, Pius Lukong and wife, Ernestine who lodged me during my field work in Yaounde and financed various phases of the study. I also extend gratitude to Prof. V.G. Fanso who read the final draft and willingly agreed to provide the foreword.

My immense appreciation also goes to my friends, Dr Bongyu Moye, Mr Jude Moye, Mr Yong Bongfen, Mr Patrice Yonkeu, Mr Etienne Dor, Mr Joe Ndikintum and Ms Jane Maih for their unwavering moral, material or financial support. I also extend gratitude to Mr Adi Fonte, Mrs Elizabeth Ngala, Mr Richard Kometa and Mr and Mrs Simaah. I am grateful to Mr Evan Vensu and Miss Lillian Vensu who typed parts of the manuscript, to Mr Gilbert Bamboye for drawing the maps, and to Edna, Reina, Chelsea, Percy, Goddy, Desmond and Marceline who cheered me up. To all I might have overlooked and whose names do not appear here, I say thank you. However, I am fully responsible for all the errors of interpretation and other shortcomings still to be found in this work.

H. V. Lukong

Abbreviations and Acronyms

AER	Rural Electrification Agency
AFD	French Development Agency
ARSEL	Electricity Sector Regulatory Agency
ASF	African Standing Force
AU	African Union
BIR	Rapid Intervention Brigade
BOSCAM	Société Bouggues Offshore Cameroun
CEMAC	Economic and Monetary Community of Central African States
CFSP	Common Foreign and Security Policy
CISSA	Committee of Intelligence and Security Services of Africa
CLB	Continental Logistic Base
CNU	Cameroon National Union
CRTV	Cameroon Radio Television
DO	Divisional Officer
ECCAS	Economic Community of Central African States
ECOWAS	Economic Community of West African States
EDC	Electricity Development Corporation
EDF	European Development Fund
EU	European Union
FCFA	Communauté Financière Africaine Franc
GGC	Gulf of Guinea Commission
ICJ	International Court of Justice
IGN-FI	Institut Géographique National France International
IGOs	International Governmental Organisations
IRAD	Institute of Agricultural Research for Development
IRIC	International Relations Institute of Cameroon
JICA	Japan International Cooperation Agency
JTT	Joint Technical Team
LCBC	Lake Chad Basin Commission
NBA	Niger Basin Authority
MINREX	Ministry of External Relations
MNCs	Multinational Corporations

MOU	Memorandum of Understanding
MW	Megawatts
NM	Nautical Miles
NGOs	Non Governmental Organisations
NIOMR	Nigerian Institute of Oceanography and Marine Research
NSAs	Non State Actors
OAU	Organisation of African Unity
PDP	Peoples' Democratic Party
PHCN	Power Holding Company of Nigeria
SDO	Senior Divisional Officer
SGBC	Société Générale de Banques au Cameroun
SNH	National Hydrocarbons Corporation
SONARA	National Refinery Corporation
UDEAC	Customs and Economic Union of Central African States
UK	United Kingdom
UNO	United Nations Organisation
USA	United States of America
UTM	Universal Traverse Mercator

Introduction

Cameroon and Nigeria share a boundary of some 1950 kilometres (km) from Lake Chad in the north to the Gulf of Guinea in the south; the longest compared to that shared by each of them with any of their neighbours. The two countries gained independence in 1960 and established relations at the ambassadorial level in November the same year.[1] From that time, the bulk of bilateral relations have been conducted according to the procedure of standard diplomacy notably through the negotiation and conclusion of agreements and treaties.

As founding fathers of the defunct Organisation of African Unity (OAU) in 1963, President Ahmadou Ahidjo of Cameroon and Prime Minister Sir Abubakar Tafewa Balewa of Nigeria attended the first conference of Heads of State and Government in Cairo in 1964 where the notion of the intangibility of colonial frontiers was adopted. Cameroon and Nigeria adhered to this *uti possedetis juris* principle by inheriting the colonial administrative borders whose delineation in some parts was either imperfect or not demarcated or both. The two countries therefore tried to correct these anomalies. As a consequence, on October 11, 1965, Cameroonian and Nigerian authorities met at Ikom, Nigeria, where they took acquaintance with the border problems.[2] Later in 1970, the two countries decided to create a Mixed Boundary Commission to tidy up these imperfections.

---

1. It was the French sector of Cameroon under French Trusteeship which got her independence on January 1, 1960 and took a new name of the Republic of Cameroon. It became a member of the United Nations (UN) on September 20, 1960 and on October 1, 1961, it merged with the British Southern Cameroons which voted in a UN organised plebiscite on February 11, 1961 to achieve her independence through reunification with the Republic of Cameroon. The Northern half of British Cameroons voted on February 11 and 12 to achieve her independence by joining the Federal Republic of Nigeria which got her independence from Britain on October 1, 1960 and acquired the UN membership on October 7, 1960. Northern Cameroons joined Nigeria on June 1, 1961.

2. Ndifontah Mo Nyamndi, "Cameroon-Nigeria Relations (1958/1978)," MA Dissertation, University of Yaounde, IRIC, 1979, p.175.

The Commission set to work and together with high-level initiatives at the Presidential level; various legal declarations on the precision of the frontier were reached by 1975. These include: the Yaounde I Declaration of August 14, 1970 which stipulated that the mapping of the frontier be in stages; the Yaounde II Declaration of April 4, 1971 wherein the Maritime Boundary was delimited on twelve numbered points; the Lagos Declaration of June 21, 1971 extending the demarcation of the Maritime Border; the Kano Declaration of September 1,1974 establishing a buffer corridor of 4km where oil prospection and exploitation was forbidden; and the Maroua Declaration of June 1, 1975, modified by the Exchange of Letters by the Heads of State of Cameroon and Nigeria in July 1975,delimiting the Maritime Boundary on eight numbered points. At the sidelines of these declarations was confidence building measures between the two countries in other spheres.[3]

From 1977, Nigeria developed a culture of persistently repudiating these border agreements. The result was of course confusion and suspicion between the two countries as far as the delimitation and demarcation of their border was concerned. More often than not, high-level talks on this issue provoked sentiments, emotions and tension. Meanwhile, along the border, repeated instances of misunderstanding and tension cropped up. In January 1981, Nigerian soldiers arrested and detained the Divisional Officer (DO) of Idabato, Esabe Simon Timeh, together with eight Cameroonians for one week. This situation created tension between Cameroonian and Nigerian coast guards culminating into the exchange of fire on May 16, 1981. Five Nigerians were killed and

---

3. The two countries signed several agreements and treaties in the 1960s, 1970s and early 80s pertaining to economic, scientific and technical cooperation, socio-cultural matters, and air services and on police and judicial matters. See Jean Emmanuel Pondi and Laurent Zang, "The Cameroon-Nigeria Border Cooperation: Presentation and Analysis of Bilateral Agreements and Treaties" *Cameroon Review of International Studies* (volume V, 1998 n°1-2, May 2000) Presses universitaires de Yaoundé, pp.169-186.

three others wounded. This first real[4] instance of tension on the Cameroon-Nigeria border brought the two countries to the brink of war.Aggrieved Nigerians in Lagos sacked the Cameroonian Embassy and some demanded a military invasion of Cameroon. Lagos[5] reacted to the incident in strong diplomatic language demanding "excuses without reservation" within a week, punishment on the Cameroonian soldiers who were involved and complete compensation to the affected Nigerian families. This was a sort of ultimatum that prepared a stage for a full scale war. But through diplomatic interventions, the incident was bilaterally solved by Yaounde and Lagos.

But later, many other border misunderstandings cropped up; foremost of them being the ones of 1993 and 94. On December 21, 1993 Nigeria unilaterally abrogated all accords and declarations between the two countries pertaining to the delimitation of their frontier by invading the Cameroon territories of Jabane and Diamond Island in the Bakassi Peninsula. This military occupation of Cameroonian territories provoked serious tension and movement of both Cameroonian and Nigerian troops to the peninsula. Again, on

---

4. Before the May 16, 1981 incident, there were some tribal conflicts of little national or international character such as the 1965 war between the people of Ikom in the Cross River State of Nigeria and those of Boundam, Mamfe, Cameroon. There were also clashes between local inhabitants of Baha in Cameroon and Nigeria border villages around the Lake Chad region over the use of the fertile land of the area for cultivation.

5. Lagos was the Nigerian capital up to 1983 when it was transferred to Abuja. The steps to transfer the capital from Lagos to Abuja started on August 9, 1975, during the reign of Murtala Muhammed (July 29, 1975- February 13, 1976) when a panel headed by Dr Justice T. Akinola Aguda was formed to study the site for the new Nigerian capital. The Aguda panel submitted its report on December 10, 1975 and recommended Abuja comprising land from Niger, Plateau and Kwara States. A Presidential Decree, no. 6 of February 4, 1976, then established Nigeria's Federal Capital Territory in the area. Traditional Abuja was renamed Suleja. The master plan was approved in late 1979.When President Shehu Shagari assumed office in October 1979,he announced a tentative scheduled for the movement of the first batch of the Federal Government to the new site in 1982/83 and the final movement in 1986/87. See *Africa Construction*, no. 2 , 1981, pp. 8- 9 and16; *Africa*, no.10 2, February 1980, p. 2.

February 18 and 19, 1994, the Nigerians launched a series of attacks on Cameroonian army units in a desperate attempt to move northwards and occupy Akwa Island and the entire peninsula. These attacks met with stiff resistance from Cameroonian troops leading to the lost of lives and material damages on both sides.

The December 1993 and the February 1994 incidents prompted Yaounde to shift from the bilateral management and resolution of the border conflict which had been pursued since the 1960s, to multilateral management and resolution. In so doing, three international bodies to which both Cameroon and Nigeria belonged were petitioned: the United Nations (UN) Security Council, the International Court of Justice (ICJ) and the OAU. While pursuing these multilateral initiatives, various efforts were still undertaken by Cameroon and Nigeria for an amicable settlement of the border dispute.

In Africa, border incidents like those that cropped up between Cameroon and Nigeria in the 1980s and 90s, have often degenerated into war. This was the case with the Morocco-Algeria war of 1963, when Morocco encircled Tindouf and Algeria, Figuig at the western and eastern ends of their border respectively; the 1977-79 Ogaden war between Somalia and Ethiopia and the Libyan-Chadian war over the Aozou strip in northern Chad in the 1980s. But the protracted incidents between Cameroon and Nigeria did not result to war. Instead, the border incidents were peacefully resolved making it a reference and model for the UN and other stakeholders involved in the management and resolution of interstate conflicts.Therefore, the objective of this study is to provide answers to the following questions. What mechanisms were put in place to prevent the protracted border incidents between Cameroon and Nigeria from escalating into war and how was the problem eventually resolved and by whom? How far has the border dispute been resolved and how have efforts to improve bilateral relations between the two countries been sustained and improved?

Through a meticulous exploitation of available data and the use of international relations concepts and theories on power, diplomacy, international law, geopolitics, and geostrategy and on conflict management and resolution, an attempt is made in this book to

4

answer these questions, and suggest new frontiers of imagination to Nigerian and Cameroonian authorities grappling with it.

Conflict management and resolution falls within the realm of the big challenges of African diplomacy in the 21st Century. The occurrence of both intrastate and interstate conflicts in the continent remains a stumbling block to achieving the world's anti-poverty Millennium Development Goals (MDGs) set by the UN in the year 2000 to be attained by 2015.[6] In July 2004, the African Union (AU) during its third Summit in Addis Ababa revealed that since 1960 conflicts have cost Africa 7 million lives and 250 billion dollars. Therefore, better management and resolution of Africa's conflicts can enable African governments to re-direct the resources put into the purchase of arms and caring for war victims into veritable development circuits. A study on conflict management and resolution like these therefore could be a contributor to the policy orientations of other African governments in the management and resolution of border disputes in particular and conflicts in general. This is so because conflict resolution can be played back comparatively. That is, to follow the process taken by another country to handle a similar situation.

In order to forestall confusion and misunderstanding, a number of terms are here defined as they are used in the framework of the study. These basic terms equally form the corpus of the analysis. We will first look at dispute, a term on which the study hinges. Dispute is first and foremost a disagreement which could be between people, groups or countries. Barrister Ndifiembeu defines dispute as, "a disagreement over a point of law or fact, a conflict of legal views of interest between two or more states."[7] Dispute is cognate with conflict and remains shrouded in usage with concepts like crisis and

---

6. These goals are : 1)eradicate extreme poverty and hunger, 2) achieve universal primary education, 3) promote gender equality and empower women 4) reduce child mortality, 5) improve maternal health, 6) combat HIV/AIDS,malaria and other diseases 7) ensure environmental sustainability, and 8) develop a global partnership for development.

7. Buba Ndifiembeu, "Why Nigeria must obey and let ICJ judgement implemented." *Insight Newsmagazine*, February 2003, p.9.

war. Holsti defines conflict as, "the set of attitudes and predispositions such as distrust and suspicion that populations and policy makers hold towards any other party."[8] Zartman on his part sees conflict as, "an incompatibility...inherent in multi-issue and multiparty situations...or [the] expression of that incompatibility."[9] These two definitions have one common denominator; that conflict is a disagreement between parties. Therefore, in this study, dispute and conflict are used interchangeably although the term dispute is systematically applied when referring to legal questions.Holsti also distinguishes crisis from conflict by regarding crisis as a stage in conflict.[10] Zartman agrees with Holsti, when he term crisis as the active outbreak of armed hostilities.[11] In this study, crisis is used with reference to the occupation of the Bakassi Peninsula by Nigeria from 1993 to 2008 when her forces completely disengaged from the peninsula. Meanwhile, dispute is used at any period of the study.

The notion of border, frontier or boundary has also been the object of international law and requires some clarifications. Border, boundary or frontier has a two-pronged meaning. It is an imaginary line separating two sovereign states. Geopolitically, it is defined as a line of demarcation between states.[12] This definition brings to focus

8. Kal J. Holsti, *International Politics: A Framework for Analysis* 4th ed. (Englewood Cliffs, New Jersey: Prentice Hall, 1983), p.450.

9. I. William Zartman "Conflict Resolution: Prevention, Management and Resolution," *in Conflict Resolution in Africa ed* Francis M. Deng and I. William Zartman (Washington D.C.: The Brookings Institution, 1991), p.300.

10. Holsti, *International Politics*, p.450.

11. I. William Zartman, *Ripe for Resolution: Conflict and Intervention in Africa* (New York: Oxford University Press 1985), p.8.

12. *Dictionnaire de Droit International Public*, Bruxelles : Bruylant, 2001, Cited in Mikoas Joseph Wylphrid, "Les Mécanismes de Gestion des Frontières Terrestres entre le Cameroun et les Etats Voisins", DESS Dissertation, University of Yaounde II, IRIC 2008, p. 538.

the notion of delimitation and demarcation. Delimitation refers to the process by which the course of a boundary is described in words or maps in a legal instrument. The ICJ's verdict on the Cameroon-Nigeria border case contains the delimitation of the frontier. Meanwhile, demarcation is the process by which the course of a boundary so described is marked out on the ground. The demarcation of the Cameroon-Nigeria boundary which kicked start in 2002 witnessed the first emplacement of boundary pillars in the localities of Banki (Nigeria) and Amchide (Cameroon) in the Lake Chad region on December 14, 2009.

The management of disputes implies reducing the pressures and preoccupations of hostilities that block creative measures on resolution. It gives the parties time to refocus on ways out of their dispute.[13] In this study, dispute management is discussed at the bilateral and multilateral levels. That is, the role played by the disputing parties, Cameroon and Nigeria and the international community.The resolution of disputes refers to concerted effort to eliminate the causes of the underlying dispute generally with the agreement of the parties.[14] Zartman posits that the resolution of disputes should be taken to mean the satisfaction of apparent demands rather than the total eradication of the underlying sentiments, memories and interests.[15] The dispute was settled through adjudication by the ICJ from March 1994 when Cameroon seised the Court till October 10, 2002, when the Court passed its verdict. The implementation of the Court's verdict from 2002 to 2011 under the aegis of the UN system constitutes part of the resolution process. The resolution equally involved mechanisms to eliminate the causes of the dispute as well as machinery for dealing with foreseeable problems and confidence building.

---

13. Zartman, "Conflict Resolution: Prevention, Management and Resolution," p.299.

14._____ , Ripe *for Resolution*, p.8.

15._____ ,"Conflict Resolution,"p.299.

The book is split into six chapters. Chapter one deals with the stakes and causes of the dispute. Chapter two focuses on the role played by Cameroon and Nigeria in the management of the dispute .Chapter three treats the role of third parties in the management of the dispute either through mediation, conciliation or through the collective effort by regional and international organisations to push the conflicting parties to refocus on the way out of the dispute. Chapter four examines the settlement of the dispute through adjudication by the ICJ. Chapter five chronicles the establishment of sovereignty on disputed border territories by Cameroon and Nigeria in conformity with the ICJ verdict, and the process of the demarcation of the Land and Maritime Boundary in synergy with the UN. Finally, chapter six brings out the confidence building measures between Nigeria and Cameroon from 2002-2011 as part of the resolution process.

Chapter 1

Stakes and Causes of the Border Dispute

At independence, Cameroon and Nigeria kicked start the delimitation of their common boundary built on a foundation laid down by European colonizers—Britain, Germany, and France—from 1885 to 1931. As a consequence, in 1964, the two countries adhered to the OAU doctrine of *uti possedetis juris* by inheriting the colonial administrative borders whose delineation in some parts was either imperfect or not demarcated or both. The two countries therefore tried to correct these anomalies.But, such efforts were later thwarted by incessant geostrategic and dilatory tactics in the seventies and eighties that persisted and resurfaced in the nineties with a more determined posture. The result was of course dispute over many border areas from the Lake Chad region in the North, through the Land Boundary area to the Maritime Zone in the South.

In the Lake Chad region, there was dispute in over 33 villages notably Naga'a, Tchika, Toro Liman, Darack, Dambore and their environs. Along the Land Boundary from Lake Chad to astride the Bakassi Peninsula, there was dispute in 17 sectors. From north to south, this concerned the localities of Limani, River Keraua, River Kohom, from Ngosi to Humsiki, from Mount Kuli to Bourha, Kotcha (Kontcha), the source of River Tsikakiri, from pillar 6 to Wammi Budungo, Maio Senche, Jimbare and Sapeo, Nomberou-Banglang, Tipsan, the Mayo Yim passes, the region of Mount Hambere, from Mount Hambere to River Mburi, Bissaula-Tosso and River Sama. In the Maritime Zone, there was dispute over the Bakassi Peninsula and on the Maritime Frontier (see map 1).

These disputes had socio-economic, geostrategic and historico-diplomatic underpinnings. The socio-economic considerations concerned the quest for subsistence by frontier populations which orchestrated constant population movements across the frontier thereby making the enforcement of frontier regulations difficult. It also concerned the geoeconomic positioning by Cameroon and Nigeria; all of which had resultant border repercussions. The security and strategic considerations, notably the quest for national cohesion and the security needs of the two countries were equally instrumental in sparking off the border dispute. Finally, international politics during the era of the colonization and decolonization of Africa and the non application of bilateral border agreements contracted by the disputing parties after independence equally contributed to the persistent border misunderstandings between the two countries.

Historico-Diplomatic Causes

The roots of the Cameroon- Nigeria border dispute can be traced as far back to the Berlin West African Conference of 1884-85 when European colonizers partitioned the African continent without taking into consideration the ethnological and socio- historical realities of the continent. This was further complicated in the years ahead by constant boundary changes which were sometimes not effectively implemented on the ground. In the same vein, bilateral border agreements reached by Cameroon and Nigeria after independence were equally not implemented on the ground.

Constant boundary changes between colonial masters

The boundary between Cameroon and Nigeria was the object of negotiation between the colonial master of Nigeria, Britain, and that of Cameroon, Germany, from 1885-1913. These negotiations ended in treaties whose subsequent modifications especially when they had not been given effect on the ground breed confusion and dispute.

In the South, Britain and Germany in 1885 began negotiations on the Cameroon-Nigeria boundary in London. These negotiations were carried out by Martin Gosselin and Sir George Taubman for Britain, and Herr Ernest Vohsen and Dr Paul Kayser for Germany. The negotiations were sanctioned by the Exchange of Letters dated April 29, 1885 and May 7, 1885.[1]

---

1. C. Weladji, "The Cameroon-Nigeria Border (contd)," *ABBIA* 29-30 (1975), p. 163.

Map 1. Disputed Zones on the Cameroon-Nigeria Border

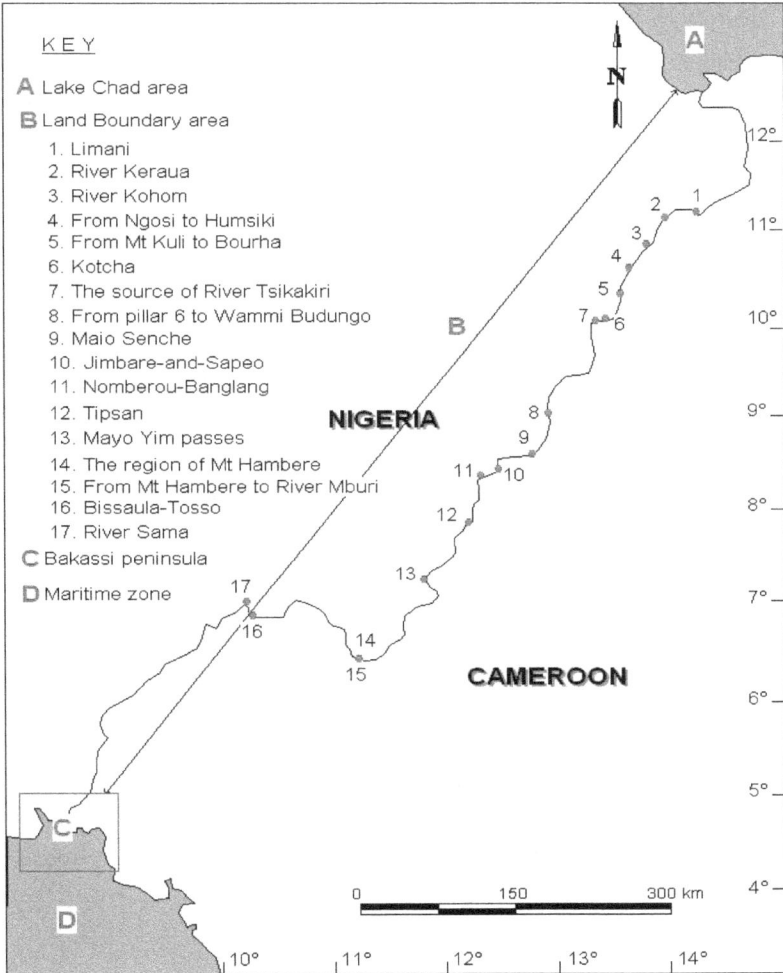

KEY

A Lake Chad area

B Land Boundary area
1. Limani
2. River Keraua
3. River Kohom
4. From Ngosi to Humsiki
5. From Mt Kuli to Bourha
6. Kotcha
7. The source of River Tsikakiri
8. From pillar 6 to Wammi Budungo
9. Maio Senche
10. Jimbare-and-Sapeo
11. Nomberou-Banglang
12. Tipsan
13. Mayo Yim passes
14. The region of Mt Hambere
15. From Mt Hambere to River Mburi
16. Bissaula-Tosso
17. River Sama

C Bakassi peninsula

D Maritime zone

NIGERIA

CAMEROON

0   150   300 km

Source: Adapted from the ICJ Verdict of October 10, 2002 on the Cameroon-Nigeria Border Dispute Case, _http://www.icj-cij.org_.,retrieved on 24/07/2010 and from _United Nations, Résumé, avis consultatifs et Ordonnances de la Cour Internationale de Justice, 1997-2002_ (New York: 2006), p. 273.

11

The outcome of these negotiations was notably the establishment of the Cameroon-Nigeria boundary at the Rio del Rey thereby placing the Bakassi Peninsula in Nigeria. Lt Von Besser, a German representative, toured the area in May-June, 1885, and a Mixed Boundary Commission led by Captain C. F. Close and Lt Besser surveyed the area and Exchanged Notes in confirmation. Later in January 1889, the German warship, *Habicht,* surveyed and mapped the area between the Cross River and the Cameroon Mountain and discovered that the Rio del Rey was not a river but a creek. They also discovered that the Akwayafe River (Akpakorum) was the only big river in the area.[2]

Although the Anglo-German Agreement of April 14, 1893 confirmed the boundary at the Rio del Rey, R. Moor, the High Commissioner for Southern Nigeria and Von Puttkamer, Governor of German Kamerun met in Buea on April 16, 1901 and reached a new agreement fixing the boundary at the Akwayafe River thereby placing the Bakassi Peninsula in Cameroon. This agreement was however not ratified. But from 1905-1906, a Mixed Anglo-German Boundary Commission respectively led by A.J. Woodroffe and Hauptmann Herrman confirmed the boundary at the Akwayafe River.[3] Subsequent boundary agreements notably the Anglo-German Accord of March 11, 1913 signed in London delimiting the boundary from Yola to the sea and regulating navigation on the Cross River confirmed the boundary at the Akwayafe River thereby maintaining Bakassi in Cameroon. Article 20 of this agreement specifies that the Bakassi Peninsula would remain Cameroon even if the waters of the Akwayafe River came to change its course to move towards the Rio del Rey.

---

2. C. Weladji, "The Cameroon-Nigeria Border (contd)," *ABBIA* 29-30 (1975), p. 176.

3. Bruno Simma, Counsel/Advocate for Cameroon during the hearing of the border dispute case at The Hague, verbatim, February 20, 2002. http://www.icj-cij.com., retrieved on 24/07/10.

Unfortunately, this agreement was not implemented on the ground because of the outbreak of the First World War in Cameroon in August 1914. The outcome of the war was German defeat and the partition of German Kamerun in 1916 by the victor Powers, France and Britain with the former taking four-fifths of the territory and the latter, the remaining fifth. This partition was finalized on July 10, 1919 by Lord Milner, British Secretary of State for Colonies, and Henry Simon, French Minister for Colonies. The partition received international recognition and legitimacy in 1922 under the League of Nations Mandate System. Britain acquired her slender territory of Cameroon and divided it into two non-contiguous segments: Northern Cameroons administered as part of the Northern Region of Nigeria, and Southern Cameroons, administered as part of the Eastern Region of Nigeria (see map 2). As a consequence, very little was done to tidy the borderline. Zartman had posited that, "generally, boundaries within the territory of a single colonizer are more likely to provoke disputes than the boundaries between colonizers because demarcation was less usual in the former.[4]

The problem of the Bakassi residents was equally not addressed. Article 27 of the Anglo-German Treaty of March 11, 1913 states that within six months from the date of making the boundary, natives living near the boundary line may if they so desire cross over to live on the other side and may take with them, their portable property and harvested crops. The non implementation of this Article, and the cultural links of the Bakassi inhabitants and continuous interaction, made the people to live as if they were nationals of the same country. As a consequence, when Nigeria as from 1991 started claiming the area, positing that the 1913 Anglo-German Treaty was null and void, as it was never given effect, the Bakassi inhabitants who were predominantly Nigerians came to believe such manoevres. This issue was even complicated when Nigeria sought to demonstrate that the Anglo-German Accord of 1913 was not valid in international law. Her arguments were hinged on the fact that neither the British nor the Germans had conquered the Calabar people of Eastern Nigeria as to have the moral right to partition their territory. According to

---

4. Zartman, *Ripe for Resolution*, p. 14.

Nigeria, she acquired the title of Bakassi from the Kings and Chiefs of Old Calabar who possessed international personality with the capacity to conclude international treaties like the one they concluded with the British on September 10, 1884. Although this treaty was one among the more than 350 treaties signed by the British with the Kings and Chiefs of the area; and not of the status of international protectorship;[5] the confusion gained currency because Cameroon over the years neglected the Bakassi Peninsula. Therefore, although Nigeria had accepted the Anglo-German Treaty of March 1913 as a point of reference in all her bilateral border negotiations with Cameroon, these new manoevres created confusion, consternation and dispute which were expressed violently in 1993 and 1994.

Furthermore, these dilatory and diversionary tactics by Nigeria was in contravention to the fundamental principles of the respect of frontiers inherited from colonialism.[6] The result of this manipulation was the tendency by Nigeria to behave as if such agreements did not exist. As a conesquence, when Nigeria occupied Jabane and Diamond Islands in the Bakassi Peninsula in1993, the spokes person in the Nigerian Ministry of Foreign Affairs, Fred Chijuka, trenchantly declared that it was not a manifestation of Nigerian expansionism but normal movement of troops on Nigerian soil. He went further to explain that following Cameroon's incursions in these areas, Nigeria wanted to assure the population there that they have not been abandoned.[7] This Nigerian stance was maintained until 2002 when the ICJ passed its verdict on the border dispute case.

---

5. One of the characteristics of international protectorship is the frequent discussions between the protector power and the leaders of the local protectorate. Such relations did not exist between Britain and the Kings and Chiefs of Old Calabar.

6. In 1964, two states without however challenging the doctrine itself declared their own case to be an exception. They included the Sharifian Empire of Morocco and the nation-state of Somalia. See Zartman, Ripe for Resolution, p. 14.

7. *Le Messanger*, no. 343, 10 Janvier 1994.

Map 2. The Evolution of Cameroon-Nigeria Boundary, 1916-1961

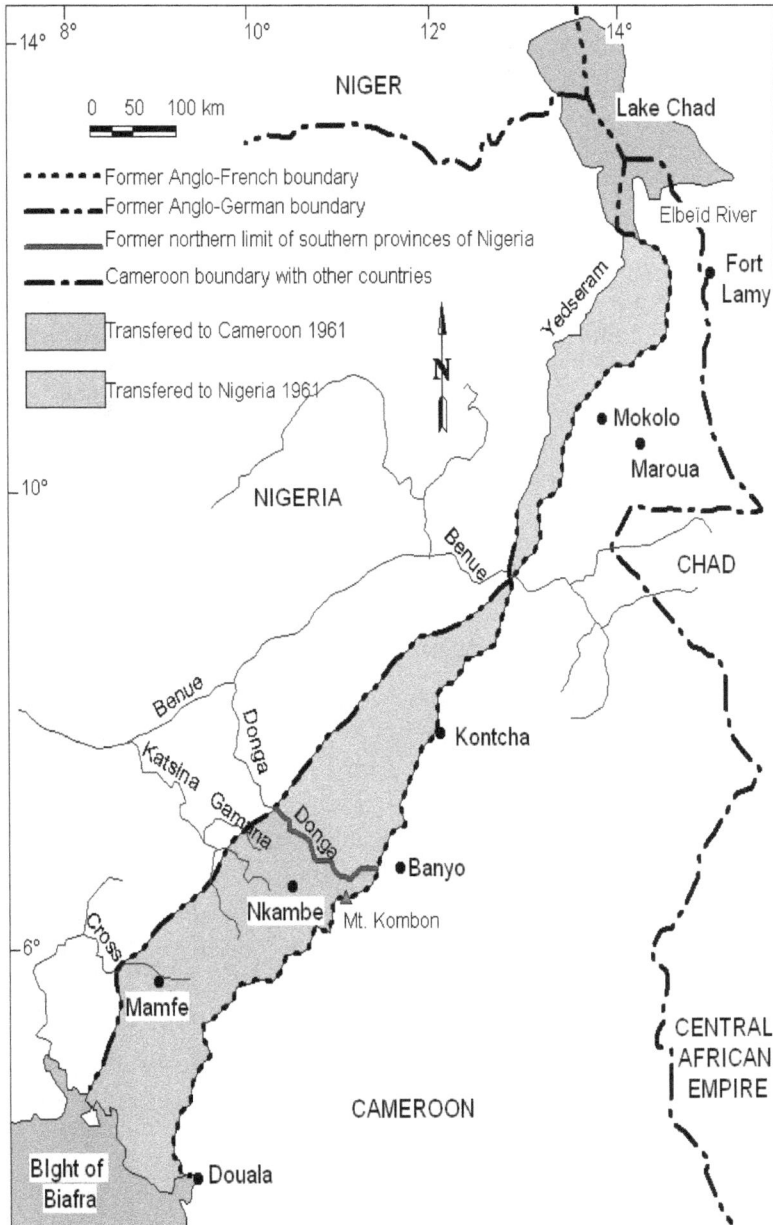

0   50   100 km

· · · · · Former Anglo-French boundary
– · · – Former Anglo-German boundary
―――― Former northern limit of southern provinces of Nigeria
– · – · Cameroon boundary with other countries

Transfered to Cameroon 1961

Transfered to Nigeria 1961

NIGER

Lake Chad

Elbeïd River

Fort Lamy

Yedseram

Mokolo

Maroua

N

NIGERIA

Benue

CHAD

Benue

Donga

Kontcha

Katsina

Gamana

Donga

Banyo

Nkambe   Mt. Kombon

Cross

Mamfe

CENTRAL AFRICAN EMPIRE

CAMEROON

Bight of Biafra

Douala

Source: Adapted from Ian Brownlie, African Boundaries, A legal and Diplomatic Encyclopaedia, University of Carlifornia Press, Los Angeles, 1979, p.554

In the North, the story was different. After the First World War, Britain, represented by Sir Graeme Thomson, Governor of the Colony and Protectorate of Nigeria, and France, represented by Paul Marchand, Commissioner of French Cameroon, established an agreement on December 29, 1929 and January 31, 1930 precising the boundary thereby confirming the Milner-Simon Boundary Declaration of July 10, 1919. The Thomson-Marchand Declaration was annexed in the Exchange of Notes between Arthur Henderson, British Foreign Minister and A. de Fleuriau, French Ambassador to London, on January 9, 1931.[8] The agreement left in the hands of Cameroon; Darack, Toro Liman, Naga'a, Tchika and their environs, later claimed by Nigeria in the post independence era. Later, on August 2, 1946, the British issued an Order in Council fixing the administrative boundary between Northern Cameroons and Southern Cameroons at the precincts of River Donga (see map 2). Therefore, when in February 1961, the British Northern Cameroonians voted in a UN organized plebiscite to gain their independence through integration with Nigeria, the Franco-British borderline as agreed in the Exchange of Notes as well as the administrative line established by the British Order in council automatically became the borderline between Cameroon and Nigeria.

The February 1961 plebiscite in British Northern Cameroons; marred by irregularities condoned and abetted by British officials as Chem-Langhëë has demonstrated,[9] created tension between the Republic of Cameroon—which lost the territory—and the Federal Republic of Nigeria—the beneficiary state. This equally had serious border repercussions on the two states (to be discussed presently). The plebiscite results for British Southern Cameroons whose returns favoured the Republic of Cameroon equally had serious border repercussions as the border regulations on the international boundary across the Bakassi Peninsula which throughout the Mandate and

---

8. Weladji, "The Cameroon-Nigeria Border: 1914 and After," *ABBIA* 38, 39, 40 (May 1982), pp. 246-248.

9. Bongfen Chem-Langhëë, "The British and the Northern Kamerun Problem 1919-1961," *ABBIA* 38, 39, 40 (May 1982). See especially pp. 315-327.

Trusteeship periods meant nothing to both Nigerians and Cameroonians had to be reinforced by the governments of Nigeria and Cameroon.

Such enforcements especially by Cameroon in the Bakassi Peninsula regarding immigration issues sparked off conflicts between Cameroon and Nigeria because it was interpreted by Lagos, much later, Abuja as an unacceptable violation of the human rights of their nationals.[10] Further, in consonance with the plebiscite results, British Northern Cameroons on June 1, 1961 got her independence by joining Nigeria, while British Southern Cameroons on October 1, 1961 got her own independence through reunification with the Republic of Cameroon to form a federation. To express its indignation on the manner the plebiscite was conducted in British Northern Cameoons, the Cameroon government declared June 1 as a Day of National Mourning in Cameroon and observed it as such until 1966.[11] Cameroon equally deposited a case file at The Hague challenging the plebiscite results in British Northern Cameroons. But, on December 2, 1963, the Court declared it incompetent to hear the case.

The scenario painted above is an indication that international politics, especially within the UN system had its own fair share in contributing to subsequent border skirmishes between Cameroon and Nigeria. One manifestation of such world politics had to do with the manner the boundary was mapped. The mapping was done based on natural elements and this later posed problems when these natural landmarks came to change. Seasonal changes in the Ebeji River and its bifurcation for example posed a problem as far as the mapping of the boundary in the Lake Chad region was concerned. The provisions of the Thomson-Marchand Declaration of 1929-30; incorporated into the Henderson-Fleuriau Exchange of Notes of 1931, traced the boundary from the Cameroon-Nigeria-Chad tripoint; and follows a

---

10. Francis Nguendi Ikome, "The Cameroon-Nigeria Maritime Border and Territorial Conflict: Would the Verdict of the ICJ Engender Lasting Peace," *Juridis Periodique: Revue de Droit et de Science Politique*, Numéro 54, Yaoundé, Cameroun (Avril-Mai-Juin 2003), p. 80.

11. Nyamndi, "Cameroon-Nigeria Relations (1958/1978," p. 121.

straight line to the mouth of River Ebeji as it was in 1931, and then run in a straight line to the point where the river today divides into two branches. But, the Ebeji bifurcation varies from season to season thereby posing the problem of which branch to be taken as the principal one. This technical problem was a contributing factor to the dispute between Cameroon and Nigeria in the Lake Chad region in 1983; that invited the Lake Chad Basin Commission (LCBC) into the scene. In 1984, the LCBC commissioned a French company, Institut Géographique National France International (IGN-FI) to demarcate the area. From 1988-90, the IGN-FI effectively demarcated the area but in 1996, Nigeria refused to ratify the outcome of the work which she participated. As a consequence, the border dispute in this region and on the Land Boundary area where earlier delimitation was faulty remained unresolved till 2002.

Non application of bilateral border agreements

After independence, Cameroon and Nigeria deployed much effort to perfect the delimitation of some border areas. But, such efforts were later thwarted by incessant geostrategic reckoning and dilatory tactics by Nigerian authorities. As a consequence, almost all the agreements reached were either contested by Nigeria or not implemented. This therefore generated dispute over some border territories along the common boundary.

From 1970-75, five important agreements were reached by the two countries on the precision of their common frontier. These included: the Yaounde I Declaration of August 14, 1970 which stipulates that the delimitation and demarcation of the common frontier be undertaken in three stages—Maritime Boundary, through Land Boundary and ending in the boundary in the Lake Chad region; the Yaounde II Declaration of April 4, 1971 in which the Heads of State of Cameroon and Nigeria, respectively Ahmadou Ahidjo and Yakubu Gowon, accepted a "compromise line" reported in the British Admiralty Map no. 3433 delimiting the Maritime Boundary along 12 numbered points (see map 3); the Lagos Declaration of June 21, 1971, extending the demarcation of the Maritime Border up to 17.7 nautical miles (NM) from the 3 NM agreed in Yaounde in April

1971; the Kano Declaration of September 1, 1974 in which the Heads of State of Cameroon and Nigeria established a buffer corridor of 4km, 2km on both sides of the border where oil prospection and exploitation was forbidden; and finally, the Maroua Declaration of June 1, 1975, modified by the Exchange of Letters by the Heads of State of Cameroon and Nigeria in July 1975 pertaining to the delimitation of the Maritime Boundary on 8 numbered points—A, A1, B, C, D, E, F, G[12] (see map 3).

Map 3. Disputed Bakassi Peninsula and Maritime Frontier

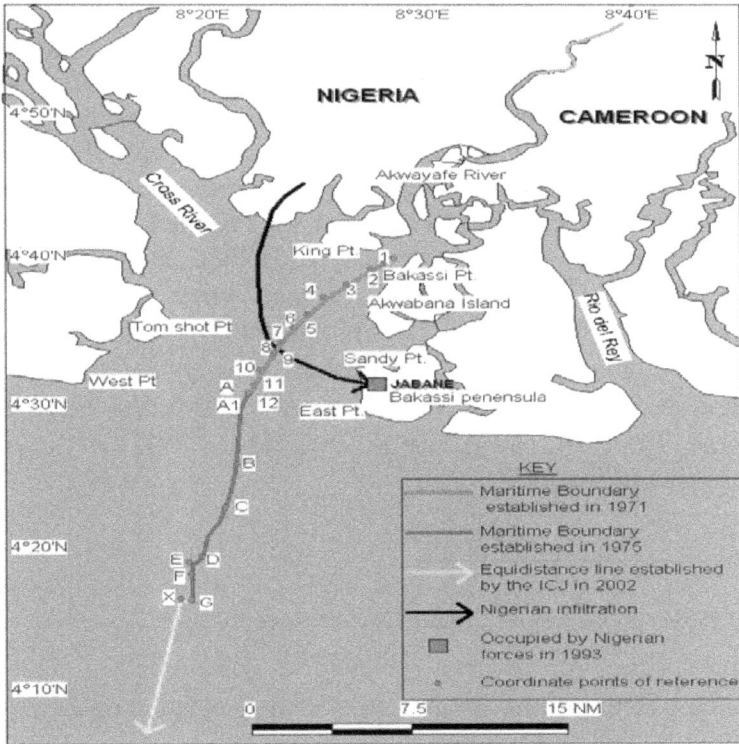

12. The Government of Cameroon, *Document on the Bakassi Peninsula Border Dispute*, Yaounde, n.d., passim; ICJ verdict on the Cameroon-Nigeria Border Dispute Case, October 10, 2002. http://www.icj-cij.com., retrieved on 24/07/10.

A little over a year after the two countries drew up the Yaounde II Declaration on April 4, 1971, Nigeria put to question this declaration during the meeting of the Mixed Boundary Commission in May and August 1972 in Garoua. During the meeting, the Nigerian delegation averred that their President had declared that the decision was unacceptable. Later on August 23, 1974, the Nigerian Head of State, Gowon, in a letter addressed to his Cameroonian counterpart, Ahidjo, confirmed this Nigerian position.[13] Then, from 1977 onwards, Nigeria developed a culture of persistently repudiating the border agreements reached with Cameroon each time she estimated that they no longer served her national interests. This is an indication that national interests are a key factor in international relations. According to Frankel; national interests' amounts to the sum total of the entire national values.[14] Cameroon and Nigeria therefore disagreed on the frontier issue when their interests were threatened.

From 1977 onwards, Nigeria systematically rejected the Maroua Declaration of 1975 on the pretext that it's President, Gowon, who contracted the declaration with President Ahidjo, did so without the approval of the Supreme Military Council which constituted the government of Nigeria and which equally failed to ratify this declaration.[15] This position was openly expressed by the Nigerian delegation to the Mixed Boundary Commission meeting in Yaounde in August 1991, and in Abuja in December 1991 and again in Yaounde in August 1993.[16]

---

13. ICJ verdict on the Border Dispute Case, October 10, 2002.

14. J. Frankel, *International Relations in a Changing World* (Oxford: Oxford University Press, 1979), p. 85.

15. On January 15, 1966, a mutiny by young army officers instituted military rule in Nigeria. The military remained in power alternating in a type of game of the dancing chairs from 1966-2007, save for a brief interregnum of civilian rule from 1979-83, and less than three months in 1993.

16. The Government of Cameroon, *Document on the Bakassi Dispute*, pp. 14-15.

By not respecting her legal engagements, Nigeria therefore created confusion and suspicion between the two countries as far as the delimitation and demarcation of their common frontier was concerned. Contrary to the border demarcation that was visible on former Nigerian and international land and maritime maps, Nigeria in 1991drew up a new administrative map on which it unilaterally changed the Maritime Border and placed it at the Rio del Rey. The result was therefore dispute with Cameroon over these border territories in the Bakassi Peninsula and maritime area; on both the delimited and undelimited sectors.

Security and Strategic Considerations

The geostrategic importance of some border areas and geopolitical positioning in the quest for national cohesion equally contributed to the border misunderstandings between Nigeria and Cameroon.

Security imperatives and geostrategic importance of some border areas

Most border misunderstandings between Nigeria and Cameroon sparked off as a result of disagreements between Cameroonian law enforcement officers and Nigerian residents on the issue of the implementation of immigration laws as well as over border territories considered strategic for the defence of the two countries. This particularly concerned Cameroonian territories in the Lake Chad region and in the Bakassi Peninsula. The manner of enforcement of immigration policies by Cameroonian gendarmes in her border territories occupied in the majority by Nigerians was interpreted by Nigeria as an unacceptable violation of the human rights of their nationals. This paradox stemmed from the fact that these Nigerian nationals had lived in these areas unperturbed by such obligatory obligations for generations. This was particularly so because these areas were administered for over 45 years (1916-61) by Britain as integral parts of her territory of Nigeria. This was further compounded by the fact that many of these border territories were neglected by the Cameroon government especially as far as the provision of basic social needs like potable water, electricity, health facilities, and quality education was concerned. As a consequence, the Nigerian government stepped into these areas on the pretext of protecting their nationals that were either being menaced by Cameroonian gendarmes or ostensibly to provide social amenities to her nationals which Cameroon failed to provide.

Although the action of the Nigerian government was in contravention to international law, this scenario generated conflict between Nigeria and Cameroon in these border territories. For example, in November 1987, the Nigerian army occupied the Cameroon Islands of Faransia, Darack I and II near Lake Chad with the official excuse that the troops were there to protect Nigerian citizens.[17] Again, on December 21, 1993, Nigerian authorities decided to send units of their army to Jabane and Diamond Island in the Bakassi Peninsula on the pretext of protecting their population which was being menaced by Cameroonian gendarmes. Nigeria equally claimed that their forces by-passed the frontier in order to maintain peace and order in the State of Akwa Ibom and Cross River and at the same time fighting against contraband. [18]

From the strategic standpoint, conflict cropped up in the Bakassi Peninsula because of its strategic importance in the security needs of Cameroon and Nigeria. Generally, the Bakassi Peninsula was strategic for the two countries because it is the gateway to the West-Central African coast in the Gulf of Guinea and constitutes a point of observation and surveillance of navigation in the Gulf of Guinea. Apart from this general importance, the peninsula equally served as an asset for Nigerian security in several ways. First, more than 90 percent of the population in Bakassi were Nigerians and Abuja wanted to acquire sovereignty over it as adverse policies from the Cameroon government in the area could lead to emigration of the Nigerian population there and swell the already high population in Nigeria estimated in the 1990s at 140 million; second, Nigeria could use the peninsula for the security of its oil fields in the Niger Delta

---

17. *Cameroon Tribune*, no. 5554/1843, Wednesday, March 16, 1994.

18. _____ ,no. 5541/1830, Wednesday, February 23, 1994.

which are found only 2km from the zone; and finally, sovereignty over it could ease access to the Nigerian port of Calabar and could serve as an excellent sea route for the distribution of onshore oil from the south to the northern states.

It was as a result of this geostrategic importance of Bakassi to Cameroon and Nigeria that dispute cropped over it between the two countries. Instances abound. In the heart of the Nigerian civil war (1967-70) the Nigerian President, Gowon solicited from Cameroon and obtained provisional utilization of Jabane in the peninsula where the Nigerian armed forces used it for surveillance and were able to hold back supplies to Biafran rebels through Calabar. Nigeria therefore realized the strategic importance of Bakassi and after the war, the Commander of Their Marine Commando, "Black Scorpion," then Colonel Benjamin Adenkule occupied the peninsula after the liberation of Calabar. He only withdrew in 1970 following protest from the Cameroon President, Ahidjo and instructions from President Gowon.[19] After then, there was Nigeria's unrepentant resolve to renegotiate its ownership. As a result, in 1991, she produced maps placing Bakassi in Nigeria thereby giving the impression to border authorities that Bakassi was part of Nigeria. This belief was later fueled in the later part of the nineties and beyond, by elected officials from the Cross River State, where Bakassi was said to be part of it. On December 21,1993, Nigerian troops actually penetrated into Diamond Island and Jabane and did not only begin putting up permanent structures there but even went ahead to rename the towns.. Thus, Diamond Island and Jabane were renamed respectively as Atabong and Abana.

This quest to acquire Bakassi even became more important as sovereignty over the continental shelf was a guarantee to the acquisition of the maritime zone which up to the nineties was partially delimited; a delimitation that was even still contested by Nigeria as discussed earlier. Cameroon which in 1981 expressed the geostrategic importance of the peninsula by naming its largest sea vessel as Bakassi could not quiver in the face of these Nigerian intrigues. Cameroon instead jostled to consolidate her position in the

---

19. *Cameroon Tribune*, no. 5541/1830, Wednesday, February 23, 1994.

peninsula as the basis of the maritime title given the fact that the land dominates the sea. This geostrategic positioning even became more glaring for Cameroon as the concavity of the Gulf of Guinea in the southern coast of Cameroon, in the sector facing the Island of Bioko in Equatorial Guinea handicaps Cameroon. All these geostrategic positioning; by Cameroon and Nigeria therefore breed dispute over Bakassi.

The prioritization of state security falls under the realists' school of thought who stresses the fact that the international system is anarchic; thereby making states to prioritize survival, using a self help dynamic. Therefore, personal morality cannot determine national interest because states do not face one another as individuals but as sovereign nation states. Realists believe that states are inherently aggressive (offensive realism) and/or obsessed with security (defensive realism).Since realism focuses on state security and power, these variables pushed Nigeria to invade Cameroonian territories. And since realists equally postulate that mankind is not inherently benevolent but rather self centred and competitive, Cameroon stood firm in the face of this Nigerian aggression. This resolute build-up by Cameroon and Nigeria in Bakassi over security concerns therefore led to a security dilemma which realists explain as a situation whereby increasing ones security can lead to greater instability as the opponent builds up its own security in response.

The quest for national cohesion

The quest for national cohesion was one of the cause of the Cameroon-Nigeria border dispute over the Bakassi Peninsula especially from 1993-94. Following the derailment of the democratic process in Nigeria in 1993 and the ensuing loss of confidence in the Abacha regime that usurped power; only a face-lifting act such as the successful annexation of foreign territory could improve on its reputation. Linkage politics which establishes a connection between the domestic setting of a nation and the resultant external behavior could be used to analyze how the quest for national cohesion prompted Nigeria to occupy Cameroon's Bakassi Peninsula in 1993/94. According to Rosenau, linkage is any recurrent sequence of behavior that originates in one system and is reacted in another.[20] This means that the actions of a state at the international level could be an extension of domestic politics.Nigerian invasion of Bakassi in 1993 and 1994, effectively had roots in her domestic politics.

On November 17, 1993, General Sani Abacha put aside the short-lived interim administration of President Ernest Shonekan henpecked by the military following the confusion that ensued in the country after the annulled Presidential election of June 12, 1993.[21] When Abacha came to power, he suspended the Constitution adopted on May 13, 1989. Terror reigned under the military junta as there was widespread human rights abuse. The presumed winner of the June 12, 1993 annulled Presidential election, Chief Moshood Abiola, was imprisoned for declaring himself President. Former President, retired General Olusegun Obasanjo and the second in command of Obasanjo's regime, retired General Shehu Musa Yar'Adua and later on, Abacha's own second in command, Major-General Oladipo Diya and others were imprisoned for their roles in alleged coup d'états against General Abacha.[22] As a result of these policies, there were monstrous anti-government demonstrations and

---

20. James Rosenau, ed., *Linkage Politics: Essays on the Convergence of National and International Systems* (London: Collier Macmillan, 1969), p.45. Enoh contends that according to some observers, Dr Chester Crocker, former US under Secretary for African Affairs is the brainchild of this policy. And that the policy came into the limelight of international relations in 1981. See Besong Samuel Enoh, "Conflict Resolution in the Post-Cold War Era: A Case Study of the Angolan Civil War" Doctorat de 3ème Cycle Thesis, University of Yaounde II, IRIC, 1994, p. 73.

21. Richard Sklar, "An Elusive Target: Nigeria Fends off Sanctions," *Polis* vol. 4, no. 2, (1997), p. 19. Cited in Aji James, "The Dynamics of Cameroon-Nigeria Relations, 1993-2002", DESS Dissertation, University of Yaounde II, IRIC, 2003, p.45.The political situation in Nigeria was set into confusion when President Babangida (August 27, 1985- August 26, 1993) in an attempt to reintroduce democracy and civilian rule in the country organized and cancelled the June 12, 1993 Presidential election which Chief Moshood Abiola, candidate of the National Republican Convention, was presumed to have won. He obtained 58% of the total votes as required for the first ballot victory and equally had at least 1/3 of the votes in 20 of the 30 states as required by law.

22. Ibid., p. 19.

growing international isolation. Given this potentially explosive situation in Nigeria, the government sought to divert the growing anger of the population by successfully annexing foreign territory as a face-lifting act. Annexing such territories was equally a ploy to muster public domestic support by appealing on patriotic sentiments for unity in the effort to defend their territorial integrity.

As a result of these considerations, Abacha marched his troops into Cameroon's Bakassi Peninsula on December 21, 1993, a little over one month after taking over power in Nigeria. Following the occupation of Bakassi, there were anti government demonstrations in Lagos on March 16, 1994 against this intrusion into Bakassi. But the Abacha regime continued to hang on the territory for survival especially as the socio-political situation in the country continued to deteriorate. For example, on November 10, 1995, human rights activist, Ken Saror Wiwa and eight other leaders of the Movement for the Survival of Ogoni People were hanged despite international appeals, especially from the Commonwealth whose summit was in session in Auckland, New Zealand.

For Cameroon whose sovereignty over the peninsula was clear in colonial treaties and maps, unanimity during the conflict was simply the commitment of a people willing to preserve its territorial integrity. This was evidenced by the stationing of soldiers in the peninsula to beat up Nigerian further incursions. Equally, during the march pass on Cameroon's National Day on May 20, 1994, tanks and amoured vehicles of the Cameroonian army bore in legible characters, names of localities of the disputed peninsula with inscriptions that Bakassi is Cameroon and non-negotiable.These inscriptions were equally carried in the government newspaper, *Cameroon Tribune,* on pages the paper reserved for write-ups on the Bakassi saga. This determination by Cameroon irked the predominantly Nigerian population in Bakassi who had been indoctrinated—at least from 1991—that Bakassi was Nigerian territory. Elected officials from the Cross River State, under which Bakassi was said to fall like Senators Bassey Ewa Henshaw and Florence Ita-Giwa (Mami Bakassi), Governor Donald Duke and the self proclaimed paramount ruler of Bakassi, Okon Edet, carried a fierce campaign ensuring the Bakassi inhabitants of Nigerian sovereignty of the area. These antagonistic positioning by Cameroon and Nigeria over Bakassi, therefore intensified conflict between the two countries.

Socio-Economic Considerations

Constant population movements across the frontier made the enforcement of frontier regulations difficult especially given the fact that these people moved across the border to meet their kith and kin separated by the arbitrary partition of the 19th century. This was further compounded by the quest for subsistence by the frontier populations as well as the geoeconomic positioning by Nigeria and Cameroon in the quest for economic take off.

Population movements across the frontier

The Cameroon-Nigeria borderline drawn up in the 19th century and its subsequent modifications divided people with the same language, culture, history and ancestry. For example, the Keyaka, Banyang and Ekoi in the South and political setups like the Yola Emirate in the North. Drawn without the slightest consideration for the real bonds uniting the populations, these artificial lines did not prevent the continuous interaction of frontier populations thereby making the implementation of border regulations difficult. This was further compounded by the fact that the Fulani cattle rearers carried out transhumance without respecting borders. The result was of course conflict between border authorities on the one hand and between the migrant population and law enforcement officers of the receiving country on the other. From the Lake Chad region through the Land Boundary area down to the coast, trans-frontier movements especially because of socio-economic imperatives were very profound. From available data, the movement seemed to have been predominantly from Nigeria to Cameroon. A few illustrations and their resultant repercussions on the frontier misunderstandings will suffice.

In the North, from the Lake Chad region down to the Adamawa plateau, draught was central in causing the movement of people from

Nigeria to Cameroon. The Great Draught in West Africa in the 1970s led to crop failure in the Region while pastures dried up over large expanses of Senegal, Mauritania, Mali, Upper Volta [now Burkina Faso], Niger, Chad, the Northern States of Nigeria and parts of Ivory Coast, Ghana, Togo and Dahomey [now Benin].[23] As a consequence, the Fulani nomads of Nigeria who were reduced to destitution succumbed their emaciated cattle on a long trek to river valleys and to the Lake Chad region. This draught equally affected many households in Northern Nigeria in the 1970s. The result was that over 500 peasant families in the Nigerian locality of Bouladega, Maiduguri expressed the desire to migrate to the Lamidat of Maroua, Cameroon in the 1970s.[24]

Some of these emigrants settled in the Cameroonian Islands in the Lake Chad region like Faransia, Darack I and II, Blangoua, and Kate-Kime where the Nigerian government later sought to occupy. Nigeria later claimed these villages and even administered some with only mild protest from Cameroon. In 2002, Nigeria postulated that these villages date 20-40 years; the oldest of the villages being Katte-Kime created 40 years ago and the very recent, Murdas, aged 13 years; all administered by the Ngala Local Government Authority.[25] The situation of the founding of these villages some 40 years ago corresponds to the period of the migration and settlement of Nigerian nationals in these Cameroonian villages in the 1970s. These wrangling and geopolitical positioning by Cameroon and Nigeria generated dispute in the region. In November 1987 for example, there was a border skirmish between Cameroon and Nigeria over Faransia, Darack I and II and in May 1989, another skirmish cropped up over Blangoua.

---

23. Jonathan Derrick, "The Great Hunger," Africa, no. 23, July 1973, p. 23.

24. Correspondence no. 02667/DGSN/DST/RG from the Delegate General for National Security, P. Pondi to the Minister of Foreign Affairs [Jean Keutcha], November 30, 1971, MINREX Archives, file no. 5490/4B300,Contentieux avec le Nigeria, 1973.

25. Ian Brownlie, Counsel/Advocate for Nigeria, verbatim, March 6, 2002.

In the South, from southern Adamawa to the coast, the Nigerian civil war of 1967-70 and the search for pasture provoked these uncontrolled trans-frontier movements that later provoked frontier misunderstandings. During the Nigerian civil war, there was a spectacular influx of Nigerians into the Bakassi Peninsula and other areas in the present day South West Region[26] of Cameroon like Bamusso, Ubenekang, Kumba, Lobe, Mbonge, Tiko, Mutengene and Victoria [now Limbe].[27] Between 1968 and 1970, as many as 25.000 Ibos fled into West Cameroon.[28] In a correspondence dated December 21, 1967, from the Federal Inspector of Administration for West Cameroon, Jean-Claude Ngoh, to the Minister of Foreign Affairs, [Benoit Bindzi] in which he relayed information received from Marine Commandant No.255 on December 14, 1967; he complained about this influx of Nigerians into Cameroon. Hear him:

> Nigerian troops and those called Biafrans occupied islands belonging to Cameroon in the Bakassi Peninsula where we have launched the search for petrol and this has rendered the search difficult. It is important that we should maintain our presence there in order to prove to the inhabitants who are almost all Nigerians that the land belongs to us; and equally to support the work of the researchers so that they could realize a petrol project in Cameroon. Nigerian authorities should be informed about this state of things.[29]

---

26. The appellation Region was instituted by Presidential Decree no. 2008/376 of November 12, 2008 replacing the appellation Province, instituted in 1972. The Decree was in accordance with Article 61 of the 1996 Constitution.

27. MINREX Archives, file no. 5490/4B300, Contentieux avec le Nigeria, 1963-1970.

28. Victor T. LeVine, *The Cameroon Federal Republic* (London: Cornell University Press, 1971), p. 175.

29. MINREX Archives, file no. 5488/4B300, Contentieux avec le Nigeria, 1970-1972. The translation is mine.

In all of these areas, the Nigerian government complained of harassment of Nigerian citizens. In a highly warded letter from the Nigerian Ambassador to Cameroon, Alhaji Bello Malabu, to Cameroon's Minister of Foreign Affairs, Simon Nko'o Etoungou dated February 16, 1968, the Ambassador complained about the harassment of Nigerians in these areas.[30] In another correspondence dated June 1, 1971 from the Nigerian Ambassador, to Cameroon's Minister of Foreign Affairs [Jean Keutcha], the Ambassador complained of the arrest of about 2.000 Nigerians in Tiko, 500 in Mutengene and 500 in Victoria [now Limbe] on May 20, 1971.[31] Since the Nigerian population continued to increase in leaps and bounds, estimated at the beginning of the 1980s at 80 million,[32] the Nigerian influx to Cameroon continued in earnest. Meanwhile, Nigerian pastoralists especially from Obudu, grazed across the frontier to areas like Akwaya, Manyu Division in the then South West Province of Cameroon and Nwa in Donga Mantung Division in the then North West Province of Cameroon.[33] These movements did not only make the implementation of border regulations difficult; but such implementation was interpreted by Lagos, much later Abuja, as a violation of the rights of Nigerian nationals thereby sparking off dispute between the two countries.

Economic needs of Nigeria and Cameroon

At independence, Nigeria and Cameroon strove to develop their scarce resources for economic take off. Some of these resources were found along border territories which were ill-defined. With time,

---

30. MINREX Archives, file no. 5490/4B300, Contentieux avec le Nigeria, 1963-1970.

31. Ibid.

32. The November 25, 1973 population census in Nigeria gave the figure of 79.7 million but the results were cancelled by the Gowon government in May 1974. See *NewAfrican*, no. 146, October 1979, p.37.

33. *Cameroon Tribune*, no. 5554/1843, Wednesday, March 16, 1994.

these efforts witnessed substantial attenuations especially because of economic crises in the 1980s. This therefore orchestrated geoeconomic and geostrategic reckoning over rich frontier territories whose potentials could be exploited for economic development. The fight for the economic pie over these border territories therefore sparked off disputes.

The Cameroon-Nigeria protracted dispute over the Bakassi Peninsula had economic underpinnings. A detail examination of the geoeconomic importance of Bakassi for the economies of Cameroon and Nigeria can better explain why dispute cropped up over it. The 700 sq km peninsula was highly coveted because of its numerous potentials. The peninsula is rich in aquatic fauna and flora respectively fish and mangrove forest. The area was equally speculated to contain many types of plants with medicinal value that could be extracted for the manufacture of pharmaceutical products. It was equally speculated that its subsoil contained mineral resources like gas and petrol. Such speculations were later confirmed. A study conducted by the Nigerian Institute of Oceanography and Marine Research (NIOMR) revealed that, "the continental shelf in the South-Eastern sector is the broadest along the Nigerian coastline highly rich in both fisheries and mineral resources.[34] Meanwhile, the Cameroon government announced the discovery of gas and oil in Bakassi.[35]

Although it was revealed that in 1971, Cameroon's fishing industry employed some 900 people and yielded over 1.6 million dollars annually,[36] and claimed that "20.000 Nigerians migrate into Bakassi seasonally, catch fish and sell to their country amounting to

---

34. J.L. Okon Ekpenyon, "The Potentials of Nigerian Corridors as Sources of International Economic Conflict," in A.I. Asiwaju and P.O. Adeniyi ed. *Borderlands in Africa* (Lagos: University of Lagos Press, 1989), Cited in Francis Nguendi Ikome, "The Cameroon-Nigeria Maritime Border and Territorial Conflict," p. 82.

35. The Government of Cameroon, *Document on the Bakassi Dispute*, p.5.

36. *Africa Contemporary Record, 1973-74*, Cited in Nyamndi, "Cameroon-Nigeria Relations (1958/1978)" p. 156.

FCFA 20 billion yearly,"[37] the stakes over Bakassi because of its fishing potentials and mangrove forest remained minimal. This is so because though fishing was the predominant activity in the area for many years, the industry remained primitive. It was only with the discovery of oil in the peninsula that Nigeria and Cameroon started the geoeconomic positioning over it. According to Sinjoun; "interstate conflicts over territories are often because of the richness of the soil or the subsoil which are factors of power for the state."[38] The stakes over the peninsula were different for the two countries.

For Nigeria, the stakes over the peninsula remained very high especially as oil prospection and exploitation was concerned. From a modest 1.9 million barrels in 1958, crude oil production in Nigeria increased rapidly to over 750 million in 1973. In monetary terms, the value of petroleum exports increased from N1.8 million in 1958 to N1.842 million in 1973.[39] When oil prices quadrupled as a result of the first oil shock in 1973,[40] there was a short-lived 'oil boom' from

---

37. *Cameroon Tribune*, no. 9496/5697, Monday, December14, 2009.

38. Luc Sinjoun, *Sociologie des Relations Internationales Africaines* (Paris: Editions Karthala, 2002), p. 156.

39. G. O. Nwankwo and Efiong Essien, "Oil and Nigerian Economy," *Africa*, no. 39, November 1974, p. 83.

40. In 1973, three successive events contributed to an oil shock: first, the decision by Arab members of the Organisation of Petroleum Exporting Countries (OPEC) to stop the shipment of petroleum to nations that had supported Israel during the October 1973 Yom Kippur War in the Middle East; second, the decision by OPEC Ministers in a summit meeting in Teheran, Iran in December 1973 to increase the market price of OPEC crude oil from US$3.60 to US $11.65, per barrel, a threefold increase that was to take effect from January 1, 1974; and finally, a cut in the production of oil by OPEC members to the tune of 5 percent from September's output, and to continue to cut production over time in 5 percent increments until their economic and political objectives were met. These dramatic events therefore inaugurated a period of recession in 1974-75, the deepest and most widespread since the Great Depression of the 1930s. See *http://en.Wikipedia.org/wiki/1973* oil crises, retrieved on 10/04/10, and Richard N. Cooper, *Economic Stabilization and Debt in Developing Countries* (London: The Massachusetts Institute of Technology Press, 1992), p. 39.

1973-76.[41] But, the withdrawal of buyers of oil, who mainly had short contracts, led to a sharp fall in foreign exchange earnings and a natural economic recession ensued during the 1977/78 financial year.[42] This economic malaise continued in the 1979/80 financial year especially as there was a slight dimming of Nigeria's oil prospects arising from a glut in the world market for light crude as a result of new sources of supply from Mexico, the Northern Sea and Alaska. Oil revenue in Nigeria was therefore expected to fall from about 20 percent less than in the previous year.[43] In the early eighties, Nigeria was producing 2.5million barrels of oil per day at official rates and oil accounted for 90 percent of the country's total revenue. In the same period, the price of crude oil had multiplied to a record 36 dollars per barrel and was climbing higher. This was because of the second oil shock that started in 1979.[44]

The annual foreign exchange yield for Nigeria was well over two billion dollars.[45] Nigeria's oil wealth that accounted for about 90 percent of the country's foreign exchange earnings was exploited predominantly along the Nigerian coastline, an area that extends from 10 NM off the coast of Calabar; and closed to the Bakassi Peninsula. Some of her most important oil installations (oil rigs,

---

41. Godwin Matatu, "Soap-box promises won't do," Africa, no. 90, February 1979, p. 39.

42. Anonymous, "Nigeria's oil business," West Africa, no. 3563, December 9, 1985, p. 2599.

43. Godwin Matatu, "Soap-box promises won't do," Africa, no. 90, February 1979, p. 39.

44. The 1979 shock to the oil market was orchestrated by a strike action in Iran by oil-field workers in December 1978.This culminated into an Islamic Revolution in 1979 which saw the advent of an anti-American theocratic regime led by Ayatollah Ruhollah Khomeini who toppled Reza Shah Pahlavi.

45. Eddie Iroh, "The 'oil-gate' scandal," Africa, no. 107, July 1980, p. 39. These figures should be taken with a pinch of salt because a five-man team ordered by President Shehu Shagari in early 1980 to probe into the export sales and management of Nigeria's crude oil revealed that Nigeria's oil "experts" did not know the actual volume of daily crude oil in the country.

tanker terminals and refineries) are located within the vicinity of the Bakassi Peninsula.[46] Therefore, given the centrality of oil in Nigeria's economic life, it became necessary to secure her oil installations by occupying Bakassi which was under grave neglect by the Cameroon government. Probably, it was this quest to secure oil installations that Nigerian police and customs left Ikang and penetrated deep into Cameroon's territorial waters in Jabane in the Bakassi Peninsula in July 1972. This incident occurred at the time that Cameroon had intensified the search for submarine oil deposits at Rio del Rey and Yamkeke-Ine Okoy creek. As a consequence, these Nigerians were detained for one night and competent authorities contacted.[47] Again, in May 1981, the Nigerian military patrol penetrated the Bakassi Peninsula up to the Rio del Rey. This created tension between Cameroonian and Nigerian security forces who exchanged fire on May 16, 1981.

The advantage for Nigeria to have sovereignty over the oil rich Bakassi Peninsula became even more important following revelations about Nigeria's oil reserves and the growing interest of the western Multinational Corporations (MNCs) in oil exploitation in the Gulf of Guinea. During an oil seminar in Warri, Nigeria, organized by the Shell Petroleum Development Company (Nigeria), for senior journalists in 1985, the Western Divisional Manager of the company, Dr Emmanuel Daykoru told participants that Nigeria's crude oil reserves of about 16.7 billion barrels could last for the next 37 years at current rates of production.[48] Although the estimates were unofficial, it implied that by about 2022, Nigeria's oil wells could dry up. As a consequence, Nigeria jostled for sovereignty over Bakassi where oil had been discovered, especially as there was the growing

---

46. J. L. Okon Ekpenyon, "The Potentials of Nigerian Corridors," Cited in Ikome, "The Cameroon-Nigeria Maritime Border and Territorial Conflict," p. 82.

47. Confidential Correspondence from Sadou Daodou, Cameroon's Minister of State in charge of Armed Forces to the Minister of Foreign Affairs [Jean Keutcha], MINREX Archives, file no. 5488/4B300, Contentieux avec le Nigeria, 1970-1972.

48. Anonymous, "Nigeria's oil business," *West Africa,* no. 3563, December 9, 1985, p. 2599.

interest in western industrialized countries like the United States of America (USA), Britain, France and Japan in the Gulf of Guinea in the quest for oil following repeated wars and insecurity in the Middle East with its very narrow and easy to disrupt shipping lanes.

For Cameroon, the stakes over Bakassi especially for oil exploitation were equally high following the discovery of oil deposits in the Missellele swamps near Tiko and at Kole by 1976.[49] With this modest discovery, in the aftermath of the 1973 oil shock, Cameroon continued to search for more discoveries notably in the Sanaga, on land and along the coast and creeks in the Bakassi Peninsula. Work for the construction of Cameroon's National Refinery Corporation (SONARA) at Cape Limbo, Victoria (now Limbe), also kicked start on September 16, 1978. Constructed by a French company, Société Francaise Procofrance; the FCFA 70 billion refinery with a capacity of 2 million tonnes per year was completed and inaugurated on May 16, 1981 by Cameroon's Head of State, Ahmadou Ahidjo. Meanwhile, on March 21, 1980, the National Hydrocarbons Corporation (SNH) was created and on July 9, studies were launched to put in place a Cameroonian Natural Gas Corporation which saw the light of day on December 16, 1980 with the creation of the Société Bouggues Offshore Cameroun (BOSCAM).

With these initiatives, in 1978, Cameroon was already producing 0.8 million tonnes of oil annually and in 1979, the figure stood at 1.7 tonnes.[50] During the Cameroon National Union (CNU) Congress in Bafoussam in 1980, President Ahidjo revealed that Cameroon was already producing 2 million tonnes of oil annually; the equivalent of the capacity of SONARA. Meanwhile, in 1985, oil accounted for 40

---

49. Anonymous, "Cameroon: search for oil," *Africa*, no. 48, August 1975, p. 60. In 1975, there were 8 countries producing oil in Africa: Nigeria, Libya, Algeria, Egypt, Gabon, Angola, Tunisia and Congo .From 1976, new discoveries were made in Zaire [now, Democratic Republic of Congo] and Cameroon, and in the 1980s, in Ghana, Ivory Coast and Benin. Therefore, only 13 countries of the 51 that counted the OAU at the time were producers of oil. See *Cameroon Tribune*, no. 2077 (French edition), Samedi 16 Mai 1981.

50. *Cameroon Tribune*, no. 2077 (French edition), Samedi 16 Mai 1981.

percent of Cameroon's income and represented nearly 70 percent of all income from exports.[51] By this time too, the Cameroon economy was witnessing a nose dive. From 1975 to the early eighties, Cameroon's foreign trade was showing a deficit because of the heavy expenditure on equipment. The country equally started witnessing the primary symptoms of an economic malaise which became reality in 1987. As a consequence, the 1987/88 budget was slashed by some 20 percent from FCFA 800 billion to FCFA 650 billion.[52]

Therefore, the government embarked on more oil exploration in the various blocks along the coast including the Bakassi Peninsula as one way of solving these economic problems. This geopolitico-economic initiative by Cameroon clashed with those of Nigeria who had devised plans to occupy the area. In 1992 for example, Nigerian forces prevented Cameroonian technicians from executing development and equipment projects in Jabane in the Bakassi Peninsula. The materials and equipment set up there were stolen and taken to Nigeria. At the same time, Nigeria put up an identification plaque on which they wrote: "Welcome to Abana Clan Akpa Buyo Local Government Area, Cross River State, Federal Republic of Nigeria."[53] Then, in 1994, Nigeria launched a series of attacks in a desperate attempt to occupy the entire peninsula.

These repeated border misunderstandings between Cameroon and Nigeria preoccupied the Yaounde and Lagos, (much later Abuja) authorities who deployed statecraft, stewardship and diplomacy to manage these protracted border incidents that cropped up from culminating into war. Such efforts paid dividends, but because the issues that sparked the dispute remained unresolved, the conflict raged on thereby inviting other actors into the scene.

---

51. Inga Nagel, "Cameroon: what can be done about the crisis in the economy?" *Africa*, 5-6, 1988, p. 22.

52. Inga Nagel, "Cameroon: what can be done about the crisis in the economy?" *Africa*, 5-6, 1988, p. 22.

53. The Government of Cameroon, *Document on the Bakassi Dispute*, p. 13.

Chapter 2

Bilateral Management of the Border Dispute, 1981 – 2002

Before the 1981 skirmishes on the Cameroon–Nigeria border, the two countries had put up structures where border issues were handled. This included the Joint Commission set up in 1963 and the Mixed Boundary Commission set up in 1970. There were equally avenues like the Seminar workshop on frontier matters in 1992 and myriad high-level talks and declarations on the border issue to beef up these initiatives.

The Role of the Cameroon–Nigeria Mixed Boundary Commission, 1991–93

A Mixed Boundary Commission of Cameroon and Nigeria was set up in 1970 under the framework of the Yaounde I Declaration of August 14, 1970.[1] This Mixed Boundary Commission was later given the mandate to proceed to delimit the Maritime Frontier in conformity with the Yaounde II Declaration of April 4, 1971. The Commission met in Lagos from October 15-22, 1971 and in Garoua in May and August, 1972, but failed to complete its mandate because Nigeria put to question the Yaounde II Declaration.[2] The Commission later met in 1975 and again in 1978 and went into inactivity until 1991. From 1991 to 1993, the Commission met three times; in Yaounde from August 27–30, 1991, in Abuja from

---

1. Maurice Kamto, Co-Agent/Advocate for Cameroon during the oral pleadings of the Cameroon – Nigeria border dispute case at The Hague, verbatim, February 22, 2002, http : // www.icj-cij.org., retrieved on 23/07/10. It was only in 1985 that the Cameroon government created a veritable structure to manage frontier issues. See Decree n⁰ 85/305 of March 7, 1985 creating the National Commission on Frontiers which was reorganized by Decree n⁰ 2001/208 of July 27, 2001.

2. ICJ Judgment on the Cameroon – Nigeria Border Dispute Case of October 10, 2002, http : // www.icj-cij.org. , retrieved on 24/07/10.

December 19, 1991 and again in Yaounde from August 11–14, 1993. During such meetings, the border authorities made recommendations for the peaceful settlement of border questions and on ways to foster peaceful co-existence and bilateral cooperation.

Promotion of trans-frontier cooperation

The meetings of the Mixed Boundary Commission provided a forum for the two countries to discuss frontier issues void of sentiments and emotions. It was in this spirit of objectivity and optimism that the Nigerian delegation to the Commission's meeting in Yaounde in August 1993 recognized that the denunciation of the 1975 Maroua Accord was because of internal problems in Nigeria and not because of the technical problems relating to the demarcation of the boundary. The Mixed Commission was also instrumental in the assessment of the manner in which the natural resources like oil and gas fields straddling the frontier or along it could be exploited by the two countries. During the Mixed Commission's meeting in Yaounde in August 1993, the issue of the communal exploitation of resources straddling the common frontier or along it was examined and a platform proposed to that effect.

Promotion of bilateral relations and sub – regional integration

The Mixed Boundary Commission equally strove to improve bilateral relations and sub– regional integration. Meeting in Yaounde in August 1991 the 53 member Cameroonian delegation led by her Minister of External Relations, Jacques-Roger Booh Booh and that of Nigeria made up of 20 members and led by Major–General Ike Omar Sanda Nwachukwo, Foreign Minister and President of the Technical Committee of the National Commission on Frontiers had as theme for discussion; frontier questions, bilateral cooperation and the project for the creation of a Commission for the Gulf of Guinea. Through this initiative by Cameroon and Nigeria, the Gulf of Guinea Commission (GGC) was later created in 1999. In 2010, the GGC was made up of Equatorial Guinea, Cameroon, Nigeria, Gabon, Sao Tome and Principe, Republic of Congo, Democratic Republic of

Congo and Angola. Its headquarters is in Luanda, Angola. Its objective is to preserve peace, security and stability in the sub-region. Its first summit was in Libreville, Gabon on August 26, 2006 and the second in Luanda, Angola on November 25, 2008.

The Yola Seminar Workshop, May 25 – 29, 1992

On May 25, 1992, Cameroon and Nigeria launched a new approach to trans-frontier cooperation through the organization of a seminar workshop in Yola, Adamawa State, Nigeria. The Cameroon delegation was led by its National Assembly President, Cavaye Yeguie Djibril while that of Nigeria was led by its Vice President who also doubled as the President of the National Commission on Frontiers, Admiral Augustus Aikhomu. The seminar workshop also brought together the Governors of the frontier States and Provinces, as well as resource persons from the two countries with diverse backgrounds. This first seminar workshop on frontier issues between Cameroon and Nigeria had myriad objectives.

Objectives

It was intended to promote peaceful relations through a better understanding of Cameroon–Nigeria relations particularly on frontier matters. The understanding of such relations was deemed necessary because there were certain socio-economic relations that tended to orchestrate conflict among frontier populations. It was also intended to promote security, cooperation and friendliness between the two countries by identifying impediments to such cordial relationship and suggesting new frontiers of imagination to Cameroonian and Nigerian authorities. Such recommendations were to serve as a guide to ameliorate trans-frontier cooperation and safeguard security in the sub region in particular and Africa in general. This spirit was conveyed vividly by the Cameroon delegation leader to the seminar workshop, Cavaye Yeguie Djibril when he declared that the seminar was intended to; "look for ways and means susceptible to trans-frontier politics between Cameroon and Nigeria …. [and] to make recommendations to our respective governments which they will put into practice."[3] The seminar workshop was also aimed at putting into focus the socio-economic links between the two countries and equally to brainstorm on the manner of exploiting these potentials for the goodwill of all.

Thirty five papers were presented during the seminar workshop. The papers were on varied themes: population movements across the frontier, trans-frontier languages, inter-ethnic relations, development of frontier agglomerations, trans-frontier business, environmental protection along the frontier and frontier security. After the paper presentations, five Commissions were formed to discuss in detail the challenges of frontier and trans-frontier issues. They included: the Commission on Culture, Frontier Economics, Frontier Administration, Frontier Security and finally that on Frontier Laws. After five days of painstaking discussions, the participants identified nine problem areas faced by frontier populations and pondered on how these problems could be solved.

Identified problems and recommended solutions

First, the participants postulated that differences in social infrastructures and development patterns were at the root cause of tension among frontier populations. As a solution to this problem, they recommended to the governments of Cameroon and Nigeria to coordinate the planning and development of their common frontier. Second, they identified the lack of the coordination of economic activities between the two countries thereby encouraging criminal activities and contraband trade along the common frontier. On this take, the seminar participants proposed that there should be the establishment of a management framework to coordinate and follow up trans-frontier economic transactions.

The third problem identified concerned the inexistence of consultations pertaining to the problems of the administration of trans-frontier resources thereby encouraging insecurity, looting and

---

3. Cavaye Yeguie Djibril, interview, Badjang ba Nken, *Cameroon Tribune*, n⁰ 5441(French edition), Dimanche 31 Mai–Lundi 1 Juin, 1992. The translation is mine.

under exploitation of these resources. In some instances; the participants posited, this insecurity often degenerates into conflicts, culminating into the destruction of property and loss of lives. On this score, they recommended as solution, the establishment of a management framework to oversee the exploitation of common resources straddling or along the common frontier. Fourth, the participants identified the problem of negative and provocative commentaries on the media which tended to aggravate tension and hostility on frontier problems.[4] As a solution to this problem, the participants recommended that there should be the sensitization of the media on the effects of inflammatory statements and sensational commentaries on frontier questions.

The fifth problem identified was the abuses of frontier security agents who tend to interfere in the free circulation of persons and in the interaction of persons across the common frontier. On this issue, the participants recommended that there should be the conscientisation of security agents on the rights and obligations of frontier communities. Sixth, they identified the lack of collaboration between the security services of the two countries relating to the fight against crime along the common border. On this take, they recommended that there should be the elaboration of appropriate legal instruments on trans-frontier cooperation especially by borrowing from what other countries had implemented on this issue so that the security needs of frontier communities could be tackled.

The seventh problem identified was the non application of existing accords and treaties thereby retarding cooperation initiatives by the two countries. On this score, they recommended the ratification and putting into application the existing accords and treaties signed by the two countries. Eighth, was the problem of the non standardization of frontier languages which tend to hinder communication among the frontier populations. Finally, there was

---

4. Following the May 16, 1981 skirmishes between Cameroonian and Nigerian coast guards which left five Nigerians dead, the bodies of these people were presented on Nigerian television and print media with such sensitive comments that it provoked certain emotions in Lagos sparking off agitation from irate persons who sacked the Cameroon Embassy in Lagos.

the problem of the incomplete demarcation of the common frontier. They recommended that there should be concerted effort to standardize frontier languages as well as the completion of the demarcation work and production of maps indicating the common frontier.[5]

These recommendations were made amidst Nigerian contest in some of the commissions notably in the Legal, Security and Frontier Administration Commissions; on the validity of former instruments reached on the delimitation of the Cameroon-Nigeria Boundary. This spirit was captured vividly by Mpouel Balla Lazare, President of the Security Commission:

> There are delegates who want to put to question what was already accepted and signed at a higher level by the two governments. In my Commission, the delimitation of the frontier was not discussed in a consensual manner. For Cameroonians, this frontier was already mapped and what is left now is to intensify the pillar demarcation; but for Nigeria, the tendency is to ignore what was already done and to put to question these accords notably that of Maroua in 1975. To them, these accords should not be evoked as they have to be revised.[6]

Meeting in Yaounde in August 1993, the Cameroon-Nigeria Mixed Boundary Commission recommended that there should be the effective implementation of the recommendations of the Yola Seminar workshop. The issue of the implementation of recommendations became serious impediment to the sustenance of trans-frontier peaceful relations and bilateral cooperation. The practical implementation of these recommendations hinged on the

---

5. *Cameroon Tribune*, n[0] 5143(French edition), Mardi 2 Juin 1992.

6. Mpouel Balla Lazare, President of the Security Commission, Yola Seminar Workshop, May 25 – 29, 1992, interview, Badjang ba Nken, *Cameroon Tribune*, n[0] 5144 (French edition), Mercredi 3 Juin, 1992. The translation is mine.

will of the Heads of State and Government of the two countries who were either slow or cautious to do so.

The Role of the Cameroon-Nigeria Joint Commission, 1987-2002

Joint Commissions are used to effect bilateral diplomatic relations when such relations attain a certain intensive degree that traditional diplomatic instruments like the use of Permanent Missions becomes insufficient. Created on February 6, 1963, the first session of the Cameroon-Nigeria Joint Commission was held in August 1987 in Yaounde, the second in Abuja in November 1993 and the third planned for Yaounde in 1995 was short-circuited following Nigeria's invasion of Cameroon's Bakassi Peninsula; but finally held in Abuja in September/October 2002; few days to the ICJ verdict on the Cameroon-Nigeria border dispute case. The Commission met in Yaounde in October 2008 and in Abuja in November 2010. The Joint Commission is constituted of politicians, diplomats and experts in diverse fields who meet to discuss bilateral cooperation strategies and propose to their respective governments to implement. The Joint Commission has been very instrumental in the promotion of trans-frontier cooperation and bilateral relations.

Promotion of trans-frontier cooperation

Articles 3, 4 and 7 of the 1963 Bilateral Cooperation Agreement; which set up the Joint Commission, outline the domains of cooperation touching on trans-frontier issues. Such issues include; economic, financial and customs matters, border exchanges, free movement of persons and goods and cultural, technical and legal matters.[7] Trans-frontier problems were identified during the various sessions of the Joint Commission and solutions proposed to such problems. Meeting in Yaounde in 1987, the Commission members examined and adopted decisions touching on trans-frontier issues notably on judicial problems, consular problems, commerce, fishing, animal husbandry and technology, transport, post and

---

7. Pondi and Zang, "The Cameroon-Nigeria Border Cooperation", p. 174.

telecommunication, energy and water resources. Furthermore, during the third session of the Joint Commission in Abuja in 2002, it decided that a joint security committee be established to check cross-border crimes. This recommendation was revisited in the subsequent sessions of the Joint Commission; notably during the fourth session in Yaounde in October 2008 and during its fifth session in Abuja in November 2010.

Promotion of bilateral relations

The preamble of the 1963 agreement defining the scope of cooperation between Cameroon and Nigeria stresses brotherhood as the basis for cooperation between the two countries. While Article 1 stresses the principle of sovereign equality on the basis of mutual interest and the respect for laws and regulations in force in the two countries.[8] These dispositions permitted the Joint Commission to identify and adopt the modus operandi for other confidence building measures between the two countries including the negotiation of a Memorandum of Understanding (MOU) on bilateral consultations between the two Foreign Ministries, exchange of official visits, construction and maintenance of roads, security, promotion of amicable media relations, joint scientific research and cooperation in sporting and youth activities. It was as a result of such ambitious projects that the Head of the Nigerian delegation to the first session of the Joint Commission, Dr. Kalu I. Kalu, Federal Planning Minister declared with optimism that Cameroon occupies a strategic position in Nigeria's foreign relations since it is the largest of all her neighbours

High-Level Talks and Declarations on the Border Issue, 1981-2002

Talks, decisions or declarations that hinged on frontier problems and trans-frontier relations were at the Presidential and Ministerial levels. Such talks and declarations more often than not followed a misunderstanding on the common border. Such talks were very

---

8. Pondi and Zang, "The Cameroon-Nigeria Border Cooperation", pp. 173-175.

instrumental in dissipating tension over frontier and trans-frontier problems.

Reconciliation process following the May 16, 1981 border incident

On May 16, 1981, five Nigerians were killed in a border skirmish between Cameroonian and Nigerian coast guards orchestrating a diplomatic row that both parties tried to resolve. Lagos reacted to the incident in strong diplomatic language demanding "excuses without reservation" within a week, punishment on the Cameroonian soldiers who were involved and complete compensation to the affected Nigerian families. This was a sort of ultimatum that prepared a stage for a full scale war. But through diplomatic interventions, the incident was bilaterally resolved by Yaounde and Lagos.

Following the incident, the Cameroon Head of State, Ahmadou Ahidjo sent a special mission to Lagos led by his Minister of State in charge of Foreign Affairs, Paul Dontsop. The mission left Yaounde on May 24, to present to the government of Nigeria and the affected families, the condolences of the Cameroon government and people. While in Lagos, the mission proposed to the Federal Government that a Mixed Commission of Nigeria and Cameroon be constituted to investigate the matter. This Mixed Commission was formed and it investigated the problem and decided that Cameroon should compensate the affected families while Nigeria repair the damages caused by irate demonstrators on the Cameroon Embassy in Lagos. The normalization of relations was followed by intensive high level talks on border issues.

Talks and Declarations before Nigerian invasion of Bakassi in 1994

The normalization of relations between the two countries was followed by the invitation by President Shehu Shagari for the new Cameroon President, Paul Biya to pay an official visit to Nigeria after his (Shagari's) to Cameroon from January 19-22, 1981, on the invitation of President Ahidjo. Shehu Shagari equally congratulated Biya following his accession to Supreme Leadership in Cameroon on November 6, 1982 after the resignation of Ahidjo on November 4.

Meanwhile, the Cameroon Prime Minister, Bello Bouba Maigari was dispatched by President Biya to Lagos on November 30, with a message to his Nigerian counterpart.

President Biya paid a three day official visit to Nigeria on April 19, 20 and 21, 1983. The presence of the Governors of the border Provinces with Nigeria in his delegation showed the importance attached to border issues during the visit. These Governors included Ousmane Mey of the then North Province and Yakum Ntaw of the then South West Province. In the Joint Communiqué that sanctioned the visit, issued on April 21, the two Presidents affirmed their desire and determination to intensify and consolidate cooperation ties in all fields particularly on economic, technical and scientific matters. For this purpose, an agreement on Economic, Scientific and Technical Cooperation was signed. In the preamble of this agreement; the two parties affirmed their renewed desire to promote and enlarge their mutual economic, scientific and technical cooperation. Meanwhile, Article 1 of the agreement stresses the need for the respect of the laws and regulations of the host country by residents of the two countries. The fields of cooperation are defined in Article 22 of the agreement, which was ratified by Cameroon in July 1985. The two Presidents equally deplored the increasing interference and intervention in the internal affairs of African states in violation of the objectives and ideals of the UN and OAU. Thus, they upheld the OAU principle of the intangibility of frontiers inherited from colonialism as well as condemned the existing state of permanent crisis in the continent.

At the end of the visit, President Biya invited President Shagari to visit Cameroon. President Shagari could not effect the visit because on December 27, 1983, he was ousted in a military coup and replaced by General Mohammadu Buhari. Like the Shagari civilian regime before them, the military opted for the expulsion of illegal immigrants from Nigeria; many of them Cameroonians. Over 700.000 people were eligible for expulsion.[9] The short-lived military government of General Buhari (December 27, 1983-August 27, 1985) was quite hostile to Cameroon as "there were threats and

9. Aidan Meehan, "The Nigerian Nightmare," *AfricAsia,* no. 18, June 1985, p. 8.

intimidation relative to border closure, deployment of troops along the common border and building of military bases in states sharing borders with Cameroon."[10] This tense relationship culminated into a border incident in February 1987 in the Lake Chad region. Nigerians sufficiently trained and armed with matchets invaded Cameroon villages in this region and three Cameroonians were kidnapped and tortured by Nigerian authorities.[11]

This incident necessitated another high-level talk on the border issue. Therefore, on the heels of this incident, President Ibrahim Badamassi Babangida who succeeded Buhari on August 27, 1985 dispatched his Chief of Staff for Infantry Battalion, Sani Abacha to Cameroon for an official and working visit in September 1987. Abacha visited the then West, Littoral, North, Adamawa, South West and Centre Provinces of Cameroon. These Provinces had a huge agglomeration of Nigerian residents. Abacha's visit and the negotiations that ensued did not bring lasting peace in the Lake Chad region. As a result, in November 1987, the Nigerian army occupied the Cameroonian Islands of Faransia, Darack I and II near Lake Chad where they lowered the Cameroonian flag and hoisted that of Nigeria. This operation was extended to about ten other villages.[12] For example, the Nigerian army occupied the centre for the training of fishermen at Katte-Kime constructed with funds from the Japanese cooperation.[13] Nigerian soldiers equally sent away Cameroonian government authorities, traditional chiefs and ordinary citizens who refused the new Nigerian authorities.

These incidents prompted another rapprochement by Cameroonian and Nigerian authorities. From December 8-10, 1987, President Ibrahim Babangida paid an official visit to Cameroon. The

---

10. Aji James, "The Dynamics of Cameroon-Nigeria Relations" pp. 35-36.

11. The Government of Cameroon, *Document on the Bakassi Dispute*, p. 12.

12. Ibid.

13. Jean Pierre Cot, Counsel/Advocate for Cameroon during oral pleadings of the Cameroon–Nigeria border dispute case at The Hague, verbatim, February 19, 2002.

presence of the Governors of frontier States in his delegation notably captain J.D. Janc of Gongola State, Lt. Colonel A.M. Aminu of Borno State and Commander I.E. Princewill of the Cross River State was intended to make them participate actively in the discussions on frontier matters. On the Cameroon side, the Governors of frontier Provinces equally constituted part of the official delegation. They included; Fon Fossi Yakum Ntaw, Ekono Nna Albert, and Magloire Nguiamba of the then North, Far North and South West Provinces respectively. In a Joint Communiqué that sanctioned the meeting, issued on December 10, 1987, the two leaders examined their bilateral relations and promised to enforce these relations. They declared that relations between the two countries were founded on the principle of independence, sovereignty, territorial integrity, equality and non interference in the affairs of another country. The communiqué also notes that these principles constitute an important element to the peace, security and cooperation in the sub region. The two leaders equally undertook to preserve a climate of peace on the two sides of their common border and to arrive at an accord of mixed patrol in the Lake Chad region in order to guarantee peace and security in the zone. These high-level visits by Presidents Ahidjo (May 5, 1960-November 4, 1982), Shagari (October 1, 1979-December 27, 1983), Babangida (August 27, 1985-August 26, 1993), and Biya (since November 6, 1982) helped to dissipate tension along the common frontier (See plate 1).

Barely a year after the visit, another border incident occurred on May 13, 1989, in Blangoua near Lake Chad when Nigerian soldiers inspected and confiscated a Cameroonian fishing boat.[14] This and other concerns prompted President Babangida to pay another official visit to Cameroon in 1989, for the two leaders to commit themselves to solve border problems and improve on their bilateral relations. In spite of these commitments by Nigerian and Cameroonian leaders to solve their border disputes, border skirmishes continued in earnest.

---

14. The Government of Cameroon, *Document on the Bakassi Dispute*, p. 12.

Plate 1. Cameroonian and Nigerian Leaders whose Efforts were Instrumental in Dissipating Tension along the Common Border

Ahmadou Ahidjo

Shehu Shagari

Ibrahim Babangida

Paul Biya

Source: http://www.google.cm/images

In April 1990, the DO of Kombo-Abedimo and his retinue were kidnapped by Nigerian soldiers while they were on an administrative tour and tortured for several days before being released. Meanwhile, from April 1990 to April 1991, Nigerian soldiers landed on many occasions at Jabane and in one of those occasions, they put down the Cameroonian flag replacing it with theirs. They also erected a giant bill board in which they wrote: Mbo Local Government, Akwa Ibom.[15] In July 1991, the Nigerian army occupied Kotcha (Kontcha) in the then Adamawa Province of Cameroon and set up an Emi-immigration control post at Tipsan.[16] Tension again mounted between the two countries as Nigerian forces made veiled threats to occupy Cameroonian territory in the Lake Chad region under the pretext of protecting Nigerian fishermen.

These border misunderstandings were managed by the Heads of State of Cameroon and Nigeria in 1991. After attending the 27th OAU summit in Abuja in July 1991, President Biya went back to Nigeria on August 10, 1991 to relaunch negotiations on the border issue on the invitation of the Nigerian Head of State and Chairman of the OAU, Babangida. The two leaders took commitment to meet regularly and to resolve the few frontier incidents that often crop up in a friendly and diplomatic manner and to the satisfaction of the two parties. They equally agreed to reactivate the Mixed Boundary Commission which lastly met in 1978. On the heels of this visit, the Nigerian Head of State dispatched his Foreign Affairs Minister, Ike O.S. Nwachukwu to Cameroon for a four-day friendly and working visit from August 27-30, 1991.

In spite of these efforts, border misunderstandings continued in earnest. This time Nigeria officially laid claims to the Bakassi Peninsula. The tenth edition of the administrative map of Nigeria published in 1991 indicated for the first time that the international boundary between Nigeria and Cameroon was at the Rio del Rey, not the Akwayafe River as indicated in colonial and former Nigerian

---

15. The Government of Cameroon, *Document on the Bakassi Dispute*, p. 12.

16. Ibid.

maps.[17] This claim was manifested on the ground following Nigerian forces seizure of material and equipment from Cameroonian technicians who were executing development projects at Jabane; and carted away with it. They also erected giant bill boards in the locality.[18]

In spite of this perpetual confrontation on the Cameroon-Nigeria border, precautions continued to be undertaken at the higher level to manage or resolve the misunderstandings in a pacific manner. In this vein, Cameroon's Head of State dispatched an envoy to his Nigerian counterpart in May 1993 to inform him of the decision by Cameroon to embark on petroleum exploitation in the Betika West Basin found in the maritime zone with Nigeria beyond the sector that was not yet demarcated by the two countries. That is, beyond point G contained in the Maroua Declaration of June 1975. Nigeria however did not react.[19] Many reasons accounted for this silence. During the meeting of the National Borders Commissions of Cameroon and Nigeria in Yaounde in August 1991, Nigeria officially contested the Maroua Declaration. Again, during the meeting of the Mixed Boundary Commission in Yaounde in August 1993, she maintained her stand although the experts stipulated in the minutes that the denunciation by Nigeria of the Maroua Declaration was as a result of Nigerian political problems and not because of technical problems relating to the demarcation of the border.

The accession to power in Nigeria of General Sani Abacha on November 17, 1993, marked a turning point in Cameroon-Nigeria relations which attained the lowest ebb during his reign. Barely one month into office, Abacha marched his troops into Cameroon's localities of Jabane and Diamond Island in the Bakassi Peninsula on December 21, 1993. This military occupation of Cameroonian territory provoked serious tension and movement of both Cameroonian and Nigerian troops to the peninsula. On February 18

---

17. Jean Pierre Cot, Counsel/Advocate for Cameroon, verbatim, February 21, 2002.

18. The Government of Cameroon, *Document on the Bakassi Dispute*, p. 13.

19. Maurice Kamto, verbatim, February 26, 2002.

and 19, 1994, the Nigerians again launched a series of attacks on Cameroonian army units in a desperate attempt to move northwards and occupy Akwa (Archibong for Nigeria) and the entire peninsula. These attacks met with stiff resistance from Cameroonian troops leading to the loss of lives and material damages on both sides. From 1994 up to 2002 when the matter was settled by the ICJ, bilateral management of the border dispute was focused on the Bakassi Peninsula saga.

Diplomatic offensives following Nigerian invasion of Bakassi

The incidents of 1993 and 1994 in Bakassi prompted Yaounde to involve multilateral actors in the management and resolution of the border dispute—the UN, OAU and ICJ. While pursuing these multilateral initiatives, various efforts were still undertaken by Cameroon and Nigeria for an amicable settlement of the border dispute. This was done at the time their relations were at its lowest ebb. As a consequence, these efforts were marked by suspicion and cynicism.

On the heat of the Nigerian invasion of Bakassi in 1993, the Cameroon President, Paul Biya dispatched his Minister of External Relations, Ferdinand Leopold Oyono to Abuja on January 13, 1994 with a message of peace and conciliation to his Nigerian counterpart. While in Abuja, Oyono met with the Nigerian Minister of Foreign Affairs, Baba Gana Kingibe, and the two men agreed to create a Mixed Commission to visit the disputed area in Bakassi.[20] Meanwhile, from January 1994, a telephone contact was established between Presidents Biya and Abacha at the initiative of President Biya. Preparations for a joint visit to the disputed Bakassi Peninsula kicked off in earnest on February 9, 1994 when the Nigerian Foreign Minister, Kingibe, led a delegation to Yaounde to set the pace for negotiations on the matter. The delegation concerted with Cameroon's Minister of Foreign Affairs, Ferdinand Oyono and planned a field trip of a joint delegation of Cameroon and Nigeria to

---

20. Aji James, "The Dynamics of Cameroon-Nigeria Relations", p. 49.

Bakassi. But, this visit was foiled by the Nigerians when the delegation reached Buea, Cameroon; as she continued to reiterate her ownership of Bakassi.[21]

In spite of the failure of the joint visit to Bakassi, diplomatic contacts continued.On February 23, 1994, Cameroon's Vice Prime Minister in charge of Housing and Habitats, Hamadou Moustapha led a Cameroon delegation to Nigeria to prepare the stage for negotiations on the matter. These renewed bilateral contacts were made amidst suspicion between the two countries. For example, on March 2, 1994, Abuja in a communiqué alleged that Yaounde was making a census of Nigerian citizens in Cameroon and had ordered the control of their bank accounts; allegations that were refuted by Yaounde authorities. In spite of the suspicion, the first round of negotiations between Cameroonian and Nigerian authorities on the Bakassi Peninsula issue kicked start in Yaounde from March 9-10, 1994. The Cameroon delegation was led by her Minister of External Relations, Ferdinand Oyono and that of Nigeria by her Foreign Minister, Baba Gana kingibe. During the talks, Cameroon insisted on a goodwill gesture from the Nigerian government notably to pull her troops out of Bakassi before she could accept the request from the Nigerian delegation leader that President Paul Biya should go to Maiduguri for talks with President Abacha. Yaounde however posited that if her conditions were met, the talks could only be held in a neutral territory. As a consequence, the Nigerian Foreign Minister later shifted the venue to Cairo, Egypt unilaterally without consulting Yaounde.

Though talks by the two leaders as a result of bilateral initiative were not held; the fact that both parties embraced the idea of a peaceful settlement to the dispute was commendable. However, the reticence with which the two parties embraced the peaceful initiatives points to the fact that the moment was not yet ripe for bilateral settlement as the mutual stalemate in the Bakassi Peninsula was not yet the sufficient condition that could spur the parties to prevent the

---

21. Zacharie Ngniman, *Nigeria-Cameroun, La Guerre Permanente?* Yaoundé : Editions Clé, 1996, p. 15.

dispute from escalating into war. As a consequence, the two parties preferred diplomatic offensives in the international arena to explain their sides of the case and canvass for support.

Cameroon sent sensitization missions to Europe led by Kontchou Kouomegni and Joseph Owona and another to African states led by Francis Nkwain. The Nkwain delegation visited Kenya and Uganda in March 1994 and Tanzania and Zimbabwe in April 1994.[22] Nigeria equally sent a delegation to African states led by her Foreign Minister, Anthony Ani. The delegation visited Gabon, Uganda, Zimbabwe, Kenya and Zambia.[23] The new Nigerian Foreign Minister, Tom Ikimi equally visited Ghana, Togo and Benin.[24] He equally visited Cameroon on April 11, 1995, as bearer of a special message from the Nigerian Head of State, General Sani Abacha.

Through declarations and coordination of their good offices, some states in the international arena like the USA, Britain, the Republic of South Africa, Kenya, Zimbabwe and Tanzania officially made their opinion on the dispute. Generally, these countries reminded the belligerents that they were at The Hague to look for a peaceful settlement to the dispute, and should therefore suspend hostilities and wait for the ICJ verdict. On the heels of these reactions from the international community, another skirmish between Nigerian and Cameroonian troops was reported near Idabato in the disputed Bakassi Peninsula on February 3, 1996, with several casualties on both sides. This prompted the Cameroon Minister of External Relations, Ferdinand Oyono, to summon the Nigerian Ambassador to Cameroon, George Bello, on February 5, 1996 for consultation.

---

22. Mgbale Mgbatou Hamadou," La Politique Camerounaise de Résolution Pacifique de la Crise de Bakassi" Doctorat de 3ème cycle Thesis, University of Yaounde II, IRIC, 2001, p. 97.

23. *West Africa*, March 28-April 3, 1994, p. 541, cited in Aji James, "The Dynamics of Cameroon-Nigeria Relations", p. 50.

24. *Cameroon Tribune*, no. 5826/2115, Wednesday, April 12, 1995.

This new incident and international public opinion on the matter influenced Cameroon greatly; as she shifted more and more away from settling the border dispute through bilateral means. This is exemplified by the following declaration during a press conference in February 1996, by Douala Moutome, Cameroon's Minister of Justice and Agent to the ICJ. Answering a question on why Nigeria was in favour of settling the dispute bilaterally; he retorted that it was all over in that line. He went on to reiterate that Nigeria had shown the limits of her faithfulness and comprehension and that neither President Eyadema of Togo nor President Bongo of Gabon succeeded in this line. Therefore, he went on; it will not be a mistake if President Biya who was always available for negotiation back out. Six years later, this Cameroonian stance was again reiterated by her new Agent in the case, Amadou Ali when he declared succinctly as follows: " We have, all too often, seen our hopes dashed each time we have negotiated; we do no longer believe in the virtues of bilateralism with regard to this particular case."[25]

A critical examination of the ingredients within the above declarations and the stance of the parties would enable us analyze the stumbling blocks that were on the way to the bilateral resolution of the border dispute. Three obvious obstacles immediately presents itself: first, that the conflicting parties wanted to maintain their honour intact as they pursued negotiations for a final settlement; second, that the resolution of the dispute did not only require ending its violent expression but equally required resolving the issues that prompted it; and finally, that the international community impacted greatly on the parties.

The issue of the parties maintaining their honour intact as they pursued negotiations became very important considering the stakes involved and the declarations already made. For Nigeria, the Bakassi Peninsula was her territory and she even produced maps in 1991 placing it in Nigeria. Therefore, successful reconciliation with

---

25. Amadou Ali, Cameroon's Agent during the hearing of the border dispute case, verbatim, March 12, 2002. See *Cameroon Tribune*, no. 7553/3842, Wednesday, March 13, 2002. Amadou Ali replaced Laurent Esso who succeeded Douala Moutome.

Cameroon required that Cameroon shifted from her insistence that Nigeria should pull out from Bakassi as a condition for the parties to engage in talks at the Presidential level. Nigeria continuously employed dilatory and diversionary tactics to gain time and play a "win-win" game[26] wherein there could be a renegotiation of former agreements. Clues of this Nigerian stance are gotten from her memoire deposited at The Hague and from her position during the oral pleadings of the case in February/March 2002, wherein she posited that former treaties and conventions be invalidated. This stance was obvious as Nigerian residents in Bakassi had been made to believe that they were in Nigerian territory.

For Cameroon, the former conventions on the common boundary recognized her sovereignty of Bakassi and therefore accepting to negotiate with Nigeria when her troops were still in her territory was suicidal. This consideration even became more discernable following two abortive attempts for a joint commission of Cameroon and Nigeria to the peninsula on February 9, 1994 and a tripartite joint team of Cameroon, Nigeria and the OAU on April 27, 1994; all foiled by Nigeria. From the above analysis, one can comfortably join Zartman in concluding that; "successful conciliation produces a shift from a winning mentality to a conciliating mentality on the part of both sides."[27] This did not occur during the bilateral negotiations for a peaceful settlement of the border dispute; even temporarily.

The issue relating to the resolution of the problem that sparked off the dispute and not only ending its violent phase was equally another stumbling block to bilateral negotiations. During the bilateral negotiations from 1994-96, the socio-economic, security and strategic concerns that provoked the dispute did not constitute an integral part of the negotiations. Therefore, successful negotiation at this juncture that was only limited to Nigeria's acceptance to pull out of Bakassi would have disadvantaged Nigeria since Cameroon could later freely

---

26. "Win-Win" game is a concept of the game theory developed by Karl Deutsch and Thomas Shelling.

27. Zartman, *Ripe for Resolution*, p. 232.

undertake measures that could negatively affect Nigerian residents in Bakassi in particular and in Cameroon in general. This consideration therefore complicated the bilateral resolution process.

Finally, the position of the international community on the dispute equally impacted greatly on the parties. In 1996, France, a World Power, made sensitive declarations with regard to the conflict which directly impinged on the parties. In February 1996, the Chief of the French Military Cooperation in Douala, Cameroon, General Rigot while reacting to rumours that France will prefer her interests in Nigeria against her friendship with Cameroon declared that between interest and friends, France will choose friends. This is what Zartman refers to in conflict management as "a pox on one of your houses."[28] That is, taking sides in conflict against one of the parties. This declaration came on the heels of the arrival of French parachutists in Yaounde for military manoevres said to have been scheduled for a long time. As a result of these developments, Cameroon became more confident in the face of the conflict. Cameroon even felt more secured because she had a Defence Accord with France signed on February 21, 1974 which allows Cameroon to call in French troops to ensure its defence and even maintain internal peace.[29] Another World Power, the USA requested the conflicting parties to accept the immediate sending to Bakassi of an investigative mission of the UN or any other organ which will be mutually acceptable to evaluate the situation. Pressure was therefore brought to bear on Nigeria and she accepted the UN Security Council fact finding mission to Bakassi in September 1996.

The preceding analysis is a pointer to the fact that the post cold war international conjuncture wherein conflict resolution has became more peaceful, conciliatory and defensive rather than militaristic, aggressive and offensive manifested itself during the process of the

---

28. Zartman, "Conflict Resolution: Prevention, Management and Resolution," p. 312.

29. In a visit to Cameroon on May 20, 2009, the French Prime Minister, François Fillon signed a new accord of military partnership with Cameroon in line with the new orientations of relations between African countries and France defined by President Nicolas Sarkozy in 2008. From Cameroon, Fillon proceeded to Nigeria.

resolution of the Cameroon-Nigeria border dispute. This is an indication that the current international system is characterized by growing interdependence; mutual responsibility and dependency on others. Aware of this interdependence which is more economic, though with inevitable psychological and cultural counterparts like the sense of belonging together, sharing values and discovering mutual interests,[30] Cameroon and Nigeria were bound to cooperate during this period of conflict.

Bilateral Cooperation at the time of Crisis

Cameroon and Nigeria maintained their diplomatic representation in each other's territory while cooperation continued between the two countries during the period of the crisis. In 1997, Cameroon's largest Diplomatic Mission in Africa in terms of personnel was Lagos with a manpower of 30; 9 from the Ministry of External Relations (MINREX) in Yaounde, 4 military personnel and 17 recruited on the ground. Meanwhile, the consulate in Calabar had 10; 6 from MINREX in Yaounde, 1 military personnel and 3 recruited on the ground.[31] Other Cameroon missions in Africa had less than half this number. For example, Bangui had 11, Brazzaville 11, Libreville 11, Malabo 11 and N'Djamena 9.[32] Nigeria on her part maintained her High Commissioner in Yaounde and the consulates in Buea and Douala.[33] Although Cameroon continued to work in Nigeria at the Chargé d'Affairs level since 1994 and equally failed to

---

30. Hylke Tromp, "Interdependence, Security and Peace Research", in James Rosenau and Hylke Tromp ed. *Interdependence and Conflict in World Politics* (England: Gower House, 1989), p. 8. Cited in Aji James, "The Dynamics of Cameroon-Nigeria Relations," p. 9.

31. Yves Alexandre Chouala, " Le Monde Selon Yaoundé: Lecture Géopolitique de la Distribution Mondiale des Services Exterièurs du Ministère des Relations Extérièures du Cameroun, " Rapport du Stage Diplomatique, University of Yaounde II, IRIC, 1998, p. 11.

32. Ibid.

33. Ibid. The only other country where Nigeria had three missions was the USA.

58

move her High commission to Abuja, the new Nigerian capital, after repeated appeals from Nigerian authorities to do so, Cameroon-Nigeria relations warmed up following the change of leadership in Nigeria in 1998.

On June 8, 1998, General Abacha died and was replaced by Abdusallami Abubakar (June 8, 1998-May 29, 1999), himself succeeded by President Olusegun Obasanjo (February 13, 1976-October 1, 1979 and May 29, 1999-May 29, 2007). Under these two leaders, politico-diplomatic exchanges between Cameroon and Nigeria increased. Cameroon dispatched a delegation led by the President of the National Assembly, Cavaye Yeguie Djibril to condole with the Nigerian people following the death of President Sani Abacha. Meanwhile, a Nigerian delegation was dispatched to give medicines and gifts to the victims of the Nsam fire disaster of February 1998 and repeated for the Limbe flood victims of August 2001.

Through the initiative of President Abdusalami Abubakar, Cameroon and Nigeria on November 24, 1998 exchanged prisoners of war with the assistance of the International Red Cross. This initiative was however interpreted by Cameroonian authorities as Nigerian manoevre to gain favour from France and entice her to arrange a meeting between the Heads of State of Cameroon and Nigeria during the Africa-France summit of November 26-28, 1998 in France so that France could influence Cameroon to withdraw her suit against Nigeria at The Hague.[34] These relations again witnessed a nose dive following Nigeria's organization of local elections in the Bakassi Peninsula on December 5 and 6, 1998 in contravention of the ICJ conservatory measures of March 15, 1996 which called on the parties to halt all hostilities in the Bakassi Peninsula. Cameroon protested against this Nigerian action by addressing correspondences to the UN General Assembly President and to the Secretary Generals of the UN, Commonwealth, the organization of the Islamic

---

34. Correspondence no. 00781/DIPL/CAB/D3 from Cameroon's Minister of External Relations, Augustin Kontchou Kouomegni dated November 23, 1998 to the Secretary General of the Presidency of the Republic, MINREX Archives, file no. 191.

Conference, OAU, Francophonie and to the Regional Delegate of the Red Cross in Yaounde.[35]

Although the Nigerian President-elect, Olusegun Obasanjo made a stop-over in Yaounde on March 16, 1999 and held talks with President Paul Biya and outgoing President, Abdusalami Abubakar paid a working visit to Cameroon on May 17, 1999; Cameroon-Nigeria relations were only revamped at the behest of the UN Secretary General, Kofi Annan. Through his efforts, the Cameroon-Nigeria Joint Commission reconvened in September 2002. These relations however remained low keyed until after the ICJ verdict on the border dispute case. Before the verdict, multilateral diplomacy on the border dispute begun since 1981 continued in earnest.

---

35. Correspondence no. 00810/DIPL/CAB from Cameroon's Minister of External Relations, Augustin Kontchou Kouomegni, denouncing the organization of local elections by Nigeria in the Cameroon territory they were occupying. MINREX Archives, file no. 191.

Chapter 3

Multilateral Management of the Border Dispute, 1981-2002

Multilateral management of disputes here refers either to the use of third parties to negotiate and arbitrate in what is known as mediation or concerted effort under the banner of regional and international organizations through the provision of necessary good offices to push the conflicting parties to refocus on the way out of their dispute. Multilateral institutions managed the border dispute through the recognition of the mediation and conciliatory efforts by third parties, the scheduling of meetings to discuss the situation, making recommendations to the parties to reach settlement by peaceful means, investigating the situation and by acting as a channel for quiet diplomacy. In this chapter, focus is on the mediation and conciliatory efforts of Togo and France and the role performed by regional and international bodies notably the UNO, OAU, EU, the Customs and Economic Union of Central African States (UDEAC) and the LCBC.

The Role of the Lake Chad Basin Commission

The LCBC was created by Nigeria, Niger, Chad and Cameroon on May 22, 1964 at Fort Lamy (old appellation for N'Djamena), Chad.[1] Article VII of its statute stipulates that member states commit themselves to maximally facilitate navigation and transportation in the Lake and to ensure the navigability, security and control of the Basin.

Following incidents between Cameroon and Nigeria in the Lake Chad region in 1983, an extraordinary summit of the LCBC was summoned in Lagos from July 21-23, 1983; at the initiative of the Heads of State of Nigeria and Cameroon; Shehu Shagari and Paul

---

1. In July 2011, the LCBC was composed of six member states—Cameroon, Central African Republic, Chad, Libya, Niger, and Nigeria.

Biya respectively. At the meeting, the Heads of State conferred on the LCBC the power to treat certain security and frontier questions and that the Commission should meet regularly to treat such matters.[2] Two Sub Commissions were created to study security and frontier problems in the region. The experts studied the matter and proposed that there should be the demarcation of the Cameroon – Nigeria frontier in the Lake Chad region.[3]

The demarcation process kicked off in 1984 but in 1987, other trans-frontier incidents cropped up between Nigeria and Cameroon in the region. In February 1987, Cameroonian villages along Lake Chad were invaded by Nigerians sufficiently trained and armed with machetes and in November 1987, the Nigerian army occupied the Cameroonian Islands of Faransia, Darack I and II near Lake Chad.[4]

These incidents did not deter the LCBC from continuing with the demarcation process. The mapping and pillar emplacement were undertaken by the IGN – FI under the auspices of the Commission. Seven principal pillars and 68 secondary pillars were planted.[5] The results of the work were presented at the 7th conference of Heads of State and Government of the LCBC in 1990 but, because of some lapses in the work done, the experts were asked to go back to the field. There was a problem in the determination of the average point at the Ebeji River whose bifurcation varies from season to season. As a consequence, Cameroon and Nigeria were in dispute over which branch should be taken as the principal one. In a bid to reach a compromise, the LCBC experts fixed the mouth of the Ebeji River at a point situated at equal distance from the two channels of the river with the participation of Nigerian and Cameroonian representatives.

During the 8th summit of the LCBC in Abuja, Nigeria on March 23, 1994, the Heads of State were informed of the completion of the

---

2. ICJ Judgement of June 11, 1998 on Nigerian Preliminary Objections, *http: // www. icj-cij.com.*, retrieved on 23/07/10.

3. Ibid.

4. The Government of Cameroon, *Document on the Bakassi Dispute*, p. 12.

5. ICJ Judgement of June 11, 1998.

work on the field. The demarcation documents were to be ratified by Cameroon and Nigeria. But in 1996, Nigeria refused to ratify the outcome of the work. Cameroon on her part deposited an instrument of ratification on December 22, 1997. As a result of Nigerian non ratification of the work, the Heads of State and Government Summit of the Commission in N'jamena, Chad on July 28, 2000, did not have the question of frontier delimitation in the Lake Chad region in its agenda. The refusal by Nigeria to ratify the final report produced by experts commissioned by the LCBC to demarcate the Cameroon–Nigeria boundary in the Lake Chad region did not however invalidate the documents which she participated in preparing. These demarcation documents therefore constituted the legal bases for the two parties with regard to the mapping of their common boundary. This is more important given that the experts of the LCBC relied on former instruments notably the Thomson – Marchand Declaration of 1929 – 30; annexed to the Henderson – Fleuriau Exchange of Notes of 1931. In its judgement of October 10, 2002, the ICJ recognized the work of the LCBC done with the accord of Nigeria and Cameroon.

The Role of the Organization of African Unity

The OAU intervened in the border dispute in 1981 following the clash between Cameroonian and Nigerian coast guards and in 1994 following Nigeria's invasion of the Bakassi Peninsula. Following the May 16, 1981 border misunderstandings between Cameroon and Nigeria, the Nigerian government decided to report the matter to the OAU. The OAU Commission of Mediation, Conciliation and Arbitration established by Article 19 of the OAU Charter and signed by 33 states in 1964 was to hear the case. The matter was however not brought before the Commission. Therefore in protest, the Nigerian President, Shehu Shagari boycotted the 18th OAU summit in Nairobi, Kenya in July 1981. At the summit, the matter was not officially tabled for discussion. Some Heads of State like Abdou Diouf of Senegal, Sekou Toure of Guinea, Gnassingbe Eyadema of Togo and Felix Houphouet Boigny of Ivory Coast proposed that a Commission of five states be constituted to mediate between

Cameroon and Nigeria. Cameroon welcomed the proposal but Nigeria was against such an initiative. With this deadlock, a number of Heads of State proposed to mediate between Cameroon and Nigeria, but the proposal did not see the light of day.

Following the weakness of the Commission of Mediation, Conciliation and Arbitration, ad hoc Commissions of the Assembly of Heads of State and Government and the Council of Ministers substituted this original mechanism. Although the OAU continuously used these ad hoc Commissions to arbitrate on disputes; this was a deviation from the Charter provision of the organization on conflict management. With time, the use of Eminent Persons Committee, good offices of the OAU Chairman and those of the Secretary General became customary in the management and resolution of conflicts among OAU members.[6]

In the border dispute between Cameroon and Nigeria; the Chairman and Secretary General of the Organization used their good offices to reconcile the protagonists. The OAU Secretary General, Edem Kodjo shuttled between Yaounde and Lagos. Meanwhile, the Chairman, Kenyan President, Daniel Arap Moi dispatched his Minister of Foreign Affairs, Robert Ouko to Yaounde in company of Alfred Machayo, Kenyan Ambassador to Lagos and Bernard Adoundo, Director of the African Department in the Kenyan Ministry of Foreign Affairs. The delegation was received by President Ahmadou Ahidjo on July 14, 1981.[7]

Through this initiative, peace was restored and the two countries solved the matter through bilateral diplomatic means in November 1982. But, twelve years later, Nigeria marched her troops into Cameroon's Bakassi Peninsula in December 1993 and February 1994 and the OAU again intervened in the matter from 1994-96.

Following the outbreak of hostilities in the Bakassi Peninsula in 1994, Yaounde formally petitioned the OAU on February 28, 1994 in

---

6. Lukong Keneth Mengjo, "From the OAU to the AU — What Lessons from African Conflicts?" *Annales des Faculté des Sciences Juridiques et Politiques*, Université de Dschang, Tome 12, 2002, pp. 292 – 295.

7. *Cameroon Tribune*, n⁰ 2126 (French edition), Mercredi 15 Juillet 1981.

conformity with Article III(4) of the Charter pertaining to the peaceful settlement of disputes by negotiation, mediation, conciliation or arbitration. The dispute was heard by a new organ; the Mechanism of Conflict Prevention, Management and Resolution, put in place during the 29th ordinary session of the Conference of Heads of State and Government in Cairo in June 1993 to replace the Commission of Mediation, Conciliation and Arbitration.[8] In this process, the OAU Secretary General in consultation with the parties involved in the conflict had to deploy efforts and take all appropriate initiatives to prevent, manage and resolve the conflict (paragraph 22 of the Cairo Declaration). The organization mandated the Secretary General, Salim Ahmed Salim on March 11, 1994 to follow up the situation and get in contact with the conflicting parties.

On March 24 and 25, 1994, a Ministerial Meeting was scheduled in Addis Ababa under the aegis of this new organ. Cameroon was represented in the six–hours meeting by her Minister of External Relations, Ferdinand Leopold Oyono; and Nigeria by her Minister of Foreign Affairs, Baba Gana Kingibe. After the deliberations, the OAU called on Nigeria and Cameroon to bilaterally and peacefully resolve the conflict. It also demanded that Nigerian troops retreat to frontier lines inherited from colonialism and called on both parties to respect the sovereignty and territorial integrity of each state. Finally, it mandated the OAU Secretary General to report back to the Organ within a month on the level of execution of these decisions.

The OAU Secretary General, Salim Ahmed Salim, intensified diplomatic offensives after this meeting to find a definitive solution to the problem. In consonance to the prescriptions contained in the OAU Organ on the Mechanism for Prevention, Management and

---

8. The mechanism is funded from the Peace Fund set up by the OAU; to be financed from 5 % OAU regular budgetary appropriation which should not be less than 1.000.000 US dollars; and from voluntary contributions from African and non African sources. The Fund was officially launched on November 18, 1993 during the first ordinary session of the organ. See Mengjo, "From the OAU to the AU" p. 296 and Niandou Aougui, "Le Mécanisme de Prevention, de Gestion et de Règlement des conflits de l'OAU face au Conflit en Afrique: cas du Burundi, Rwanda et de Bakassi". Rapport de stage Diplomatique, university of Yaounde II, IRIC, 1997, p. 15.

Resolution of Conflicts, pertaining to the fact that the organization could deploy civil and military observation and verification missions for a limited specified period; the Secretary General dispatched a delegation on April 25, 1994 led by his deputy, Zambian born, Mapuranga, to visit Yaounde, Abuja and the Bakassi Peninsula. Her mission was to appraise the issue and report back to the organization. Other members of the OAU delegation included Mme Adoa Coleman and Salah Awad.

The mission first went to Lome, Togo and concerted with President Eyadema who was mediating in the dispute. From Togo, the mission went to Nigeria and held talks with Nigerian authorities who expressed their disagreement over the inspection visit to Bakassi.[9] The team arrived Yaounde on April 25, 1994 and the following day (April 26), it had a working session with Cameroonian authorities. It first met with authorities in the Ministry of External Relations and then continued to the National Assembly for a working session with experts notably members of the Mixed Boundary Commission of Cameroon and Nigeria, cartographic specialists, diplomats and security personnel. In attendance were the Cameroon Acting Ambassador to Nigeria, Samuel Libock Mbey, the Director of the Africa–Asia Affairs at MINREX, Basile Messobot Sep, Rear Admiral Ngouah Ngally and General James Tabe Tataw among others.

A delegation from Nigeria was to join the OAU mission and the Cameroon delegation so that the tripartite joint team proceeds to the Bakassi Peninsula on April 27, 1994. The three delegations (Nigeria-OAU-Cameroon) effectively met at Limbe, Cameroon on the agreed date for the joint visit to the peninsula. Right after lunch, the leader of the Nigerian delegation complained that 'there was no need going to Bakassi because as brothers we can solve the problem amicably.'[10] The Cameroon delegation including General James Tataw, Rear Admiral Ngally, South West Governor, Oben Peter Ashu and Cameroon's Acting Ambassador to Nigeria, Samuel Libock Mbey

---

9. Ngniman, *Nigeria-Cameroun, La Guerre Permanente?* p.143.

10. *Cameroon Tribune*, n⁰ 6184/2473, Monday, September 16, 1996.

however proceeded to the Bakassi Peninsula where they visited Idabato I. The Cameroonian military authorities in Idabato I revealed to the press that Nigerian officials did not entertain such a visit because all avenues to iron out a bilateral solution to the conflict have not yet been exhausted.The Nigerian volte face frustrated the attempt by the very first international body to visit the peninsula since its occupation by Nigerian forces on February 18, 1994. Therefore, the team was unable to prepare a comprehensive file on the affair, to be presented in the planned session of the Central Organ of the Mechanism for Prevention, Management and Resolution of Conflicts slated for May 1994. Therefore, Nigerian dilatory and diversionary tactics and confusion worked against the settlement of the dispute.

Although the OAU did not complete its mission as a result of Nigerian intransigence, tension temporarily reduced in the peninsula. This was confirmed by the OAU Secretary General, Dr. Ahmed Salim when he visited Yaounde from November 28 – 30, 1994 to assess the level of preparation by Cameroon to host the 32nd OAU summit in July 1996; a summit the Nigerian Head of State, General Abacha did not attend. Although Abacha's absence from the summit was linked to the Bakassi problem, the explosive political situation in Nigeria and growing international isolation equally made Abacha to feel unsafe to leave Abuja.

The Role of the United Nations Organization

Two UN Organs were directly involved in the management of the border dispute. They included the Security Council which was seised on the dispute and the Secretariat whose Secretary General used his good offices by taking steps publicly and in private in the interest of preventive diplomacy to prevent the dispute from escalating into war.

On February 28, 1994, Cameroon's President, Paul Biya seised the UN Security Council following the 1993 and 1994 incidents in Bakassi. This was in accordance with Article 35(1) of the UN Charter which stipulates that any member of the UN may bring any dispute to the attention of the Security Council. The Council is bestowed this responsibility in Article 24(1) of the UN Charter wherein member states confer on the Council the primary responsibility for the maintenance of international peace and security. From this Article therefore, the principal functions for the maintenance of international peace and security go to the Security Council while the residual function go to the Assembly.[11] Again, the procedural primacy which has its priority in Article 12(1) equally obliges the Assembly to abstain from making recommendations on any dispute assigned to the Security Council unless it so requests. As a consequence, during the Cameroon–Nigeria border dispute, the UN General Assembly did not make any recommendations since the Security Council did not request it to do so.

When a complaint concerning a threat to peace is brought before the Council, the Council's first action is usually to recommend that the parties try to reach agreement by peaceful means.[12] In some cases, the Council itself undertakes investigation and mediation (Article 34 of the Charter) or makes recommendations on the terms of settlement of the dispute (Article 37(2) and 38 of the Charter). The Council can also create Commissions in charge of mediation between the conflicting parties or request the Secretary General to do so or to use his good offices. It can also apply non–military actions notably economic sanctions and the severance of diplomatic relations (Article 41 of the Charter) or coercive military action (Article 42 of the Charter).

In the Cameroon–Nigeria border dispute case, the UN Security Council on February 22, 1996 expressed its position on the dispute

---

11. These functions however overlap. The UN General Assembly adopted on November 3, 1950, Resolution 377(V), entitled "Uniting for Peace", also called the Dean Acheson Resolution after its promoter, the American Secretary of State. The Resolution spells out that if the Security Council because of lack of unanimity of the Permanent Members fails to exercise its primary responsibility for the maintenance of international peace and security, the General Assembly shall consider that matter immediately in order to maintain or restore international peace and security. The resolution instituted a system of collective security which survived the Korean War (which it was designed to solve) to become a Permanent UN instrument and superimposing itself in the Charter.

12. *Basic Facts About the United Nations* (New York: UN Department of Public Information, 1992), p. 11.

following a second complaint by Cameroon to the Council after the February 3, 1996 skirmishes in the Bakassi Peninsula. The Council called on the two parties to; respect the Kara Accord reached in Togo(to be discussed later), refrain from further violence, return to positions occupied before the matter was taken to The Hague, redouble efforts to search for a peaceful settlement, welcome bilateral and regional efforts and finally called on the Secretary General to send a fact-finding mission to meet the conflicting parties, monitor the matter closely and report to the Council the results of the fact-finding mission and any other significant developments.[13] On this score, the UN Secretary General, Boutros Boutros-Ghali who had since February 5, 1996 called on Nigeria and Cameroon to peacefully settled the dispute; sent a special envoy, Assistant Secretary Charged with Special Affairs, Lakhdar Brahimi to Yaounde and Abuja in May 1996 to convince the disputing parties to avoid the use of arms and to accept the ICJ to pursue the case.

The UN Security Council equally undertook to investigate the case in consonance with Article 34 of the UN Charter which accords the right to the Council to investigate any dispute or any situation which might lead to international friction or endanger the maintenance of international peace and security. Before undertaking this investigation, the Council had to consider the procedures for settlement that have already been adopted by Cameroon and Nigeria as spelt out in Article 36(2) of the UN Charter. It should be recalled that Cameroon and Nigeria attempted to settle the dispute bilaterally, but there was no breakthrough as Cameroon continued to insist on the withdrawal of Nigerian troops from her territory of Bakassi before a summit meeting of the Heads of State of Nigeria and Cameroon; a condition Nigeria was not ready to fulfill. Equally, the mediation and conciliation efforts of Togo, France and the OAU were facing substantial attenuations. Another disposition the Council could have taken before ordering an investigation was to find out if this measure would include the demand for reports, the audition of

---

13. Paraphrase of the letter from the Security Council Chairperson, Mrs. Madeleine Albright to Presidents Abacha and Biya dated February 29, 1996. See *Cameroon Tribune*, n⁰ 6184/2473, Monday, September 16, 1996.

witnesses, and the dispatch of commissions of inquiry or other measures.

The UN Security Council launched an investigation of the dispute in September 1996. Such an investigation can either be an ordinary or a special one. An ordinary investigation requires that the Council finds out about the state of things and then analyze them while a special investigation necessitates that the Council assesses if the prolongation of the dispute or situation is likely to endanger international peace and security. The Security Council fact-finding mission to Yaounde, Abuja and the Bakassi Peninsula was a special one. Clues for this conclusion are contained in a letter from the Security Council chairperson Mrs Madeleine Albright dated February 29, 1996 and addressed to Presidents Abacha and Biya. In the letter, she insinuated that the fact-finding mission was to "monitor this matter closely and report ... any other significant developments."[14] The warding of the letter shows that the investigation was more ambitious and aimed at the qualification of the situation, a characteristic that augur well with special unlike ordinary investigations.

The UN Security Council's fact-finding mission, dispatched by its Secretary General, Boutros Boutros-Ghali in September 1996 was led by Omar Alim of Indonesian nationality. Other members of the delegation included: Willy Wanstraelen (Belgian), Mpazi Simjela (Zambian) and Mme N'Tumba Makombo (Zairean). The mission visited Yaounde, Abuja and the Bakassi Peninsula. According to Omar Alim, their mission was to know the confidence of Yaounde and Abuja in the ICJ and to try to reduce tension in the Bakassi Peninsula.[15] Meanwhile, on the invitation of the Cameroon President, Paul Biya, the new UN Secretary General, Kofi Annan, who took up service on January 1, 1997, visited Cameroon from May 1 – 3, 2000. In a press conference on May 3, 2000, he emphasized on the need for the parties in conflict to seek for a peaceful settlement to the border dispute.

---

14. *Cameroon Tribune*, n⁰ 6184/2473, Monday, September 16, 1996.

15. Ibid.

The initiatives of the UN were limited to declarations and recommendations before and after sounding the opinion of the parties in dispute. Its call on the two parties to have confidence in the ICJ, and to try to reduce tension in the peninsula did not pay dividends as tension remained high following renewed skirmishes in the peninsula in February 1996. Meanwhile, Nigeria continued to question the admissibility of the Cameroon suit and the competence of the ICJ to hear it. Therefore, the UN initiative did not have a real impact in the management of the dispute as its recommendations were not enforceable.

The Role of the European Union

The Maastricht Treaty[16] creating the EU sanctioned the role of the organization in major political initiatives in the world. This is done through one of its institutions, the European Council which inter alia deals with current international issues through the Common Foreign and Security Policy (CPSP); a mechanism devised to allow member states to align their diplomatic positions and present a united front.[17] That is, a sort of caucusing wherein a common stand is taken against the actions of countries with the intention of influencing them into the political mores and folkways of international law. The Council meets at least twice a year.

During the Cameroon–Nigeria border dispute, the EU through declarations and quiet diplomacy mounted pressure on the conflicting parties to rethink on a peaceful way out of their dispute. In March 1994, the EU adopted a Resolution on the Bakassi Peninsula affair in which it recommended a solution by arbitration or mediation, and condemned the concentration of troops on one side of the border. Though this resolution highly irritated Nigerian

---

16. The Treaty creating the EU was signed by member states in Maastricht, Austria on February 7, 1992. After a series of referenda in member states, the treaty was finally ratified and it entered into force on November 1, 1993 creating the EU. The community had 25 members as of July 2011.

17. Article 20 (1, 2) of the Single European Act; pertaining to a Common Foreign Policy.

authorities, it helped in the months ahead to cause Nigeria to face the ICJ as she saw the world gradually turning against her action.

When skirmishes broke between Nigerian and Cameroonian forces in the Bakassi Peninsula on February 3, 1996, the Cameroon Minister of External Relations, Ferdinand Leopold Oyono, wrote to the EU to inform it on the incident. He also met with the Italian Ambassador in Yaounde, Pietro Lonardo, on February 6, 1996, given that Italy was occupying the Presidency of the EU at the time.[18] In response, the EU issued a communiqué on February 20, 1996 deploring the recourse to the use of military action by the conflicting parties. The communiqué published by the Italian Embassy went ahead to make recommendations as the following paraphrase of the communiqué indicates:

> The union invites the parties in confrontation to abstain from all military intervention in abidance by the international law and particularly by the Charter of the United Nations and expresses its wish that a peaceful solution be found to the dispute through the recourse to the International Court of Justice. The European Union requests the parties to revert to the positions that they held prior to the appeal to the Court of Justice.[19]

The EU communiqué was published at the time Nigeria had succumbed to the compulsory jurisdiction of the ICJ since December 13, 1995 when she raised preliminary objections to Cameroon's suit in the place of a counter memoire. It also came at the time Cameroon had asked the Court on February 12, 1996 to indicate conservatory measures following the skirmishes in Bakassi between the armies of Cameroon and Nigeria. Therefore, the EU stance was in consonance with current developments and the respect of international law.

---

18. *Cameroon Tribune*, n⁰ 6.033/2322, Wednesday, February 7, 1996. The Presidency of the EU is held for six months beginning on January 1, and July 1, each year.

19. *Cameroon Tribune*, n⁰, 6.042/2331, Thursday, February 22, 1996.

The Role of the Customs and Economic Union of Central African States

Following the outbreak of hostilities between Cameroon and Nigeria in 1993/94, the Heads of State of UDEAC[20] met in an informal meeting in Libreville, Gabon on February 28, 1994 and called on the conflicting parties to exercise moderation and resort to the peaceful settlement of the dispute. The Heads of State designated President Omar Bongo of Gabon to mediate between Abuja and Yaounde. President Bongo however did not take any overt action to mediate between the conflicting parties.

Three probable reasons prompted President Bongo to take such a position. First, UDEAC's principal objective was economic integration. Although member states signed a convention of monetary cooperation with France in November 1972 to guarantee the external convertibility of their currency, the CFA franc; it did not act as a multidimensional Economic and Monetary Community. Therefore, unlike the Economic Community of West African States (ECOWAS) which previewed in Article 58 of its Statute the putting in place of a mechanism for security and stability in the sub region,[21] UDEAC did not have such ambitions. Therefore, the absence of such a structure prevented President Bongo from pursuing his mediation mission under the aegis of UDEAC. Second, the conflicting parties were found in two economic regions; Cameroon in UDEAC and Nigeria in ECOWAS. President Bongo from a modest Economic Union therefore found it difficult to mediate in the

---

20. The Treaty creating UDEAC was signed in Brazzaville, Congo on December 8, 1964. The founding members were; Cameroon, Central African Republic, Congo, Gabon and Chad. In 1984, Equatorial Guinea became the sixth member state. On March 16, 1994, the member states met in N'Djamena, Chad and created the Economic and Monetary Community of Central Africa (CEMAC). In their 33rd summit in February 1998, the Heads of State proclaimed the dissolution of UDEAC. The first CEMAC summit was held in Malabo, Equatorial Guinea from June 23-25, 1999.

21. Meeting in Banjul, Gambia on July 23 and 24, 1998, ECOWAS member states put in place a mechanism for Prevention, Management and Resolution of Conflicts and the Maintenance of Peace and Security.

dispute given that Nigeria was an economic giant from a preponderant Economic Union. Finally, it was probable that Bongo's mediation efforts were supplanted by those of President Eyadema of Togo.

The Mediation and Conciliation Efforts of Togo and France

Mediation is a process by which an impartial third party assists parties in a dispute to explore and understand their differences and if possible, settle them.[22] In this process, the parties, not the mediator, dictate the terms of any agreement. The job of the mediator or conciliator runs through four non sequential but reinforcing and cumulative phases: contacts, deadlock, proposal and implementation. The first phase continues after the second begins and both continue through the third and then the fourth.[23] In this process, the mediator act as a formulator, communicator and even manipulator.

The mediation efforts of Togo

Togo mediated in the dispute following the outbreak of hostilities over the Bakassi Peninsula in 1994. On March 3, 1994, the Togolese President, Gnassingbe Eyadema launched a mediation initiative. This initiative came barely 15days after the Nigerian attacks on Cameroon army units in the Bakassi Peninsula and Cameroon army riposte. President Eyadema shuttled between Yaounde and Abuja for high-level talks on the Bakassi issue. He arrived Yaounde on March 3, 1994, and left for Abuja, the same day. These formal contacts were intended to sound the opinion of both countries in order to sort out a compromise based on evidence and technical assessment. During such contacts, as Zartman has pointed out, President Eyadema equally had the task of rendering the conflict option unattractive and

---

22. John Crawley and Katherine Graham, *Mediation for Managers: Resolving Conflict and Rebuilding Relationships at Work* (London: Nicholas Brealey Publishing, 2002), p. 3.

23. Zartman, *Ripe for Resolution*, p. 238.

then deflects the parties from competing attempts to impose unilateral solutions.[24]

This mediation initiative was done early enough in conformity with the prescriptions of experts on the subject. In that line, Zartman writes; "Mediation like conflict prevention works best early, right after the first flare of the conflict and as a simple stalemate sets in. As the conflict continues, the parties become use to it."[25] President Eyadema set the stage for the mediation process and the mantle was taken by his Minister of Foreign Affairs and Cooperation, Fambare Ouattara Natchaba who shuttled between Yaounde and Abuja. He visited Yaounde on March 9, 1994, and was received in audience by President Paul Biya on March 11. After the audience, he declared that negotiations were still going on and that he was optimistic about a peaceful settlement to the conflict.During these visits, the Togolese Foreign Minister was expected to act both as a communicator and formulator. As communicator, he had to deliver to Cameroon, Nigeria's agreement to an outcome that was attractive to her, and then deliver to Nigeria, Cameroon's agreement to the outcome that was also attractive to her. As a formulator, Fambare Ouattara also tried to come out with an outcome that was attractive to both Cameroon and Nigeria. On this score, he sold to the parties the idea of bilateral settlement to the dispute.

Bilateral reconciliation as a result of Togo's mediation started in earnest during the OAU Heads of State summit in Tunis on June 13, 1994 when Presidents Paul Biya of Cameroon and Sani Abacha of Nigeria met at the Abou Nawas hotel in the presence of President Eyadema. According to the outcome of the meeting dubbed the Tunis Peace Initiative, Foreign Ministers of the two countries were to meet in the Northern Togolese city of Kara to prepare the groundwork for the Biya-Abacha summit which was slated for July 18, 1994. The Foreign Ministers of the two countries; Ferdinand Leopold Oyono for Cameroon and Baba Gana Kingibe for Nigeria

---

24. Zartman, *Ripe for Resolution*, p. 2.

25. -----------, "Conflict Resolution: Prevention, Management and Resolution," p. 315.

met in Kara from July 4-6, 1994 for the preparatory meeting with experts of Cameroon and Nigeria.

The outcome of the Kara meeting was the preparation of a five-point accord which was to be signed by the two Heads of State in Togo on July 18. The Accord code-named Kara I appeared thus: 1) the commitment of the two parties to withdraw their troops from all areas of tension and as concerns the Bakassi Peninsula, to pull them back to the positions held before December 21, 1993 in accordance with a mutually agreed calendar by the two parties; 2) the putting in place of a neutral interposition troop and surveillance force whose composition and mission will be defined in a Common Accord by the two parties; 3) peaceful return of the displaced civilian population in the Bakassi Peninsula; 4) the maintenance of the existing Cooperation Agreements with regard to navigation and free access to the various ports; and 5) the setting up of a Tripartite Technical Commission—Cameroon,Togo,Nigeria—charged with the implementation of this agreement which would meet at venues and periods to be agreed upon by the two parties.[26]

This text was never signed by the two Heads of State in Togo on July 18, 1994 as stipulated because President Abacha could not make it to Kara. This was particularly because of the deteriorating socio-political situation in his country following the annulled Presidential elections of June 12, 1993 which Chief Moshood Abiola was presumed winner. Abiola declared himself President and was imprisoned for the act. Former President retired General Olusegun Obasanjo and second in command, Major-General Oladipo Diya and many more were equally imprisoned for their roles in alleged coup d'états against General Abacha. As a result of this internal situation, it was therefore unlikely that Abacha could feel safe enough to leave Abuja for Togo.

Following the failure of the Heads of State summit in Kara on July 18, 1994, the new Togolese Minister for Foreign Affairs and Cooperation, Boumbera Alasounouma shuttled between Yaounde and Abuja to intensify mediation for the Biya-Abacha summit under

---

26. *Cameroon Tribune*, no. 6040/2329, Monday, February 19, 1996.

the aegis of Eyadema. His mission was intended to sustain the relative peace in the Bakassi Peninsula and to seek a peaceful resolution of the dispute. The two parties returned to the negotiation table probably after a realization that matters could swiftly get worse following the outbreak of another skirmish on February 3, 1996 between Nigerian and Cameroonian troops near Idabato in the disputed Bakassi Peninsula that led to several casualties on both sides. This came at the time that both countries were already feeling the pinch of keeping huge numbers of troops in Bakassi. Nigeria which in 1994; because of economic crisis, reduced her troops from the 1986 level which stood at 94.000 to 85.500 deployed 7000 soldiers in the Bakassi Peninsula.[27] Meanwhile, Cameroon which had a total of 12.000 soldiers in 1994 deployed 3.000 of these soldiers in the peninsula.[28]

The two parties returned to the negotiation table in February 1996 following appeals from Eyadema in separate correspondences to Cameroonian and Nigerian leaders to diffuse renewed tension following the February 3, 1996 skirmishes. He also exhorted the two countries to continue negotiations at resolving the dispute. In response to this invitation, the Ministers of Foreign Affairs of Nigeria, Cameroon and Togo met at Kara from February 16-17, 1996 to prepare a new accord under the auspices of President Eyadema. Chief Tom Ikimi sat for Nigeria, Ferdinand Oyono for Cameroon and Barry Moussa Barque for Togo. The two ministers of Cameroon and Nigeria were first received separately by President Eyadema, then jointly. In an accord signed on February 17, 1996 code-named Kara II, the two Ministers accepted to stop hostilities and recognized that the dispute was pending at the ICJ. They also agreed to meet again in the first week of March in order to prepare the summit of the Heads

---

27. *Jeune Afrique*, no. 1871, Novembre 13-19, 1999, Cited in Hamadou, "La Politique Camerounaise", p. 224.

28. ----------------, no. 1731, Mars 10-16, 1994. Cited in Hamadou, "La Politique Camerounaise", p. 227.

of State of Nigeria and Cameroon under the auspices of President Eyadema to continue with his mediation efforts.[29]

Eighteen months later in August 1997, the Togolese Minister for Foreign Affairs and Cooperation wrote to his Cameroonian and Nigerian counterparts to propose a summit of their respective Presidents. A draft joint declaration was even submitted in advance to the parties, with the attention of the UN for examination.[30] The summit was scheduled for September 5, 1997. But with the upcoming Presidential election in Cameroon billed for October 1997, President Biya wrote to Eyadema to express his regrets not to take part in the talks because of the election.[31] This therefore marked the end of Togo's mediation efforts for the peaceful settlement of the Cameroon-Nigeria border dispute over the Bakassi Peninsula.

Togo's mediation efforts were thwarted by a number of factors. The role of President Eyadema and his Ministers of Foreign Affairs and Cooperation was limited to that of communicators and formulators. Given Togo's clout in Africa vis-à-vis Cameroon and Nigeria, she could not act as manipulator either verbally or materially. Togo has a surface area of 56.785 sq km with a population of about 4 million inhabitants in the 1990s; being one of the smallest country in Africa. Cameroon on the other hand has a surface area of 475.442 sq km with a population of about 15million inhabitants in the 1990s while Nigeria's surface area is 923.728sq km with a population of about 130million in the 1990s, and being the most populated country in Africa. Togo's small size and modest production notably of cocoa and coffee could not permit her to mount pressure on the leaders of the conflicting parties to sign let alone implement the accords prepared by their Foreign Ministers in concert with Togolese authorities. Zartman contends that "the implementation stage [of an agreement] requires another expenditure of vigilance and perhaps

---

29. See the full text of the press release at the end of the Ministerial Meeting in Appendix 1.

30. Aji James, "The Dynamics of Cameroon-Nigeria Relations." p.51.

31. *La Nouvelle Expression*, Special Bakassi, no. 225. Cited in Hamadou,"La Politique Camerounaise", p. 201.

pressure from the conciliator."[32] This pressure can only be exercised if there is strength and will. Strength comes from the transformation of resources into capabilities. Capabilities are thought of in tangible terms—they are measurable, weighable and quantifiable assets.[33] Therefore, Togo had the will but lacked the capabilities. Togo's mediation efforts therefore had but the personal weight of President Eyadema as one of the oldest African leaders with a long experience in mediation efforts.[34]

Another impediment to Togo's mediation effort was the lack of a diplomatic presence in Yaounde. In the 1990s, Togo only had a consulate in Douala. On the other hand, Cameroon's Ambassador to Togo was non residential. Zartman has contended that "effective preemptive action requires a diplomatic presence."[35] Therefore, the lack of such a diplomatic presence in Yaounde impeded the effective use of quiet diplomacy in Togo's mediation initiative.

Finally, the failure of Togo's mediation effort was also the result of Eyadema's legitimacy. President Eyadema launched the mediation initiative at the time he was facing social unrest at home especially because of his lamentable human rights records and flawed elections. The international community treated his country as a pariah state for much of the 1990s. He was elected in 1993 and re-elected in 1998 with ballot either boycotted or contested by the opposition. He even

---

32. Zartman, *Ripe for Resolution*, p. 224.

33. Niall Ferguson, "What is Power"? http://www.hoover.org, retrieved on 21/08/10.

34. Eyadema came to power on April 14, 1967 and died in power on February 5, 2005. In 1964, he mediated between Mobutu Sesse Seko of Zaire (now Democratic Republic of Congo) and Marien Ngouabi of Congo and played the same role in the imbroglio between Presidents Houphouet-Boigny, Omar Bongo and Yakubu Gowon following the recognition of Biafra by Ivory Coast and Gabon during the Nigerian civil war of 1967-70. In 1978 at Monrovia, he took part in the reconciliation effort between Sedar Senghor, Houphouet Boigny and Sekou Toure who had had relations at low ebb for 20 years.

35. Zartman, *Ripe for Resolution*, p. 239.

missed an assassination attempt in March 1994; the month and year the mediation efforts were launched. With these problems, it was unlikely that he could have succeeded. According to Zartman, mediation is a trilateral exercise of a delicate type because mediators can be expected to have interests in the management and resolution of the dispute like maintaining or improving their own relations.[36] Eyadema paradoxically offered his services towards resolving the dispute in order to cleanse his international image and correct the crisis of legitimacy that he was suffering in his country.

In spite of the failure of the Togolese mediation to cause the cessation of hostilities in the Bakassi Peninsula, the initiative brought to the limelight the will of the disputing parties to peacefully resolve the dispute. This pacific stance was dictated by the long standing historical and socio-cultural links between the two neighbouring countries which prompted the frontier populations to continue to interact peacefully at the time of the crisis. France exploited this pacifist stance in her conciliation efforts.

The French conciliation efforts

The French conciliatory role in the dispute varied greatly. Although her conciliatory role included that of communicator, formulator and manipulator; her role as manipulator was very much discernable. This was possible given her economic might and military power at the world stage. In the eighties and nineties when the dispute was raging on, France was a Great Power alongside countries like the USA, China, Japan, the United Kingdom of Great Britain and Russia. She was therefore able to influence the conflicting parties verbally and materially through pressure, threat or use of force and economic interaction. France's role in the border dispute was very much felt as from 1994. She played this role of conciliation amidst mutual fear and suspicion between her and Nigeria nursed from Nigeria's condemnation of the French Nuclear Test in the Sahara in

---

36. Zartman, "Conflict Resolution: Prevention, Management and Resolution", p. 312.

1963 and French support of the secessionist Biafra during the Nigerian civil war of 1967-70.

When hostilities erupted between Cameroon and Nigeria in the Bakassi Peninsula in February 1994, France sent a diplomatico-military mission to Cameroon on February 26, 1994 led by General Quesnot, Private Army Chief of Staff to the French President, François Mitterand. The mission was composed of Bruno Delaye, Adviser to French President on African and Madagascar Affairs; Jean Marc Rochereau de la Sablière, Director of African affairs in the Ministry of Foreign Affairs and Colonel Bentegeat. They were accompanied to the State House by French Ambassador to Cameroon, Gilles Vidal. The mission also traveled to Nigeria and held discussions with the Nigerian Foreign Minister, Baba Gana Kingibe.[37] This French mission shuttled between Yaounde and Abuja in order to sell France's intention to mediate in the dispute but Abuja was not in favour of the proposition, ostensibly because of its suspicion that France was on Cameroon's side.

Apart from the strained relations between France and Nigeria in the sixties and seventies, Nigeria doubted the sincerity of the French offer given the fact that France and Cameroon had a Technical and Military Assistance Accord signed in November 1960 and revised in February 1974. The accord spells out that France was to ensure the training and the equipping of the Cameroon army. The accord also allowed Cameroon to call in French troops to ensure its defence and even maintain internal peace. Nigeria's suspicion later seemed to hold water following military manoevres between France and Benin Republic which started in Benin; Nigeria's western neighbour. French parachutists equally arrived Yaounde for military manoevres with the Cameroon army. Efforts by the French authorities to explain that the joint military manoevres in Benin and Yaounde had been scheduled for a long time and had nothing to do with the conflict in Bakassi could not appease Abuja. Following these military manoevres, the

---

37. *Jeune Afrique*, no. 1732, March 17-23, 1994. Cited in Hamadou, "La Politique Camerounaise", p. 183.

Nigerian Foreign Minister, Kingibe vehemently accused France that she will be held responsible for the escalation of the Bakassi affair.[38]

Amidst this suspicion, France on February 28, 1994 made her position on the dispute known. She expressed her desire for peace to reign between the two countries and averred that appropriate means be taken to settle the problem in conformity with international law in the shortest possible time.[39] By evoking international law, France was in favour of the adjudication of the dispute by the ICJ, a position she confirmed by giving an exceptional aid of 2.6 million French francs to Cameroon[40] in support of her suit against Nigeria at The Hague deposited on March 29, 1994.

Although these French moves were perceived to be playing against her proposition to mediate in the dispute; they were trial balloons aimed at threatening Nigeria to cooperate in order for a multilateral solution to be found. This paradox of "over commitment" on one side of a dispute tend to hunt many mediators. In this line of thought, Zartman writes; "the mediator must not become over committed to one side in perception or in reality. The danger is often present, and most successful mediators skirt it rather than avoiding it completely."[41]

As the French and the international community continued to mount pressure on Nigeria, Elf Group, a French multinational company involved in oil exploitation in Nigeria and Cameroon, dispatched a mission to Cameroon on March 17, 1994 led by Philippe Jaffre. The mission concerted with President Paul Biya and discussed

---

38. *Cameroon Tribune*, no. 5550/1839, March 9, 1994.

39. Ibid.

40. Hamadou, "La Politique Camerounaise", p. 184.

41. Zartman, *Ripe for Resolution*, p. 235. The US and her Western associates mediated reconciliation after Shaba in the 1970s despite their close ties with Zaire (present day Democratic Republic of Congo) and their stained relations with Angola.

the Bakassi issue with him.[42] The Elf Group was to be the great beneficiary if peace reigned between Cameroon and Nigeria as Cameroon represented 20.000 barrels of Elf daily oil production and Nigeria, more than 135.000 barrels.[43] Given that France was an economic power house in Nigeria and Cameroon; together with the help of other multilateral actors—UN, ICJ, OAU and EU—she was able to block unilateral solutions by the parties while making joint solutions conceivable. Following the ICJ ruling of June 11, 1998 declaring it competent to hear the border dispute case, Nigeria progressively found favour with the French initiative to mediate in the border dispute.

The visit of the French President, Jacques Chirac to Nigeria and Cameroon in July 1999[44] was therefore the logical manifestation of her mediation initiative. Therefore, one can comfortably join Zartman in concluding that: "only time resolves conflicts but time needs some help."[45] Unexpectedly, the Nigerian High Commissioner to Cameroon on August 17, 2001 forwarded a correspondence to the Cameroon Minister of External Relations stating Nigeria's commitments to respect the judgement of the ICJ.[46] The successes registered by the French conciliation efforts paradoxically prompted the UN Secretary General, Kofi Annan to schedule a Tripartite Summit of Presidents Biya, Obasanjo and himself in the Parisian outskirts of St. Cloud in the presence of French President, Jacques Chirac. During this meeting, the two Heads of State inter alia committed themselves to respect the outcome of the ICJ verdict on the border dispute which was expected in the coming weeks or months. The Cameroon-Nigeria Joint Commission which held in

---

42. Hamadou, "La Politique Camerounaise", pp. 185-186.

43. Ibid. pp. 177 and 185.

44. *Cameroon Tribune*, no. 6897/3186, Monday, July 26, 1999.

45. Zartman, *Ripe for Resolution*, p. 237.

46. Amadou Ali, Cameroon's Agent to the ICJ, verbatim, February 18, 2002. See *Cameroon Tribune*, no. 7538/8827, Tuesday, February 19, 2002.

Abuja in September/October 2002, was a logical follow-up of this French initiative.

All these confidence building measures psychologically prepared the parties as they waited for the ICJ verdict on the border dispute case; which lasted from 1994 when Cameroon seised the Court till 2002 when the verdict was pronounced.

Chapter 4

The Settlement of the Dispute through Adjudication by the International Court of Justice, 1994 – 2002

Dispute settlement entails the resort to an independent adjudicator like the ICJ [1] to make an official decision about who is right. This is opposed to dispute resolution which entails the elimination of the causes of the underlying dispute with the agreement of the parties. The ICJ adjudication of the border dispute took eight years; from March 29, 1994 when Cameroon seised the Court till October 10, 2002, when the Court passed its verdict.

Cameroon's Suit and Nigeria's Preliminary Objections

Following the incidents of 1993 and 1994 by Nigerian armed forces in the Bakassi Peninsula, Cameroon filed a suit at the ICJ against Nigeria in March 1994. An additional suit was filed in June 1994. Cameroon prayed the Court to examine the two cases as one. In the place of a counter suit; Nigeria presented preliminary objections which the Court handled before proceeding with the case.

Cameroon's introductory suit

On March 29, 1994, Cameroon's Agent and Minister of Justice and Keeper of the Seals, Barrister Douala Moutome in company of two senior jurists and the Cameroon Ambassador to Belgium, Mrs Isabelle Bassong formally presented Cameroon's petition to the ICJ at The Hague. By that petition, Cameroon made a complaint against Nigeria for forcefully occupying her territory in Bakassi and called on the Court to put an end to this military occupation and to determine

---

1. The ICJ was established pursuant to chapter XIV, Articles 92 – 96 of the UN Charter. Article 92 specifies that the Court is "the principal judicial organ of the UN ", and provides that the Court shall function in accordance with a statute which forms an integral part of the UN Charter.

the reparations to be paid by Nigeria for damages inflicted on Cameroon following the occupation. She also prayed the Court to specify the course of the Maritime Boundary between itself and Nigeria from the point the two countries left it in 1975; right up to the outer limit that international law imposes on them to respect. This introductory suit equally recognized the competence of the compulsory adjudication jurisdiction of the Court following Nigeria and Cameroon adherence to it on August 14, 1965 and March 3, 1994 respectively, in accordance with Article 36(2) of its statute.

On June 6, 1994, Cameroon deposited an additional suit as an amendment to the March 29 introductory suit, asking the Court to delimit definitively the course of the entire boundary from Lake Chad to the sea. This additional complaint was communicated to Nigeria by the Registrar of the Court on June 7, 1994. In this additional suit, Cameroon made a complaint against Nigeria for violating the fundamental principles of the respect of frontiers inherited from colonialism as well as her legal engagements relating to the demarcation of their common frontier in the Lake Chad region. She equally raised the problem of Nigerian occupation of parts of her territory as a violation of conventional instruments and customary rights, and that Nigeria should evacuate these areas with no delay and without conditions. In this additional suit, Cameroon averred that Nigerian invasion of her territory was a violation of international law and therefore, she should repair these damages by paying an amount to be decided by the Court.[2] Cameroon's introductory suit was in conformity with Article 38(2) of the Court's statute which requires the plaintiff to succinctly present the case and furnish the complementary elements later.

Following the deposit of this introductory suit by Cameroon, the President of the Court, French born; Gilbert Guillaume scheduled a meeting with the Agents and Defense Counsels/Advocates of the parties on June 14, 1994. The Cameroon delegation to the meeting was led by her Agent and Minister of Justice, Douala Moutome while

---

2. ICJ Judgement of June 11, 1998 and, October 10, 2002, *http://www. icj-cij. org.* ,retrieved on 23/07/10.

that of Nigeria was led by her own Agent and Minister of Justice, Alhadji Abdullahi Ibrahim. During this meeting, the Cameroon Agent precised that the additional suit by Cameroon was simply an amendment to her introductory suit; a situation the Nigerian delegation leader and the Court in general did not find any problem in merging and examining the case as one.[3]

By an order of June 16, 1994, the Court fixed March 16 and December 18, 1995 respectively as the dates for the expiration for the deposit of memoires by Cameroon and Nigeria. Cameroon deposited her 127 point memoire with six annexes on March 16, 1995. On December 13, 1995, Nigeria in place of a counter memoire instead raised preliminary objections challenging the jurisdiction of the Court and the admissibility of Cameroon's claim. Meanwhile, by a letter of February 12, 1996, Cameroon presented to the Court, a petition of conservatory measures to avoid further skirmishes in Bakassi. Through an order on March 15, 1996, the Court reacted to this letter, calling on the two parties to halt all hostilities in the Bakassi Peninsula and equally effect a mission, envisaged by the UN Secretary General to the peninsula.[4]

Nigeria's preliminary objections and Court's verdict, June 1998

In law, preliminary objections are an incident of procedure and if they are considered, the judge does not hear the case.[5] Nigeria raised eight preliminary objections and the Court had to statutorily solve this procedural problem in conformity with Article 79(3) of its statute. By an order of January 10, 1996, the Court fixed May 15, 1996 as the date of expiration in which Cameroon had to answer in writing to these objections. Cameroon responded to these objections recognizing the competence of the Court to hear the case and called

---

3. ICJ Judgement of June 11, 1998.

4. ICJ Order of March 15, 1996, http: www. icj-cij. org. Retrieved on 23/07/10.

5. Guy Roger Eba'a, *Affaire Bakassi : Genèse, Evolution et Dénouement de l'Affaire de la Frontière Terrestre et Maritime Cameroun-Nigeria (1993-2002)* Yaoundé : Presses de l'Université Catholique d'Afrique Centrale, 2008, p. 34.

on the Court to fix the deadline for the next process in the examination of the case.

Since the Court did not have a judge each from Cameroon and Nigeria as required by Article 30(3) of its statute, ad hoc judges were chosen by the parties to represent them. Cameroon chose the Senegalese, Keba Mbaye while the Nigerian, Prince Bola Ajibola sat for his country. Hearing on Nigeria's preliminary objections opened on March 2 and ended on March 11, 1998. Hearing was presided over by the American judge, Stephen Schwebel. Laurent Esso led the Cameroon legal and technical team while Abdullahi Ibrahim led that of Nigeria. Seven of the eight preliminary objections were rejected. The objections and reasons for rejection were as follows.

First, Nigeria averred that Cameroon violated Article 36(2) of the ICJ statute pertaining to the time lapse to deposit a declaration with the UN Secretary General accepting the Court's compulsory jurisdiction and the period she deposited her suit. On this complaint, the Court explained that Cameroon accepted the Court's compulsory jurisdiction through its declaration with the UN Secretary General on March 3, 1994. It also notes that Nigeria did same on August 14, 1965. The Court went further to explain that there was no time lapse between the declaration of adherence to the Court and its seisure. The Court equally averred that, Nigeria unlike Great Britain did not protect herself against surprised complaints against her in the ICJ. The judgement equally made mention of the fact that on March 4, 1994, Nigeria expressed surprise that Cameroon was internationalizing the problem following Cameroon's seisure of the UN Security Council on February 28, 1994. As a consequence, she was aware of the moves by Cameroon to involve multilateral actors in the border dispute including the ICJ. With these precisions, the motion was rejected.

Second, Nigeria was of the opinion that although Cameroon had the right to seise the Court on the matter, it was uncalled for since the two countries for over 24 years had accepted obligatorily to solve their frontier problems through bilateral means. This was rejected by the Court on account that there is no deposition in the Court's statute which stipulates that until diplomatic initiatives must have been exhausted, a country in dispute with another cannot seise the

Court. The Court went ahead to precise that Cameroon had no accord with Nigeria which compels the two countries to solve their border disputes through bilateral diplomatic means.

In the third preliminary objection, the defendant while indicating her reservation on what will be concluded on the obligatory resort to bilateral means to solve frontier problems as indicated above; complaint that the frontier dispute in the Lake Chad region fell under the exclusive competence of the LCBC. And that the procedures laid down by the Commission were obligatory for all the parties. This was rejected on account that the LCBC did not have as goal to maintain international peace and security at the regional level. As a consequence, its role in the maintenance of peace and security does not tie with the provisions of chapter VIII of the UN Charter which Cameroon and Nigeria are signatory.[6] The Court went ahead to explain that the LCBC should not be taken as a tribunal or arbitration structure since it had never received exclusive competence to pronounce judgement on territorial disputes between Cameroon and Nigeria.

The fourth preliminary objection pertained to the incompetence of the Court to hear the matter since the LCBC already had competence in the Lake Chad region tripoint and especially as the settlement would affect Chad. This was rejected on the grounds that Cameroon's additional suit did not contain a specific request for the mapping of the tripoint in the Lake Chad region and the Lake itself. The judgement equally specified that the two countries were not contesting the frontier between Cameroon and Chad in the Lake and therefore the absence of Chad Could not disturb the Court from hearing the matter.[7]

In the fifth objection, Nigeria averred that without prejudging the question on the owner of the Bakassi Peninsula, Darack and the other islands inhabited by Nigerians in the Lake Chad region; there

---

6. Chapter VIII of the UN Charter refers to the specific powers granted to the Security Council for the maintenance of international peace and security.

7. The case between Libya and Chad over the Aozou strip was heard by the Court in 1994 in the absence of Niger.

was no dispute on the delimitation of the entire boundary from Lake Chad tripoint to the sea. She also stated that there was also no problem with the delimitation from the Lake Chad tripoint to Mount Kombon in the precincts of Bankim and from pillar 64 in the vicinity of Furu–Awa and then from pillar 64 to the sea. The Court rejected this count on the grounds that there were border conflicts in Darack and neighbouring islands and in Tipsan and the Bakassi Peninsula. According to the Court, the Bakassi conflict was to influence the Maritime Frontier between the two countries. The Court went ahead to precise that by contesting these areas, Nigeria put to cause the validity of the instruments mapping the frontier. Nigeria equally failed to answer satisfactorily on judicial bases the question from the President of the Court, Gilbert Guillaume, who wanted to know if there was another area she contested outside Darack and Bakassi as proof that they accepted the geo-coordinates in the rest of the boundary. As a result of these lapses in her defense, the Court rejected this fifth Nigeria's preliminary objection.

The sixth preliminary objection was focused on Nigerian international responsibility for damages inflicted on Cameroon following her military occupation of the Cameroon territory. Nigeria postulated the fact that because there was no precision on the dates, presumed incursions, incidents and dates they occurred; this count should be rejected. The Court ruled against this motion on account that Cameroon could still bring complementary elements as per Article 38(2) of the Court's statute.

In the seventh preliminary objection, Nigeria posited that there was no legal dispute concerning the delimitation of the Maritime Frontier between the two countries and consequently it was impossible to determine the Maritime Frontier before the hearing of the Bakassi case. To her, the delimitation of the Maritime Boundary can be done by the parties through an accord in conformity with international law. The Court rejected this complaint on account that the two countries undertook negotiations on the delimitation of their Maritime Boundary from 1970-75 culminating in the Maroua Declaration which had been recognized by Cameroon and rejected by Nigeria. The Court therefore concluded that the two countries were in dispute with regard to the Maritime Frontier.

Finally in the eighth complaint, Nigeria averred that the delimitation of the Maritime Boundary was to affect the rights and interests of third parties; referring to Equatorial Guinea and Sao Tome and Principe in the Gulf of Guinea. The Court concluded that from point G where negotiations had so far been reached by the two countries; the prolongation of the boundary seawards was definitely to affect the interests and rights of third parties. Therefore, the Court accepted this complaint so that the problem could be examined in detail during the hearing.

In its judgement on Nigeria's preliminary objections made public on June 11, 1998, the Court declared itself competent to hear the case and equally found the case admissible. Nigeria however requested the Court to interpret the judgement and this prompted the Court to issue a statement on March 25, 1999 noting that its preceding decision was perfectly clear and was not subject to interpretation. Therefore, on June 30, 1998, the Court went ahead and fixed March 31, 1999 as the new date of expiration for Nigeria to deposit its counter memoire. This deadline was extended to May 31, 1999 by an order issued by the Court on March 3, 1999. Nigeria deposited its counter memoire on May 26, 1999. Then, on June 30, 1999, the Court through an order acknowledged the receipt of the memoire. The Court then went ahead and fixed by order, April 4, 2000 as the deadline for Cameroon's replication to Nigeria's memoire and January 4, 2001 for Nigeria's rejoinder.

With these precisions, the Court fixed February 18, 2002 as the beginning date for oral proceedings. The detail calendar was also made available to the parties. The documents produced were also made accessible to the public. The hearing was in phases. The first phase lasted from February 18 – March 2, 2002. Cameroon presented her defense during this first phase on February 18, 19, 20, 21, 22, 25, and 26, 2002 while Nigeria presented her own defense on February 28, March 1, 4, 5, 6, 7, and 8, 2002. The second phase of hearing took 4 days. Cameroon took to the rostrum on March 11 and 12 and Nigeria followed on March 14 and 15, 2002. Equatorial Guinea then intervened on March 18 and made concluding statements on March 20, 2002. The last observations by Cameroon and Nigeria especially to react to Equatorial Guinea's intervention and making a summary of their stance took place on March 19, 20, and 21, 2002. The hearing was presided over by the President of the Court, Gilbert Guillaume. The Cameroon delegation was led by her Agent and Minister of Justice, Amadou Ali and that of Nigeria by her own Agent and Minister of Justice, Musa Elaya Abdullahi.

The Stance of Cameroon and Nigeria during the Oral Pleadings

The stance of Cameroon was contained in her memoire deposited at The Hague in March 1995 and that of Nigeria in her counter memoire deposited in May 1999. These memoires were exploited by the defense lawyers, experts and officials of the two countries during the public hearing of the case in February and March 2002. The border dispute concerned four sectors: the Lake Chad region, the Land Boundary area from Mount Kombon through pillar 64 to the sea, the Bakassi Peninsula and the Maritime Boundary area. In each of these sectors, the two countries presented diverse views and interpretations of legal instruments in place that either delimited or demarcated these areas. The two parties equally expressed varying opinions on the issue of Nigeria's international liability.

Dispute in the Lake Chad region up to Mount Kombon

Cameroon postulated that the delimitation of the zone was done during the period of the British rule in Nigeria and the Franco-British rule of their sectors of Cameroon from 1919 to 1931. On this score, Cameroon posited that the boundary in the Lake Chad region was delimited by Milner, British Secretary of State for Colonies and Henry Simon, French Minister for Colonies, on July 10, 1919 during the partition of German Cameroon after the First World War. This came to be known as the Milner-Simon Boundary Declaration. This boundary was later precised by Sir Graeme Thomson, Governor of the Colony and Protectorate of Nigeria and Paul Marchand, Commissioner of French Cameroon, on December 29, 1929 and

January 31, 1930.[8] Article 3-60 of this Thomson–Marchand Declaration defined the coordinates of the boundary delimitation as situated at longitude 14° 12' 11" 7 East and latitude 12° 32' 17" 4 North.[9] This Thomson-Marchand Declaration was annexed in the Exchange of Notes between Authur Henderson, British Foreign Minister and A. de Fleuriau, French Ambassador to London, on January 9, 1931.[10]

Nigeria on her part recognized the existence of these colonial treaties but averred that they were not sufficient to delimit the frontier in this region because of their ambiguity and inexactitude.[11] Nigeria justified this thesis by pointing out that in the Thomson-Marchand Declaration; their point of departure was the Ebeji River bifurcation which unfortunately varies from season to season thereby posing the problem of which branch should be taken as the principal one. Even further south; Nigeria averred, the delimitation in the locality of Jimbare, Mberogo, Sapeo, River Sama and Tipsan was faulty.[12]

In response to this Nigerian stance, Cameroon explained that even if the instruments were imperfect, they constituted the legal bases and rights of the two parties with regards to the delimitation of the common frontier between the two countries. Cameroon went ahead to precise that the LCBC which was conferred the mission to demarcate the frontier in the Lake Chad region determined an average point between the sector disputed by Cameroon and Nigeria at the Ebeji River. The operation which ran from 1988-90 was carried by the IGN-FI. And that in 1996, Nigeria refused to ratify the

---

8. Jean Pierre Cot, Counsel/ Advocate for Cameroon, verbatim February, 19, 2002, http:// www.icj-cij. org.; retrieved on 24/07/10. The verbatim pleadings are available in this ICJ website.

9. Cameroon's memoire at the I.C.J, cited by Eba'a, *Affaire Bakassi*, p. 35.

10. Jean Pierre Cot, verbatim, February 19, 2002.

11. Georges Abi Saab, Counsel/Advocate for Nigeria, verbatim, March 4, 2002.

12. Sir Arthur Watts, Counsel/Advocate for Nigeria, verbatim, March 4, 2002.

outcome of the work in which she participated. According to Cameroon, this refusal however did not put to question the former instruments of delimitation.[13] Cameroon went ahead to explain that 61km in the Lake Chad region was already demarcated.[14]

In response to this Cameroonian postulation, Nigeria precised that the IGN-FI from 1988–90 delimited and demarcated the Lake Chad area, whose results were presented at the 7th conference of the Heads of State of the LCBC in 1990. But because of the weakness of the work done, it was demanded that the experts go back to the field. To her, successive summits of the LCBC failed in their efforts to endorse the conclusion of the experts especially as decision making by the LCBC was by unanimity.[15] Therefore, Nigeria refused to sign the report and later rejected it during a meeting in June 1991. According to Nigeria; that is why the 10th summit of the Heads of State and Government of the LCBC in N'Djamena on July 28, 2000; did not have the problem of frontier delimitation in its agenda.[16] As a consequence, Nigeria concluded that the frontier problems here were not resolved by the LCBC.

Cameroon went ahead to precise that the Cameroon-Nigeria boundary in this region remained as such till independence in 1960. Therefore, Darack and other areas in the Lake Chad region claimed by Nigeria belonged to Cameroon. To buttress her point, Cameroon cited the Nigerian military occupation of the centre for the training of fishermen at Katte Kime, constructed with funds from the Japanese Cooperation.[17] At this juncture, Nigeria qualified Cameroon's defense as exaggerated and undignified especially when she talked of Nigerian

---

13. Jean Pierre Cot, verbatim, February 19, 2002.

14. Alain Pellet, Counsel/Advocate for Cameroon, verbatim, February 18, 2002.

15. Ian Brownlie, Counsel/Advocate for Nigeria, verbatim, March 6, 2002.

16. Ibid.

17. Jean Pierre Cot, verbatim, February 19, 2002.

aggression and invasion.[18] Nigeria debunked this Cameroonian position postulating that she occupied Darack since 1386 and Cameroon had never contested. According to her, the oldest of the villages in the Lake Chad area was Katte Kime, created 40 years ago and that the very recent was Murdas, aged 13 years. These villages, she posited; date 20 – 40 years and had been administered by the Ngala Local Government Authority with no least protest from Cameroon.[19]

Nigeria equally rejected the thesis propounded by Cameroon, that in February 1987, Cameroonian villages in the Lake Chad region were invaded by the Nigerian army and civilians armed with machetes, followed by a military occupation on May 2, 1987. She instead talked of intrusion by Cameroonian soldiers and agents into Nigerian territory,[20] where 60.000 Nigerians live.[21] Nigeria averred that administrative activities like the payment of taxes, public order, population censuses, justice, education, health, electoral lists, matriculation of fishing boats, regulation of business, immigration and assistance to development was done by Nigeria. And that, Cameroon does not give any prove of her administration of the 15 villages which Nigeria claimed or protested before April 11, 1994.[22] Cameroon reacted to this Nigerian claim by positing that Nigeria had no map indicating the frontier that she was contesting in the Lake Chad region. According to Cameroon, she had produced 39 maps indicating the frontier contested in the Lake Chad region.[23]

---

18. Musa E. Abdullahi, Agent for Nigeria, verbatim, February 28, 2002.

19. Ian Brownlie, verbatim, March 6, 2002.

20. Ibid.

21. Musa E. Abdallahi, Agent of Nigeria, verbatim, February 28, 2002.

22. Ian Brownlie, verbatim, March 6, 2002.

23. Jean Pierre Cot, verbatim, February 21, 2002.

Dispute along the Land Boundary area from Mount Kombon through pillar 64 to the sea

Cameroon maintained that the sector from Mount Kombon to pillar 64 in the vicinity of Furu-Awa was delimited by part 12 of the Anglo-German Accord of April 12, 1913 signed at Obokum, Nigeria and by the British Order in Council of August 2, 1946; precisely section 61 of this order. She also precised that this Order was confirmed later by the Definition of Boundaries Proclamation of Nigeria's Northern, Western and Eastern Regions. Cameroon equally precised that this line separated British Northern Cameroons from British Southern Cameroons and was accepted by the UN in the 1959 and 1961 plebiscites in Cameroon.[24] This line constituted therefore the frontier between Nigeria and Cameroon when Northern Cameroons joined Nigeria and Southern Cameroons joined the Republic of Cameroon in 1961. Cameroon averred that; this frontier was fixed by the administrative power and accepted internationally.[25]

From pillar 64, Cameroon maintained that the boundary was mapped by paragraph 13 and 21 of the Obokum Accord up to pillar 114 on the Cross River.[26] Meanwhile, the line of delimitation was prolonged up to the point marked in the Gulf of Guinea by Article 18 of the Anglo-German Treaty of March 11, 1913. Equally, Articles 22 and 23 prolonged this line up to the estuary of the Cross River.

---

24. Alain Pellet, verbatim, February 18, 2002; Jean-Marie Bipoun Woum, Special Adviser/Advocate for Cameroon, verbatim, February 21, 2002. The UN organized a plebiscite in British Northern Cameroons in November 1959 to determine whether the people would like to join Nigeria or to decide their future on a later date. About 64% of the electorate (men only) voted to decide their future later .The UN equally organized separate plebiscites in British Northern and Southern Cameroons in February 1961 to decide whether they should achieve their independence by joining Nigeria or the Republic.of Cameroon.

25. Malcom Shaw, Counsel/Advocate for Cameroon, verbatim, February 19, 2002.

26. Cameroon's memoire, cited in Eba'a, *Affaire Bakassi*, p.35.

According to Cameroon, the Southern part of this frontier was delimited by the Anglo-German Accords of March 11 and April 12, 1913. She also maintained that Article 23 of the March 11, 1913 Treaty delimited the frontier from the thalweg of the Akwayafe River and relating also to navigation in the Cross River.[27]

In response, Nigeria especially to drive home her proposal for the invalidation of instruments delimiting the boundary, postulated that from Lake Chad to Bakassi, there was dispute on 22 localities or points totaling 140 miles [87.5km] where delimitation was either defective or put to question by Cameroon.[28] Following this Nigerian presentation, Cameroon averred that the methods used to map the frontier were based on natural elements and this posed a problem when this had to be concretised on the ground. According to her, rivers might have dried up or changed their course; but this did not invalidate the legal instruments in place. In reaction to this thesis propounded by Cameroon, Nigeria cited incorrect watershed reproduced in a map by the German, Max Moisel between 1908 and 1913 on the Land Boundary area. She continued and cited the Itang Hill (Mount Kombon) which is displaced by 18 km in the map. As a consequence, Nigeria condemned the lackadaisical approach of Cameroon towards these instruments. She cited the zones of Lip and Yang as defective. Nigeria equally averred that the position of Cameroon on Bissaula-Tosso and in Mount Mandara was illogical and unjustified.[29]

Cameroon continued to defend her thesis by evoking that the principles and methods of the delimitation of the Land Boundary

---

27. Bruno Simma, Counsel/Advocate for Cameroon, verbatim, February 18, 2002.

28. Georges Abi Saab, Counsel/Advocate for Nigeria, verbatim, March 4, 2002.

29. Alastair Mac Donald, Counsel/Advocate for Nigeria, verbatim, March 5, 2002. A land surveyor and former Director of the Ordnance Survey of Britain who in the late 50s and early 60s worked in the Southern Cameroons and therefore claimed to be not only very knowledgeable about the cartographic situation of the boundary area, but has also helped draw maps for several other parts of Africa. See *Cameroon Tribune*, n° 7548/3837, Wednesday, March 6, 2002.

between Cameroon and Nigeria was based on the *uti possidetis juris* adopted by the defunct OAU in a resolution in Cairo on July 21, 1964. That is, the inheriting of colonial frontiers at independence. And that this principle was used in the Burkina Faso-Mali case by the ICJ on December 22, 1986.[30] Meanwhile, Nigeria castigated the principle *of uti possedetis juris* as a defensive colonial instrument which has its origin in the 19th century in America under Spanish domination.[31]

Dispute over the Bakassi Peninsula

Cameroon maintained that negotiations on this sector of the boundary were begun in 1901 between Moor, British High Commissioner for Southern Nigeria and Von Puttkamer, German Governor to Cameroon. Article 3 of their preliminary project of April 16, 1901 placed Bakassi in Cameroon under German administration; although the document was not ratified. Cameroon then went ahead to explain that from 1905-06, the demarcation was effected by the Woodroffe-Hermann Commission. This Commission placed the Cameroon-Nigeria Boundary at the Akwayafe River. Therefore, the Bakassi boundary at the Rio del Rey claimed by Nigeria was a product of pure fantasy as their arguments did not have a legal foundation.[32] Cameroon went further to explain that this sector was delimited by paragraph 16 and 21 of the Anglo-German Accord of March 11, 1913.[33] And that the Germans published it in the colonial collection, *Deutsches Kolonial blatt* volume 24 on page 430 and the British in *Treaties Series* 1913, Number 13.[34]

---

30. Peter Ntamark, Co-Agent for Cameroon, verbatim, February 18, 2002.

31. Georges Abi Saab, verbatim, March 4, 2002.

32. Bruno Simma, verbatim, February 20, 2002.

33. Cameroon's memoire, cited in Eba'a, Affaire Bakassi, p.35.

34. Christian Tomuschat, Counse/Advocate for Cameroon, verbatim, February 20, 2002.

Nigeria in response; this time did not evoke the defects of the treaties delimiting or demarcating this sector of the boundary but instead put forward the thesis that she acquired the title of Bakassi from the Kings and Chiefs of Old Calabar. According to her, there was no Nigeria in the 1800 but Old Calabar, administered by Kings and Chiefs. And that Old Calabar later became Nigeria and Bakassi part of it. Nigeria went further to explain that these Kings and Chiefs possessed international personality and in particular, the capacity to conclude treaties. As a consequence, Britain had no power to give Bakassi to Germany following the Treaty of March 11, 1913 since it did not belong to her. Answering a question from the judge—kooijmans—if the incorporation of Old Calabar into the Niger District of Nigeria did not put an end to the international personality of these Kings and Chiefs; Nigeria posited that information on that was not available. But added that the end of their personal international status was in 1960 when Nigeria acceded to independence.[35]

Cameroon debunked this Nigerian claim by recalling how these same Kings and Chiefs submitted themselves to the authority of colonial Britain while some were even appointed by the British colonial authorities. Cameroon also saddled her argument on Article 20 of the London Agreement which postulated that even if the course of the Akwayafe River—which is the official boundary between the two countries—came to change its course to move towards the Rio del Rey, the Bakassi Peninsula would remain German.[36] Cameroon equally went ahead to argue that if the treaties with the Kings and Chiefs of Old Calabar are considered to have international status; that should have been the same thing with the Protectorate of Lagos (colony) which was never abrogated at

---

35. Sir Arthur Watts, Counsel/Advocate for Nigeria, verbatim, March 14, 2002.

36. Joseph Marie Bipoun Woum, Special Adviser/Advocate for Cameroon, verbatim, February 20, 2002.

independence. Therefore, the presence of Nigerian troops in Lagos and Old Calabar constituted an invasion.[37]

Cameroon went ahead to buttress her point by explaining that the Germans created administrative structures in Bakassi and equally collected taxes on the bases of the colonial law of February 22, 1913 which entered into force on April 1, 1913. Cameroon postulated that; eight months after the start of the First World War, Britain and her Allies imposed a maritime blockage to stop supplies to the German forces on the sea at the mouth of the Akwayafe River. According to her, if Germany was not the owner of Bakassi, Britain would have naturally design her point of departure from the Rio del Rey. And that, even during the war, Britain did not raise eye brows concerning the ownership of Bakassi.[38] According to her, with the departure of the Germans in 1916, Bakassi remained part of British Southern Cameroons. A report by the British administrative authority, F.B. Carr in 1922 relating to fishing activities in the Rio del Rey, says he had never had problems from British authorities concerning the ownership of Bakassi by Cameroon under the Mandate and Trusteeship periods, which was annexed to Cameroon pursuant to the March 1913 Treaty. Cameroon went further to explain that in the partitioning of the plebiscite districts in British Southern Cameroons in 1961; the Victoria South West district was divided into 14 zones and included Bakassi.[39]

Nigeria reacted to the issue of Bakassi inhabitants participating in the plebiscite by declaring that there was no documental proof that during the 1961 plebiscite, Victoria South West electoral district included Bakassi; same as there was no evidence that the people of Bakassi participated in the plebiscite. To her, the bases of Nigerian sovereignty of Bakassi were on long occupation by Nigeria and

---

37. Michel Aurillac, Senior Counsel/Advocate for Cameroon, verbatim, February 20, 2002.

38. Christian Tomuschat, Senior Counsel/Advocate for Cameroon, verbatim, February 20, 2002.

39. Malcom Shaw, verbatim, February 21, 2002.

effective administration with no protest from Cameroon.[40] Nigeria continued to explain that although Cameroon was now claiming sovereignty over Bakassi, it had never had title and had never acted as if she had one. And that it was Nigeria that had looked after the Bakassi inhabitants and exercised sovereignty over the land. To her, the interest of Cameroon was petrol and not the Bakassi inhabitants.[41]

According to Cameroon, the historic consolidation of this title is exemplified by a correspondence n° 570 of March 27, 1962 by the Nigerian Foreign Minister to the Cameroon Ambassador in Lagos in which he recognized that the frontier was delimited from the Cross River to the sea by the Anglo–German Treaty of March 11, 1913 thereby placing Bakassi in Cameroon. Cameroon also evoked the opinion put forward in 1972 by Taslim Elias, Nigerian Minister of Justice and former President of the ICJ who recognized the March 11, 1913 Accord.[42] Cameroon continued to explain that by 1963, permits and licenses for research and exploitation of petrol in Bakassi, military activities, collection of taxes, organization of electoral districts, appointment of DOs, opening of schools and agricultural training was undertaken by her. As such "Cameroon was the sovereign and Nigeria the interloper."[43] Cameroon equally postulated that during a visit in February 1969 to Bakassi by the Nigerian Consul to Buea, a report of the DO of Bamusso dated March 20, 1969 talks of collaboration of the Consul with Cameroonian police which was carrying investigation of the eventual participation of Nigerian soldiers in the criminal acts at Ine-Odiong, in the Bakassi Peninsula.[44] And that in a Diplomatic Note during

---

40. Ian Brownlie, verbatim, March 1, 2002.

41. Musa E. Abdallahi, verbatim, February 28, 2002.

42. Peter Ntamark, verbatim, February 18, 2002.

43. Malcom Shaw, verbatim, February 18, 2002.

44. Maurice Mendelson, Counsel/Advocate for Cameroon, verbatim, February 22, 2002.

many Consular and Ambassadorial visits, the Nigerian Minister of Justice, K.B. Olukulu in a letter dated June 6, 1985, recognized that Bakassi was found in Cameroon. As a consequence, it was a futile attempt for Nigeria to contend Cameroon's ownership of the peninsula.[45]

In response to this defense by Cameroon, Nigeria posited that up to 1972, Cameroon recognized Nigeria's administration of Bakassi and from that date, Cameroon started changing names of villages there. She went ahead to explain that Cameroonian incursions here between 1972 and 73 led to protests from the Chiefs and Kings of Old Calabar. She explained further that there was another protest in 1993 when Cameroon wanted to collect land taxes and other types of taxes. To Nigeria, Bakassi was administered in 1967 by the Akpabujo council, in 1976 by the Local Government of Akpabujo for the northern part and Oron for the south; in 1987, by the Local Government of Akpabujo for the north and Effiat/Mbo and Okobo for the south; and in 1986 by the Cross River State. To her, legislative elections, matriculation of boats, population censuses of 1953, 63 and 91 took place there under her control. And that, in 1991, Bakassi had a population of 156.000 inhabitants.[46]

Cameroon went further to appreciate Nigerian maps spelling out that Nigeria had no map indicating the frontier contested in the Bakassi Peninsula. Meanwhile, Cameroon had 58 maps on Bakassi. According to Cameroon; from pre-independence and independence period up to 1990, all maps published by the United Kingdom and later by Nigeria placed Bakassi in Cameroon. She cited the example of the 1956, 63 and 73 maps which placed Bakassi in Cameroon. Meanwhile, the 10th edition of the administrative map of Nigeria published in 1991 indicated for the first time that the international boundary between Cameroon and Nigeria was at the Rio del Rey, thereby leaving Bakassi in Nigeria.[47]

---

45. Maurice Mendelson, verbatim, March 11, 2002.

46. Ian Brownlie, verbatim, February 28, 2002.

47. Jean Pierre Cot, verbatim, February 21, 2002.

Dispute over the Maritime Boundary and Equatorial Guinea's intervention

On this sector of the boundary, the position of the two countries was on the already demarcated part as well as on the undemarcated one. Equatorial Guinea intervened in the case in order to protect her rights in the undemarcated part of the boundary; notably concerning the fixing of the tripoint. On the already demarcated part of the boundary, Cameroon postulated that three principal legal instruments demarcated this sector. They included; the Anglo– German Accord of March 11, 1913(precisely Article XXI), the Cameroon–Nigeria Accord of April 4, 1971(Yaounde II Declaration), and the Cameroon–Nigeria Accord of June 1, 1975(Maroua Declaration). To Cameroon, beginning from the intersection of the straight line joining Bakassi Point and King Point and the centre of the navigable channel of the Akwayafe River up to point 12, this part was delimited by a compromise reported in the British Admiralty map n° 3433 by the Heads of State of Nigeria and Cameroon in a Declaration in Yaounde on April 4, 1971 to map the lines from point 1 – 12 and those of A – G, defined by a Declaration signed in Maroua on June 1, 1975 precisely Article 9.[48] Cameroon equally evoked the Kano Accord of September 1, 1971 which disallowed all activities of petrol prospection in an area of 4km, that is, 2km on two sides of the border.[49]

In response, Nigeria first opined that the Maritime Boundary had never been an object of negotiation between Cameroon and Nigeria as Cameroon had failed to negotiate any of its Maritime Boundaries with any of its coastal neighbours.[50] Later, Nigeria who had rejected the Anglo – German Treaty in their pleadings focused on the Maroua Declaration. She opined that according to the Nigerian Constitution of 1963, President Yakubu Gowon could not engage his government

---

48. Cameroon's memoire, cited in Eba'a, *Affaire Bakassi*, p.36.

49. Jean Marc Thouvernin, Counsel/Advocate for Cameroon, verbatim, February 22, 2002.

50. Musa E. Abdullahi, verbatim, February 28, 2002.

without the approval of the Supreme Military Council which constituted the government of Nigeria. To her, the military legislations of 1966 and 67 did not abrogate this 1963 Constitution. Further, Nigeria explained that the Maroua Declaration was not published in the *Federal Gazette* and therefore had no force of law.[51]

Cameroon debunked the Nigerian position on the Maroua Declaration positing that it constituted a treaty in international law as it was the result of the Maroua meeting of May 30- June 1, 1975. And that following the signing of the Maroua Accord between Presidents Ahidjo and Gowon, a technical error was realized in the calculation of coordinates at point B. Then, on June 12, 1975, President Ahidjo wrote to President Gowon and proposed that there should be a correction of this mistake. As a consequence, on July 17, 1975, Gowon answered favourably to this proposition. Therefore, Nigeria recognized the validity of the Maroua Declaration. Cameroon went further to explain that there was nothing in the 1963 Nigerian Constitution relating to a disposition that could disturb President Gowon to engage his country in the international scene.[52] Cameroon cited the Vienna Convention on Treaties which stipulates in Article 7(2) that the Head of State is considered as the representative of his country and therefore Gowon had the right to represent Nigeria. On the Supreme Military Council not ratifying the accord; Cameroon maintained that it remained valid especially as it was only in 1978 during the meeting of the Mixed Boundary Commission in the Nigerian town of Joss that the Nigerian delegation expressed its intention to put to question this accord.[53]

On the undemarcated sector; from point G seawards, Cameroon maintained that it should be demarcated following the law of the sea. That is, in accordance with the Montego Bay Convention of 1987; this replaced the 1958 Vienna Convention. Cameroon equally postulated that Nigeria was responsible for the non continuation of

---

51. Ian Brouwnlie, verbatim, March 1, 2002.

52. Sir Ian Sinclair, Counsel/Advocate for Cameroon, verbatim, March 12, 2002.

53. Christian Tomuschat, verbatim, February 25, 2002.

the delimitation process from point G. For Nigeria, if the Court engaged itself in the delimitation of the Maritime Boundary, this was to touch on the interests of third parties—Equatorial Guinea and Sao Tome and Principe. Therefore, the Court was incompetent on the matter.[54] She went further to explain that the Court should first determine sovereignty over the Bakassi Peninsula especially as sovereignty over the coast was the basis of the maritime title. That is, the land dominates the sea.[55]

Cameroon further precised that even to point G, Nigeria did not present a precise boundary. And that from point G, the line of delimitation moves south west to point H with coordinates 92^0 21' 16" East and 4^0 17' 00" North and prolonged to point I (70^0 55' 40" East and 30^0 46' 00" North) and then K (6^0 45' 22" East and 3^0 01' 05" North) represented in map R_{21} and featuring on page 407 of Cameroon's replication. Cameroon then suggested an equitable solution until the zone where international law limits Cameroon and Nigeria.[56] Cameroon equally postulated that the island of Bioko where Malabo, Capital of Equatorial Guinea is found was 18km from the Cameroon coast, 43km from the continental part of Equatorial Guinea and 30km from the Nigerian coast. Therefore, the Court can determine the equidistance line taking into consideration these distances and the concavity of the Gulf of Guinea which handicaps Cameroon. Cameroon equally regretted that the line traced by Nigeria and Equatorial Guinea in their Treaty of September 23, 2000 ignored totally the rights of Cameroon.[57] Cameroon equally opined

---

54. James Crawford, Counsel/Advocate for Nigeria, verbatim, March 6, 2002.

55. _____ , verbatim, March 6, 2002.

56. Maurice Kamto, verbatim, February 26, 2002.

57. Maurice Kamto, verbatim, February 25, 2002. Nigeria concluded a Treaty with Equatorial Guinea on September 23, 2000 and on February 21, 2001 with Sao Tome and Principe delimiting their Maritime Frontier, ignoring the rights of Cameroon.

that the Court was not competent to fix a tripoint.[58]

In response to Cameroon's proposition on the equidistance line, Nigeria averred that the zone proposed by Cameroon; a space with an area of 7.400 sq km touched on the Nigerian petrol wells where Nigeria had been exploiting petrol for over 50 years and that the Court was informed on the negotiations with Equatorial Guinea and with Sao Tome and Principe on the fixing of their international boundaries with Nigeria. She explained that Cameroon simply wanted a geopolitical vantage point in the Gulf of Guinea. Nigeria equally rejected the equidistance line presented by Cameroon and posited that if the Court must delimit this area, it should take into consideration the equidistance line proposed by Equatorial Guinea. And that between Cameroon and Nigeria, the appropriate equidistance line starts on the Rio del Rey, leaving Bakassi in Nigeria.[59] Nigeria equally propounded the idea that the Court should come out with a general legal framework for the delimitation of the Maritime Frontier which will involve the three states concerned with the tripoint—Cameroon, Nigeria and Equatorial Guinea.[60]

It was the issue of the equidistance line that invited Equatorial Guinea to intervene in the case in order to protect her rights in the Gulf of Guinea. Equatorial Guinea deposited a suit on June 30, 1999 and on October 21, 1999, the Court authorized her to intervene as a non-party to the case. It also fixed April 4, 2001 for her to make a declaration in writing and July 4, 2001 for Cameroon and Nigeria to make their observations to Equato–Guinean declarations. Equatorial Guinea defended her case on March 18, 2002 and made concluding statements on March 20. Ricardo Mangue Obama N'fube, Minister of State for Labour and Social Security was her Agent to The Hague. According to Equatorial Guinea, the equidistance line proposed by Cameroon was incorrect. She therefore prayed the Court to either

---

58. Jean Pierre Cot, verbatim, March 19, 2002.

59. James Crawford, Counsel/Advocate for Nigeria, verbatim, March 6, 2002.

60._____ , verbatim, March 15, 2002.

abstain from hearing the matter[61] or from determining the tripoint which Cameroon situated between the Bioko Island and the continent thereby leaving an area of only 34 sq km to cover the interests of Equatorial Guinea.[62]

Nigeria's international liability

Cameroon maintained that the responsibility of Nigeria resulted principally from her invasion of the Bakassi Peninsula and a large territory of Cameroon in the Lake Chad region as well as her non respect of the conservatory measures indicated by the Court on March 15, 1996.[63] Cameroon went further to explain that the occupation of her territory by Nigerian forces was a violation of conventionary and customary international rights and that Nigeria should put an end to this occupation. She prayed the Court to fix reparations for Nigeria to pay to Cameroon for the material and moral damages caused by this occupation,[64] as this was a violation of international law which stipulates that force should not be used in the resolution of disputes. She equally explained that this was a violation of the principle of non intervention and the respect of the sovereignty of states.[65] She equally evoked the non respect by Nigeria of conservatory measures put forward by the Court as she continued hostilities in Bakassi on April 21 and 24, 1996 and even created the Bakassi Council in 1996 as stated in *The Guardian* of October 1, 1996. As a result of all these, Cameroon prayed the Court to allow her to present an evaluation of indemnity which Nigeria owed her.

---

61. Pierre Marie, Deputy Counsel/Advocate for Equatorial Guinea, verbatim, March 18, 2002.

62. David Colson, Counsel/Advocate for Equatorial Guinea, verbatim, March 18, 2002.

63. Maurice Mendelson, verbatim, March 11, 2002.

64. Cameroon's memoire, cited in Eba'a, *Affaire Bakassi*, p.36.

65. Olivier Corten, Counsel/Advocate for Cameroon, verbatim, February 26, 2002.

To Nigeria, Cameroon's presentation was a model of indecision, impression and inadequacy.[66] According to her, there was no proof of the alleged incidents by Nigeria as she was in her territory in Bakassi. Nigeria therefore accused Cameroon of incursions by her gendarmes and agents in Bakassi. Nigeria went further to insinuate that Cameroon failed to bring forth proof of Nigerian responsibility in the invasion of Bakassi as she (Nigeria) could not unilaterally invade and use force against herself since she was the owner of Bakassi.[67]

With the oral pleadings over, the President of the Court, Guillaume, explained that all the written additional responses pertaining to the questions of the judges should reach the Court not later than April 4, 2002. That is, in conformity with Article 72 of the Court's statute which requires that observations concerning such responses should reach the Court within 15days after the receipt of the questions and observations. It took the Court five months, two weeks to deliberate on the matter. The verdict was pronounced on October 10, 2002.

The Verdict, October 10, 2002

The Court passed its verdict in consideration of the various conventions, treaties, declarations and decisions concluded by the colonial masters of Cameroon and Nigeria, Mandatory and Trusteeship powers of Cameroon as well as those concluded by Cameroon and Nigeria and the LCBC after independence.The Court equally took intermediate or neutral decisions to delimit some sectors on the Land Boundary area and the undelimited sector of the Maritime Frontier. The verdict equally touched on the intervention of Equatorial Guinea, Nigeria's international liability and the invalidation of former conventions.

---

66. Sir Arthur Watts, verbatim, March 8, 2002.

67. Georges Abi Saab, verbatim, March 15, 2002.

Delimitation of the boundary

The Court delimited the undelimited sector of the Maritime Boundary and some sectors along the Land Boundary area and confirmed former accords of international character delimiting and demarcating the frontier.

Lake Chad region

The Court delimited this sector of the boundary in conformity with the Milner–Simon Boundary Declaration of July 10, 1919; the Thomson–Marchand Declaration of December 29, 1929 and January 31, 1930 and annexed in the Henderson–Fleuriau Exchange of Notes of January 9, 1931. The Court precised that the LCBC for seven years (1984 –90) undertook the demarcation of the frontier in this region with the accord of Nigeria and Cameroon. And that even though Nigeria later put to question the mapping and pillar emplacement undertaken by IGN- FI under the auspices of the LCBC; this contest did not mean that international legal instruments were not applicable to her. The Court equally recognized that these former instruments were equally applicable in the area of the bifurcation of the Ebeji River thereby rejecting the thesis propounded by Cameroon that the Court should consider in tutu the propositions of the LCBC concerning the tripoint and the bifurcation of the Ebeji River as an authentic interpretation of the Milner–Simon and the Thomson–Marchand Declarations. The Court equally rejected Nigeria's claims of sovereignty over many villages in the Lake Chad area on account of her long occupation and effective administration.[68]

With these dispositions, the Cameroon–Nigerian boundary in the Lake Chad region was delimited as follows. From the tripoint situated in the Lake by longitude 14⁰ 04' 59" 9999 East, and latitude 13⁰ 05'

---

68. ICJ Judgement of October 10, 2002, http://icj-cij.org., retrieved on 24/07/10.

North; the frontier then follows a straight line up to the mouth of River Ebeji situated on longitude 14^0 12' 12" East and latitude 12^0 32' 17" North; and moves in a straight line to the bifurcation of this river in a point situated at longitude 14^0 12' 03" East and latitude 12^0 30' 14" North. Consequently, localities situated east of this frontier fall under Cameroon sovereignty and those on the west fall under the sovereignty of Nigeria.

Land boundary from the vicinity of lake Chad to astride the Bakassi Peninsula

The Court delimited this sector in conformity with the following legal instruments: the Thomson–Marchand Declaration of 1929–30, incorporated in the Henderson–Fleuriau Exchange of Notes, notably paragraph 2 – 60 for the sector from the bifurcation of River Ebeji to Mount Tamnyar; the British Order in Council of August 2, 1946 for the sector from Mount Tamnyar to pillar 64 and the Anglo–German Accord of March 11, and April 12, 1913.

The Court made mention of the fact that Cameroon and Nigeria recognized that this sector was already an object of delimitation and equally recognized the validity of the instruments. The Court therefore examined 17 points which still posed some ambiguity and dispute. In many of these areas, the solution retained was in favour of Nigeria. This was the case with the localities around River Keraua, Mounts Mandara, Maio Senche, Jimbare and Sapeo found between Namberou and Banglang; then the area around the Akbang River and Mount Tosso. In the localities around River Kohom and the region from Mount Kuli to Bourha in Kotcha (Kontcha) village and in the zone of Mount Hambere and River Sama; the verdict was closed to the thesis propounded by Cameroon. The Court also retained intermediary and neutral solutions in the locality of Limani, around pillar 64 at Wammi Budungo, at Tipsan, Mount Hambere and River Mburi.

With these dispositions, the Cameroon–Nigeria boundary along the Land Boundary area was delimited. From the point where River Ebeji bifurcates as far as the Tamnyar peak and from this peak to pillar 64, the interpretation of the delimitation was done in the

110

manner set out in paragraphs 91, 96, 102, 114, 119, 124, 129, 134, 139, 146, 152, 155, 160, 168, 176, 184 and 189 of the October 10, 2002 judgement. Following this interpretation, Nigeria inherited Ndabakura, Bourha Wango and other patches of territory along the land boundary area while Cameroon inherited Narki and other patches of territory along the frontier.

Bakassi Peninsula

The Court passed its verdict on this sector of the boundary in conformity with Articles XVIII to XX of the Anglo–German Accord of March 11, 1913. The Court therefore rejected the thesis propounded by Nigeria that she acquired Bakassi at independence from the Kings and Chiefs of Old Calabar. According to the Court, these Kings and Chiefs concluded a Treaty with Britain in 1884 which was not of an international character as they did not possess international personality. The Court went on to precise that one of the characteristics of international protectorship is the frequent discussions between the protector power and the leaders of the local protectorate; a situation which Nigeria failed to prove. The Court equally added that in the numerous Orders in Council by the British; none mentioned such relations. The Court also averred that there was no protest from these Kings and Chiefs after the cession of their territory to Germany in 1913. Britain, the administering power of Old Calabar therefore had the right to determine her frontier with Germany in the Bakassi Peninsula. According to the Court, this frontier which left Bakassi in Cameroon was never modified by Britain as she could not do so unilaterally. The Court equally rejected Nigeria's claim of sovereignty over the peninsula on account of her long occupation and effective administration.

With these precisions, the Court decided that sovereignty over the Bakassi Peninsula lied with Cameroon. It also delimited the Cameroon–Nigeria frontier in the peninsula as follows: from the thalweg of River Akpakorum(Akwayafe) and dividing the mangrove islands near Ikang in the way shown on map TSGS 2240 and as far as the straight line joining Bakassi Point and King Point.

Maritime Boundary

It involved two sectors; the already delimited area up to a point marked G and the unmapped area; from this point seaward to the external limits of the maritime zone as defined in international law.

The delimited Sector

The Court passed its verdict on this sector in conformity with the Anglo–German Accord of March 11, 1913; the "compromise line" reported in the British Admiralty map n⁰ 3433 by the Heads of State of Nigeria and Cameroon in the Yaounde II Declaration of April 4, 1971; and the Maroua Declaration signed by the Heads of State of Cameroon and Nigeria on June 1, 1975 and modified by the Exchange of Letters by these Heads of State on June 12 and July 17, 1975.

By taking this position, the Court rejected Nigeria's contest of the above Conventions. The Court went on to precise that during the meeting of the Boundary Mixed Commission of Cameroon and Nigeria in Garoua in May and August 1972, Nigeria put to question the Yaounde II Declaration. And that, on August 23, 1974, the Nigerian Head of State in a letter addressed to his Cameroonian counterpart confirmed this position by Nigeria. The Court evoked Articles 74 and 83 of the UN Convention on the rights of the sea which does not require that negotiations on matters of territorial delimitation must be successfully carried to the end. And that modification can only be made to what was already reached only if they are of a legal character. Concerning Nigeria's position that the Maroua Declaration was not ratified by the Supreme Military Council, and therefore not valid in international law; the Court declared that it was an international accord concluded in writing by two states mapping their common frontier. It therefore constituted a treaty in the spirit of Article 7 of the Vienna Convention on the rights of treaties; a convention that Nigeria is party since 1969 and Cameroon since 1991.

The Court equally rejected Nigeria's thesis that based on the Nigerian Constitution, President Gowon could not engage his government in the signing of the accord without the approval of the Supreme Military Council which constituted the government of Nigeria. On this score, the Court evoked Article 46(1) of the Vienna Convention which stipulates that if a state engages itself in a treaty in violation of any disposition of its internal rights relating to the competence to conclude such a treaty; this could not be considered as a reason for rejecting such a treaty. The Court went ahead to explain that the Heads of State in exercising their functions are considered as representatives of their countries. The Court even observed that in June and July 1975, the Heads of State of Cameroon and Nigeria respectively made a corrigendum to the Maroua Declaration through the Exchange of Letters. And that Nigeria did not contest the validity of this Declaration before 1977.

With these precisions, the Court decided that from the continental shelf seawards and up to point G mentioned in the Yaounde II Declaration of April 4, 1971, the Maritime Boundary is delimited as follows: starting from the intersection of the centre of the navigable channel of the Akwayafe River in a straight line joining Bakassi Point and King Point and passing through 12 numbered points drawn jointly at Yaounde on April 4, 1971 by the Heads of State of Cameroon and Nigeria on the British Admiralty Chart 3433, whose coordinates it defined(see table 1a). After point 12, the frontier was delimited by the Maroua Declaration of June 1, 1975 modified by the Exchange of Letters by the Heads of State of Cameroon and Nigeria on June 12 and July 17, 1975 respectively. This line passes through 8 points (A–G) whose coordinates it defined (see table 1b).

Undelimited sector

This concern the area from point G seawards up to the external limits of the maritime zone as defined in international law. This area had never been an object of negotiation between Cameroon and Nigeria. Therefore, the Court had to delimit this sector in conformity with international instruments in force and without hurting the interests of third parties in the Gulf of Guinea; Equatorial Guinea and Sao Tome and Principe. Cameroon and Nigeria were in unison that a common Maritime Boundary should be determined between their respective countries. On this score, Cameroon proposed an equidistance line which Nigeria did not see as equitable.

The Court evoked the UN conventions of December 10, 1982 on the law of the sea ratified by Cameroon on November 19, 1985 and by Nigeria on August 14, 1986 which in its Articles 74(1) and 84(1) stipulates that in delimiting adjacent areas of states with exclusive economic zones, it should be done in the manner that there is equity. The Court quickly added that equity does not necessarily mean equality as the equidistance line has to be mapped first followed by the examination of factors which necessitates adjustment or the displacement of the line in order to reach equitable results.

The equidistance line was determined amidst rejection of Cameroon's position who posited that the Court should take into consideration the peculiarity of the coast of Guinea notably its concavity which disfavour Cameroon. The Court explained that this was not enough reason to displace the equidistance line but added that the area of the coast that was concave was the sector facing the Island of Bioko in Equatorial Guinea and not that at the area of the Cameroon–Nigeria coast. Before mapping this equidistance line, the Court noted that point G where the delimitation had so far been reached by Cameroon and Nigeria was not situated on this line, but instead to the east of it.

With these precisions, the Court delimited this sector as follows: from point G follows a loxodrome having an azimuth of 270^0 as far as the equidistance line passing through the mid point of the line joining West Point and East Point and then the boundary meets the equidistance line at a point X with coordinates of longitude 8° 21' 20" East and latitude 4^0 17' 00" North; then from point X, the boundary follows a loxodrome having an azimuth of 187^0 52' 27." The Court in order not to infringe into the rights of Equatorial Guinea limited itself with the indication of the direction of the equidistance line without fixing the tripoint—Cameroon, Nigeria, Equatorial Guinea.

114

Table1. Geo-Referencing Coordinates of the Cameroon-Nigeria Maritime Frontier Mapped in the 1971 Yaounde II and 1975 Maroua Declarations and Confirmed by the ICJ in 2002

POINT	LONGITUDE	LATITUDE	POINT	LONGITUDE	LATITUDE
1	8⁰ 30' 44" E	4⁰ 40' 28" N	A	8⁰ 24' 24" E	4⁰ 31' 30" N
2	8⁰ 30' 00" E	4⁰ 40' 00" N	A1	8⁰ 24' 24" E	4⁰ 31' 20" N
3	8⁰ 28' 50" E	4⁰ 39' 00" N	B	8⁰ 24' 10" E	4⁰ 26' 32" N
4	8⁰ 27' 52" E	4⁰ 38' 00" N	C	8⁰ 23' 42" E	4⁰ 23' 28" N
5	8⁰ 27' 09" E	4⁰ 37' 00" N	D	8⁰ 22' 41" E	4⁰ 20' 00" N
6	8⁰ 26' 36" E	4⁰ 36' 00" N	E	8⁰ 22' 17" E	4⁰ 19' 32" N
7	8⁰ 26' 03" E	4⁰ 35' 00" N	F	8⁰ 22' 19" E	4⁰ 18' 46" N
8	8⁰ 25' 42" E	4⁰ 34' 18" N	G	8⁰ 22' 19" E	4⁰ 17' 00" N
9	8⁰ 25' 35" E	4⁰ 34' 00" N			
10	8⁰ 25' 08" E	4⁰ 33' 00" N			
11	8⁰ 24' 47" E	4⁰ 32' 00" N			
12	8⁰ 24' 38" E	4⁰ 31' 26" N			

(a)   (b)

Source: ICJ Verdict of October 10, 2002, Available from *http://www.icj-cij.com,*retrieved on 24/07/10.

Withdrawal of Administration, Armed Forces and Police

The delimitation of the Cameroon–Nigeria border from the Lake Chad to the sea modified the territorial configuration of both countries as per the claims held before. Territories east of the borderline fell under Cameroon's sovereignty and those to the west fell under the sovereignty of Nigeria. As a consequence, the Court ordered the two countries to each withdraw its administration, armed forces or police from territories falling under each other's sovereignty, within the shortest possible time and without conditions. For Nigeria, this concerned the localities of Naga'a, Tchika, Toro

Liman and Darack and their environs in the Lake Chad region; Narki and other localities and territories falling under Cameroon's sovereignty along the Land Boundary area, and the Bakassi Peninsula. For Cameroon, this concerned Dambore and its environs in the Lake Chad region and Ndabakura, Bourha Wango and other localities and territories along the Land Boundary area falling under Nigeria's sovereignty.[69]

The Court equally took note of the commitment undertaken by Cameroon at the hearing of the case that; 'faithful to its traditional policy of hospitality and tolerance' it 'will continue to afford protection to Nigerians living in the [Bakassi] Peninsula and in the Lake Chad area.'[70] The Court rejected Cameroon's position on Nigeria's international responsibility because of lack of proves. It equally rejected Nigeria's counter claims.

If it took more than eight years to pass judgement on the border dispute case, it required more energy and commitment to implement the judgement as the pronouncement of the verdict was one thing and its implementation another.

---

69. The Withdrawal and Transfer of Authority Forms for Narki, Ndabakura, and Bourha Wango, precise that; "the ceremony is symbolic and representative of the overall process of withdrawal and transfer of authority of localities and territories along the Land Boundary."

70. ICJ Judgement of October 10, 2002.

Chapter 5

The Process of the Implementation of the International Court of Justice Verdict, 2002-2011

The verdict of the ICJ on the Cameroon–Nigeria border dispute case delivered on October 10, 2002 requested both countries to withdraw their administration and military or police from the areas they occupy which fall within the sovereignty of the other, immediately and unconditionally. The Court equally delimited the Cameroon-Nigeria boundary from Lake Chad through the Land and Maritime Boundary which had to be demarcated. Unlike national courts which rely on its officers to execute or enforce its judgements, it is the UN Security Council which has the right (but not obliged) to make recommendations or take measures to implement the judgement of the Court especially if one of the parties fails to obey it. In the Cameroon-Nigeria border dispute case, the good offices of the UN Secretary General were primordial in the implementation of the verdict.

Complementing Legality with UN Brokered Diplomacy

Cameroon and Nigeria committed themselves to respect the outcome of the verdict in conformity with the jurisdiction of the Court which spells out that "states may commit themselves in advance to accept the jurisdiction of the Court, either by signing a treaty or convention which provides for referral to the Court or by making a declaration to that effect."[71] On that score, the UN Secretary General used his good offices to convene a pre-verdict meeting of the Heads of State of Cameroon and Nigeria in September 2002.

---

1. *Basic Facts About the United Nations,* p. 16.

The Paris Tripartite Meeting, September 2002

On September 5, 2002, Presidents Paul Biya of Cameroon and Olusegun Obasanjo of Nigeria met in the Parisian outskirts of Saint Cloud at the invitation of the UN Secretary General, Kofi Annan. The meeting took place in the presence of French President, Jacques Chirac. The two Presidents agreed to respect whatever verdict the ICJ would pass. They also opted for confidence building measures and initiatives that favour the demilitarization of the disputed areas with the possibility of involving international observers to follow the withdrawal of all troops. With these engagements and commitments, Nigeria and Cameroon had the moral obligation to obey the Court's judgement.

In spite of these assurances, the Court's verdict was received in Cameroon with great joy and with mixed feelings in Nigeria. While Abuja was asking for time to digest the verdict, Yaounde issued an official statement on the morrow of the verdict making commitments to reinforce the friendly ties between the two countries, and promising hospitality for the millions of Nigerians living in Cameroon. As the Federal government of Nigeria was studying the verdict, pressure was being mounted on her to reject it. Cross River State Governor, Donald Duke, and the Senator of the South-South Senatorial District under which Bakassi was said to fall, Princess Florence Ita-Giwa, was some of the prominent figures who openly rejected the verdict. The Nigerian Senate even threatened to impeach President Obasanjo if he accepted the verdict.[72] After a Federal government meeting on the ICJ verdict, an official statement was issued on October 23, 2002 and signed by the Minister of Transport, Ojo Madueke, which was more or less a rejection of the verdict.[73]

It was against this backdrop that the UN Secretary General, Kofi Annan used his good offices to convene the first post verdict

---

2. Aji James, "The Dynamics of Cameroon-Nigeria Relations", p. 58.

3. Ibid., p. 59.

meeting of the Heads of State of Cameroon and Nigeria in Geneva, Switzerland on November 15, 2002 to chart a way forward.

The Geneva I Tripartite Meeting, November 2002

The Geneva I Tripartite Meeting of Biya, Annan and Obasanjo came out with what was termed the "Joint Geneva Communiqué" in which the two Presidents renewed their commitment to renounce the use of force in their bilateral engagements and to look for peaceful means to solve frontier differences. They also defined proper measures to reinforce confidence building and requested the UN Secretary General to put in place a Mixed Bilateral Commission presided over by his personal representative and charged with reflecting on ways of implementing the ICJ verdict.

After this tripartite meeting code-named Geneva I, the Nigerian President, Obasanjo, declared to the press that Nigeria has never accepted nor rejected the ICJ judgement. This wavering attitude of Obasanjo was conditioned by Nigeria's internal politics at the time and which was having an impact on her foreign policy as far as the Cameroon-Nigeria border dispute was concerned. The country was just a few months from Presidential, Governorship and National Assembly elections slated for April and May 2003. President Obasanjo was therefore pursuing a balancing act by trying to prove tough in the eyes of the people of the Cross River State where Bakassi was said to be found and where the ruling Peoples' Democratic Party (PDP) held sway, and at the same time, pandering to the dictates of international law and its instruments of implementation. Furthermore, he was simply playing for time in the face of rising sentiments in the Cross River State where its elected leaders, Governor Duke and Senator Ita-Giwa were galvanizing support for mass rejection of the verdict.

Once more, this is an indication that the preservation of "national interests" is a key concept in international relations. The pursuit of national interests falls within the realm of the realists' school of thought. Hans Morgenthau, a key proponent of the realists' school opines that international politics like any other politics is the pursuit of power. To him, "a political policy seeks to keep power, increase

119

power, or to demonstrate power."[74] Linkage politics which establishes a connection between the domestic setting of a nation and the resultant external behavior can also be used to analyse Obasanjo's stance.Rosenau explains that linkage is any recurrent sequence of behavior that has its foundation in one system and is reacted in another.[75] Obasanjo's wavering stance therefore had roots in Nigeria's domestic politics.

This Nigerian stance did not however deter the UN Secretary General from putting in place an ad hoc Mixed Commission charged with the implementation of the Court's verdict as agreed by the Heads of State of Nigeria and Cameroon in November 2002.

The role of the Cameroon – Nigeria ad hoc Mixed Commission

The Commission[76] was entrusted the task of considering all the implications of the decision of the ICJ including the need to protect the rights of the affected populations in both countries, the putting in place of the modalities for the establishment of sovereignty on disputed areas in conformity with the Court's verdict, the demarcation of the Land and Maritime Boundary between the two countries and to promote confidence building measures between the two countries. It was also intended to be an implementation organ in charge of implementing the decisions and directives emanating from the tripartite summits of the Heads of State of Nigeria and Cameroon with the UN Secretary General.

Cameroon's delegation in the Commission was led by Ahmadou Ali, Minister of State in charge of Justice and keeper of the Seals. While that of Nigeria was led by Prince Bola Ajibola, Senior

---

4. Hans Morgenthau, *Politics Among Nations: A Struggle for Power and Peace* (New York: Alfred A. Knopf, 1973), p. 42.

5. Rosenau, ed. *Linkage Politics*, p. 45.

6. The Commission is variously known as the Cameroon-Nigeria Mixed Commission; Cameroon–United Nations–Nigeria Mixed Commission; or the United Nations Mixed Commission to demarcate the Cameroon–Nigeria Land and Maritime Boundary.

Advocate of Nigeria (SAN), former Minister of Justice, former High Commissioner of Nigeria to the United Kingdom and former ad hoc judge of the ICJ. The Mauritanian born diplomat, Ahmedou Ould-Abdallah, Chairman of the Commission represented the UN Secretary General.[77] The other members of the Commission included government officials, experts in various fields and high ranking military personnel.

In the maiden meeting of the ad hoc Mixed Commission in Yaounde in December 2002, it decided that the working documents for its meetings shall consist of the ICJ judgement of October 10, 2002; the press releases issued following the Paris Tripartite Summit of September 5, 2002 as well as the joint communiqué adopted at the Geneva I Summit on November 16, 2002 as well as other documents that may be adopted at the meetings of the Commission. The Mixed Commission also created Sub-Commissions to handle specific issues notably the demarcation of the boundary and the re-establishment of sovereignty on disputed areas in conformity with the ICJ ruling.

The Process of the Establishment of Sovereignty on Disputed Territories in Conformity with the ICJ Verdict

The Sub-Commission on affected populations was directly involved with the establishment of sovereignty on disputed areas. It was set up during the ad hoc Mixed Commission's meeting in Abuja in February 2003. This Sub-Commission was charged with the evaluation of the problems of affected areas in order to propose concrete solutions to such problems. Its meeting schedules and

---

7. In 2011, Ahmadou Ali and Prince Bola Ajibola were still leaders of the Cameroon and Nigeria delegations respectively. Saddig Marafa Diggi, Director General of the Nigerian Borders Commission sat for Ajibola during the 23rd session of the Commission in Yaounde from October 9-10, 2008 and during the 25th session in Yaounde from October 8-9, 2009. He equally represented Ajibola during the first pillar emplacement on the boundary on December 14, 2009. Meanwhile, Lamine Cissé, retired Senegalese Army General was appointed in 2007 by the UN Secretary General, Ban Ki-Moon to replace Ould-Abdallah. The Algerian diplomat Said Djinnit replaced General Cissé in May 2008. He was the chairperson of the commission in 2011.

reports were approved by the Tripatite Mixed Commission in its various sessions. As the Commission get to work, the Cameroon delegation to the Mixed Commission proposed a calendar of activities for the withdrawal of administration, armed forces and police from the areas concerned. The Nigerian delegation later examined the proposal and made its own comments. During the Mixed Commission's meeting in Yaounde in August 2003, the delegates discussed the Cameroonian proposal and the comments made by the Nigeian delegation and agreed that the first phase of the withdrawal process should take place in the Lake Chad region before the end of 2003.

The process of the retrocession and transfer of sovereignty in the Lake Chad region, 2002-2003

The Sub-Commission on affected populations made a field trip to the Lake Chad area in August 2003 to appraise the situation on the ground. This was followed by an extra-ordinary meeting of the ad hoc Mixed Commission in Abuja on October 28, 2003 where the Working Group for the withdrawal and transfer of sovereignty in the Lake Chad region was put in place.[78] Another extra-ordinary meeting of the Mixed Commission took place from November 30– December 1, 2003 in Yaounde and examined the integrated operations related to the withdrawal and transfer of authority in the Lake Chad region. The delegates agreed that the withdrawal and transfer of authority in the Lake Chad region should be in December 2003. The delegates also decided that an Observation Mission be put in place to organize regular visits to the Lake Chad area and present a report one month after the definite transfer of authority. It was also agreed that this Observation Mission should subsequently submit a report after every three months for a one year period. These decisions were approved during the 7th ordinary session of the Mixed

---

8. Paragraph 13 of the press release at the end of the 1st session of the Commission's meeting stipulates that it shall meet after every two months. That is, on 1st Tuesday of the month, unless circumstances disturb. And that in consultation with the Members, the President can convene extra-ordinary meetings.

Commission in Yaounde in December, 2003. During this meeting, it was agreed that the withdrawal and transfer of authority in the Lake Chad area should take place from December 8-18, 2003.

In the Lake Chad region, the ICJ verdict stipulated that Cameroon re-establish sovereignty on Naga'a, Tchika, Toro Liman, Darack and their environs, while Nigeria was to inherit Dambore and its environs. The withdrawal concerned the army, police, customs and civil administration. The re-establishment of sovereignty was marked by the lowering of the flag of the country withdrawing from a given area or locality and then hoisting that of the country which was re-establishing sovereignty in that locality in conformity with the ICJ decision. The withdrawal was in phases; beginning with the locality of Naga'a, then Tchika, Dambore, Toro Liman and finally Darack.

Cameroon re-established sovereignty in Naga'a and its environs on December 8, 2003, at exactly 15h 8mins local time when in strict military tradition, the Nigerian flag; green-white-green was lowered and that of Cameroon; green-red-yellow hoisted. The ceremony was witnessed by the Head of the UN delegation and Legal Adviser of the Cameroon-Nigeria Mixed Commission, Jacob Haile Mariam of Ethiopian nationality. He was accompanied by Daniel Readburn, Military Adviser to the Mixed Commission. The Cameroon delegation was led by General James Tataw while that of Nigeria was led by General A.F.K. Akale.After Naga'a, the next locality that Nigeria retroceded to Cameroon was Tchika and its environs. The area was drapped in Cameroonian colours at 11h 40mins local time on December 16, 2003 in a ceremony attended by the special representative of the UN Secretary General, Ould-Abdallah, and Ahmadou Ali and Bola Ajibolah; leaders of the Cameroon and Nigeria delegations respectively.[79]

After the peaceful transfer of this locality to Cameroon, Ould-Abdallah declared that, it was an example to be followed by the whole continent. Meanwhile, Ahmadou Ali assured the population of the locality of Cameroon's commitment to assure the security of

---

9. *Cameroon Tribune*, N° 7996/4285, Wednesday, December 17, 2003.

foreigners resident in her country. For Ajibola, it was an historic moment for Africa.[80] From Tchika, the next stop was Dambore and its environs where at 17h 10mins local time, the Cameroon flag was put down and that of Nigeria hoisted. After the establishment of sovereignty in this locality, Nigeria assured Cameroon that the rights of the Cameroon population resident in the area were to be protected. In attendance was Ould-Abdallah for the UN, Ahmadou Ali for Cameroon and Bola Ajibola for Nigeria. It was in Dambore on December 16, 2003, that the official ceremony was organized (see plate 2).

From Dambore, the next stops for the transfer of sovereignty were in the localities of Toro Liman, situated at the shore of Lake Chad; and then Darack, an island in the heart of the lake. The two localities are 10km apart.[81] In attendance was Jacob Haile Mariam, Head of the UN delegation, Ambassador Cheik Oumar Diarrah, Executive Secretary of the Cameroon-Nigeria Mixed Commission and Colonel Daniel Repert of Canadian nationality; and Legal Adviser to the Mixed Commission. General A.F.K. Akale led the Nigerian delegation while General James Tataw led that of Cameroon.[82] The localities of Toro Liman and Darack were retroceded to Cameroon. The first stop was at Toro Liman. From Toro Liman, the different delegations moved to Darack where the Nigerian flag was lowered and that of Cameroon hoisted, at 12h 15mins local time. After this last stage, the three delegations—Cameroon, UN and Nigeria—met in Maga for the evaluation of the retrocession process. This was done in Camera.[83]

---

10. *Cameroon Tribune*, n° 7996/4285, Wednesday, December 17, 2003.

11. _____ , n° 7997/4286, Thursday, December 18, 2003.

12. Ibid.

13. Ibid.

Plate 2. The official Ceremony in Dambore Marking the Transfer of Sovereignty in the Lake Chad Region

Ajibola, Ould-Abdallah (centre) and Amadou Ali
signing documents at Dambore on December 16, 2003

Generals A.F.K. Akale (left) and James Tataw Shaking hands
during the retrocession ceremony

Source: *Cameroon Tribune*, n° 7999/4288, Monday, December 22, 2003.

125

Generally, Cameroon re-established sovereignty in 28 villages covering a total surface area of 888sq km and all situated in the Hile-Halfa Sub Division of the Logone and Shari Division of the then Far North Province of Cameroon. Nigeria on her part inherited territory of about 300sq km situated in the Borno State of Nigeria.

The local populations in these villages had the right to decide whether to go back to their country of origin or to remain on the spot. Meanwhile, the UN Observer Mission which was to effect regular visits to the Lake Chad area visited this area in January 2004; one month after the transfer of authority. The mission subsequently submitted a report after every three months for a one year period on the situation in the region. The first quarterly report was submitted during the 10th session of the Mixed Commission in Abuja in June 2004. The report was based on the Group's follow-up field visit to the area in May 2004. The Mixed Commission adopted the report and noted with satisfaction the general state of peace and good relations prevailing in the area in the aftermath of the transfer of authority. The Observer Personnel paid two other visits to the Lake Chad area in December 2004 and in February 2005; whose reports were considered and adopted by the Mixed Commission.

This first implementation of the ICJ verdict, barely 14 months after, was proof of the fact that Nigeria and Cameroon were committed to a peaceful implementation of the ICJ ruling. Therefore, we can comfortable join Jacob Haile Mariam, Head of the UN delegation who on December 8, 2003 at Naga'a declared that; "Cameroon and Nigeria have given a sound lesson in peaceful settlement of conflicts to the entire world."[84] Following the smooth withdrawal and re-establishment of sovereignty by Cameroon and Nigeria on disputed territories in the Lake Chad region in December 2003, it dawned on the UN Secretary General, Kofi Annan, to convene another tripartite summit with the two Presidents in order to assess the road covered so far and chart new avenues to finish the remaining tasks in the Land Boundary area and in the Bakassi Peninsula.

---

14. *Cameroon Tribune*, N° 7990/4279, Tuesday, December 9, 2003.

The Geneva II Tripartite Summit, January 2004

At the invitation of the UN Secretary General, Presidents Biya and Obasanjo met on January 31, 2004 in Geneva for the third Tripartite Meeting code-named Geneva II.The UN Secretary General and the two Presidents welcomed the significant progress achieved so far notably the smooth re-establishment of sovereignty on disputed territories in the Lake Chad area in December 2003. They also appreciated the climate reigning in the region one month after. They equally renewed their commitments to ensure the effective implementation of the ICJ verdict and reiterated the need to avoid any actions or declarations which could jeopardize the process. They also committed themselves to guarantee the security and welfare of the population affected by the Court's decision in areas under their respective sovereignty. They equally agreed to strengthen confidence building measures in myriad spheres.

Following this renewed satisfaction and commitments of Presidents Biya and Obasanjo to ensure the effective implementation of the ICJ verdict; the Mixed Commission immediately set to work to implement those decisions. Therefore, the Commission decided to undertake a tripartite field visit to the Land Boundary area—between the Lake Chad region and the Bakassi Peninsula—to assess the impediments in the implementation of the Court's decision.

The process of the retrocession and transfer of sovereignty in the Land Boundary area, 2002-2004

On the Land Boundary area, 17 sectors were affected by the ICJ decision. In many of these areas, the verdict was in favour of Nigeria. Generally, the areas concerned were in the border villages of Narki and some patches of territory along the border that were handed to Cameroon and the border villages of Bourha-Wango and Ndabakoura as well as some patches of territory along the border that went to Nigeria.

Meeting in Yaounde in April 2004, the Mixed Commission set the withdrawal of troops from the Land Boundary to run from June 15 – July 15, 2004. A Working Group was also established to oversee the transfer of authority.The Commission equally carried out a field visit to the Land Boundary area from May 15-19, 2004. The Commission visited Ndabakura and Narki in the Borno State in Nigeria or the then Far North Province in Cameroon; Bourha Wango, in the Adamawa State in Nigeria or the then Far North Province in Cameroon; Jalingo, Banyo, Dorofi, Takum and Mbererego, in Taraba State in Nigeria or the then Adamawa and North West Provinces in Cameroon. In all these localities, the Commission met with the local populations, listened to their concerns and explained to them the work of the Mixed Commission and the efforts of the two governments to enhance and further consolidate the peaceful relations between them.

Following these visits, the Commission appraised the conditions on the ground and decided to plan more visits to the Land Boundary. As a consequence, the calendar of withdrawal and transfer of authority in the Land Boundary was revised to take place from July 13-15, 2004. Members of the Working Group to oversee the establishment of sovereignty on the Land Boundary and those of the Sub-Commission on Demarcation visited the Land Boundary area in the first week of July 2004. This paved the way for the operational phase of the withdrawal and transfer of authority in the Land Boundary area.

Cameroon established sovereignty in the village of Narki and Nigeria in Bourha-Wango and Ndabakoura villages.The withdrawal and transfer of authority forms for Narki, Ndabakoura and Bourha Wango precise that the ceremony was symbolic and representative of the overall process of withdrawal and transfer of authority of localities and territories along the Land Boundary. This is so because in the mapping of the boundary, some patches of territory along the border either went to Cameroon or Nigeria.

The border village of Narki in the Mora Sub Division, Mayo Sava Division of the then Far North Province of Cameroon was on July 13, 2004, handed over by Nigerian officials to Cameroon. The Cameroon delegation to the handing over ceremony was led by Amadou Ali and that of Nigeria by Bola Ajibola. Ahmedou Ould-Abdallah represented the UN Secretary General. Alhaji Adamu Shetima Dibal, deputy Governor of the Borno State in Nigeria and

Lazare Abate Abate, Governor of the then Far North Province of Cameroon were also in attendance. Narki, with a population of about 15.000 was drapped in Cameroonian colours followed by the signing of the withdrawal and transfer of authority documents under the supervision of Ould-Abdallah.[85]

Meanwhile, Nigeria on July 14, 2004 established sovereignty in the localities of Bourha-Wango with 67 families and with about 700 inhabitants and then in Ndabakoura respectively in the Borno and Adamawa States in Nigeria. Amadou Ali led the Cameroon delegation while Ajibola led that of Nigeria. Ould-Abdallah sat in for the UN. The transfer of authority ceremonies were also witnessed by the Senior Divisional Officer (SDO) of Mayo Tsanaga of the then Far North Province of Cameroon, Hamidou Bala, the Emir of Mubi in Nigeria and the Governor of the Adamawa state in Nigeria, El Hadj Boni Haruna. The Cameroon flag was lowered in these localities and that of Nigeria hoisted and documents marking the change of sovereignty signed.[86] This equally marked an end to the withdrawal and transfer of authority in the affected areas along the Land Boundary area in the North.

The UN Observer Personnel visited the Land Boundary from November 22-23, 2004 and again from February 24-25, 2005 and from June 13-15, 2005 to appraise the situation on the ground after the transfer of sovereignty. The reports of these three visits were considered and adopted by the Mixed Commission during its 13th session in Yaounde in July 2005. The Commission noted with satisfaction the peaceful atmosphere prevailing in the Land Boundary area one year after the withdrawal and transfers of authority notably the good relations existing between the populations and the new authorities. With these assurances, attention was then focused on the Bakassi Peninsula in the South.

---

15. *Cameroon Tribune*, n° 8138/4423, Wednesday, July 14, 2004.

16. _____ , n° 8139/4424, Thursday, July 15, 2004.

The Process of the Withdrawal of the Nigerian Administration, Armed Forces and Police in the Bakassi Peninsula, 2002-2008

The Mixed Commission had the task of working out a calendar for the operational phase for the withdrawal and transfer of authority in the Bakassi Peninsula. To do this, field visits were undertaken to the peninsula to evaluate the situation on the ground. The Sub-Commission on affected populations undertook a field visit to the peninsula in February 2004 and reported back to the Mixed Commission. The report permitted the Mixed Commission to set the withdrawal of Nigerian administration and troops from the peninsula to commence from July 15 and to terminate on September 15, 2004. A working Group was also established to oversee the transfer of sovereignty. In order to tidy up all details on the field, the Tripartite Mixed Commission effected another visit to the peninsula from May 15-19, 2004. In and around the peninsula, the Commission members visited Danare, Bodam, Mamfe, Calabar, Abana/Jabane, Archibong/Akwa and Ekondo Titi, in the Cross River State of Nigeria or the then South West Province of Cameroon. The Commission members met with the local population and assured them of the efforts of the two governments to consolidate the peaceful relations between the populations of the two countries.

Following this visit, a revised working calendar for the operational phase for the withdrawal and transfer of authority in the Bakassi Peninsula was set to take place from August 20 – September 13, 2004. Meanwhile, the official ceremony to mark the transfer of sovereignty in the peninsula was fixed for September 14-15, 2004.[87] This calendar was hardly respected because at the 11th session of the Mixed Commission in Yaounde in August 2004, Nigeria wanted a clearer definition of the status of her nationals in Bakassi beyond the pledges of good treatment by the Cameroonian government as

---

17. *Cameroon Tribune*, n° 8113/4402, Wednesday, June 9, 2004.

contained in the ICJ verdict of October 10, 2002.[88] A tripartite meeting with leaders of Cameroon and Nigeria in the Commission with the Special Representative of the UN Secretary General met in Yaounde on August 29 to clarify the situation but there was no breakthrough. From that time too, the Mixed Commission's meetings witnessed a stalemate between the 12th and 13th sessions as they were interrupted for over eight months. This apparent blockage was confirmed by the Chairman of the Commission, Ould-Abdallah in an interview on November 27, 2004 during the 10th Francophonie Summit in Ouagadougou, Burkina Faso; held from November 26-27, 2004. According to Ould-Abdallah; Nigeria wanted the problem of her nationals in Bakassi to be well spelt out.[89]

The process of the establishment of sovereignty in the Bakassi Peninsula witnessed substantial setbacks because of several considerations and influences. First, Nigeria wanted a clearer definition of the fate of their nationals' resident in Bakassi. This became necessary because more than 90 percent of the inhabitants of Bakassi were Nigerians. Nigeria was therefore afraid that Cameroon would still continue to neglect the area as she had done in the past. She needed a protocol agreement that would compel Cameroon to develop the area as well as guarantee the fundamental rights of Nigerian residents. This expression of national interests stems from the fact that the Cameroon government may implement policies that could force these Nigerian residents to opt to go back home; a situation that would swell the already high population in Nigeria estimated at 150million inhabitants at the time. This could also weigh heavily on Nigerian resources. Second, the geostrategic importance of the peninsula prompted Nigeria to continue such manoeuvrings in order to renegotiate some of the clauses of the ICJ ruling in her favour through the ad hoc Mixed Commission. This Nigerian stance is also an indication that national interests is a key factor in

---

18. The Court addressed the problem of Nigerian residents in Bakassi by taking note of Cameroon's undertaking given at the hearings to continue to afford protection to Nigerians living in the Bakassi Peninsula and in the Lake Chad area.

19. *Cameroon Tribune*, n° 8234/4433, Monday, November 29, 2004.

international relations. As a consequence, Cameroon and Nigeria disagreed in the Mixed Commission when their interests were threatened.

As a result of the interruptions in the implementation of the ICJ verdict over Bakassi, the UN Secretary General, Kofi Annan convened another tripartite meeting in Geneva to repair the rupture and chart a way forward, notably by reconvening the meeting of the ad hoc Mixed Commission.

The Geneva III Tripartite Summit, May 2005

The May 10-11, 2005 meeting was attended by Presidents Obasanjo and Biya at the instance of the UN Secretary General, Kofi Annan. During the meeting, the UN Scribe and the two Presidents examined the state of advancement of the demarcation process and agreed on a new programme of the withdrawal of Nigerian troops from Bakassi. They agreed that this programme was to be communicated in the shortest time possible by the two Presidents and the UN Secretary General. They also appreciated the withdrawal and transfer of authority in the Land Boundary in July 2004 and the atmosphere existing among the populations of the two countries and their new administrators. They equally examined the question of the concerned populations in areas affected by the ICJ ruling and promised to take all measures to guarantee property and the interests of these populations.

This expression of commitment by the two Presidents was not enough to cause Nigeria to accept pulling out of Bakassi. It needed an accord to that effect. As a consequence, the UN Secretary General, Kofi Annan summoned the Heads of State of Cameroon and Nigeria, Paul Biya and Olusegun Obasanjo respectively to a meeting at Greentree near New York in the USA.

The Greentree Tripartite Summit, June 2006

The June 12, 2006 Greentree meeting in Manhasset, New York City, USA was the 5th tripartite summit of Presidents Biya and Obasanjo with the UN Secretary General. The close door summit at the Greentree estate[90] was scheduled to last 30 minutes but it went slightly beyond one hour, with no aides allowed in. The two Heads of State and the UN Secretary General reviewed the progress achieved by the Mixed Commission and noted with satisfaction the advances made in the implementation of the judgement of the ICJ of October 10, 2002. They then focused on the Bakassi Peninsula and discussed the modalities of peacefully restoring it to Cameroon in accordance with international law and with due regard for the well-being of the populations. Thereafter, the two Presidents parted ways before returning into Room B conference centre hall accompanied by their close collaborators for the signing of the much awaited agreement (see plate 3).

The Greentree Accord

This was an agreement between the Republic of Cameroon represented by its President, Paul Biya, and the Federal Republic of Nigeria, represented by its President, Olusegun Obasanjo and witnessed by the UN and representatives from the Federal Republic of Germany, the USA, the French Republic and the United Kingdom of Great Britain and Northern Ireland, concerning the modalities of withdrawal and transfer of authority in the Bakassi Peninsula.

By the terms of the agreement, Nigeria agreed to withdraw her troops from the Bakassi Peninsula within 60 days. This deadline could be extended by the UN Secretary General for a further period not exceeding a total of 30 days.[91] By this agreement, Nigeria effectively recognized the sovereignty of Cameroon over the Bakassi Peninsula in accordance with the ruling of the ICJ of October 10, 2002. By the terms of the agreement, Cameroon undertook to guarantee Nigerian nationals living in the Bakassi Peninsula the

---

20. Greentree is situated about 2hours drive from the UN building in New York. It has an area of about 1.8sq Km, very calm and dotted with green gardens. It belongs to the family of late John Hay Whitney; a millionaire diplomat and philanthropist who put the building at the disposal of the UN for special, high level meetings. See *Cameroon Tribune,* n° 8613/4812, Tuesday, June 20, 2006.

21. See Appendix 3 for the full text of the Accord.

exercise of their fundamental rights and freedoms. Besides the strengthening of bilateral relations, Cameroon also undertook to respect the culture, language and beliefs of Nigerians who chose to stay in the area; respect their right to continue their agricultural and fishing activities, and to protect their property and customary land rights as well as take measures to protect them from any harassment.

The mandate of the Follow-up Committee set up to oversee the implementation of the agreement was to span up to 2013, when the period of the special transitional regime provided in the accord to Nigerian nationals in the peninsula was to end. Article 4 of Annex I of this agreement specifies that following the transfer of authority over the peninsula to Cameroon—which took place in August 2008—the latter shall apply in the zone a special transitional regime for a non-renewable period of five years. In application of the special transitional regime, Cameroon shall: allow access by Nigerian civil authorities to the Nigerian population living in the zone; not apply its customs or immigration laws to Nigerian nationals living in the zone on their direct return from Nigeria for the purpose of exercising their activities; allow officers and uniformed personnel of the Nigerian police access to the zone, in cooperation with Cameroonian police and finally; allow innocent passage in the territorial waters of the zone to civilian ships sailing under the Nigerian flag.

The agreement was signed for the Republic of Cameroon by President Paul Biya and for the Federal Republic of Nigeria by President Olusegun Obasanjo. The UN Secretary General, Kofi Annan signed for the organization. The representatives of the witness states equally appended their signatures on the agreement. They included: Gunter Pleuger, Permanent Representative of Germany at the UN; Ms Karen Pierce, Deputy Permanent Representative of the United Kingdom (UK) at the UN; Michel Duclos, Deputy Permanent Representative of France at the UN and Ms Fakie Sanders, Ambassador and Head of the US Mission to the UN.

The acceptance by Nigeria of a close deadline to pull out of the Bakassi Peninsula was prove to the fact that pressure was being mounted on her to respect the ICJ ruling. Unlike in the past, four big powers of the UN, three of them—the US, UK and France—Permanent Members of the Security Council, were represented to

Plate 3. The Greentree Tripartite Summit, June 12, 2006

Biya, Annan and Obasanjo during the close door meeting.

Biya and Obasanjo appending their signatures on
the Greentree Agreement flanked by their collaborators
and representatives of the witness States.

Source: *Cameroon Tribune,* no.8613/4812, Tuesday, June 20,
2006.

bear witness to the agreement. This was an indication that they supported the process and will continue to mount pressure on Nigeria to accept her international engagements. Article 94 (2) of the UN Charter empowers the Security Council to take action to ensure that states conform with international obligations as decided by the outcome of legal proceedings in the ICJ.

The deadline for the withdrawal of Nigerian troops from the Bakassi Peninsula expired when the troops were still stationed there. However, after 13 years of Nigerian occupation, the Bakassi Peninsula became Cameroon on August 14, 2006 with the exception of Jabane, Idabato and Akwabana which remained on provisional Nigerian administration for a period of 2 years. During this period, Cameroon was to allow Nigeria to keep its civil administration and a police force necessary for the maintenance of peace and order in this areas.During this two-year period too, Nigeria could not conduct or allow the conduct of any activities in the Zone which would prejudice Cameroon's peace and security. Nigeria was also forbidden to carryout activities like heavily equipping of its police force and the positioning of armed forces in the Zone, the transfer or influx of Nigerian nationals into the Zone, exploitation of natural resources in the sub soil of the Zone, and the undertaking of activities harmful to the environment.Nigeria was also required to guarantee to Cameroonian nationals wishing to return to their village in the Zone the exercise of their rights and take every necessary measure to prevent any change of land property rights and not engage in any activity in the Zone which would complicate or hinder the transfer of authority to Cameroon.[92]

The August 2006 disengagement of Nigerian troops from the peninsula was marked by a ceremony in Akwa (Archibong for Nigeria) situated at the extreme north-east of Bakassi. The Nigerian flag was lowered at 12:30pm local time and the Cameroonian flag hoisted. This was under the command of the two Chiefs of Defence Staff; General Martin Luther Agwai for Nigeria and Major General Meka for Cameroon. The documents of transfer were signed by the representative of the government of Cameroon, Maurice Kamto and

22. See Appendix 3.

that of Nigeria, Chief Bayo Ojo; the representative of the UN Secretary General and President of the Follow-up Committee of the Greentree Accord, British Diplomat, Sir Kieran Prendergast as well as the representatives of the witness states of the Greentree Accord; Germany, the USA, France and Great Britain. They included; the British High Commissioner to Cameroon, Syd Madicott, French Ambassador to Nigeria, Yves Gandeul; US Chargé d'Affairs in Cameroon, Richard W. Nelson and Defence Attaché at the German Embassy in Nigeria, Lieutenant Colonel Mathias Aochhausen.[93]

The dispute ended on August 14, 2008, with a barely 40mins retrocession ceremony at the Roland Adjai Peregrino Hall, Calabar, the official Lodge of the Governor of the Cross River State of Nigeria. Five speeches were delivered during the handover ceremony. Successively taking the podium were Said Djinnit, the chair of the Cameroon-Nigeria Mixed Commission; the Rt Hon. Francis Adah, Acting Governor of the Cross River State of Nigeria; chief Michael Anodoakan, Attorney General and Minister of Justice of Nigeria; Professor Maurice Kamto, Cameroon's Minister Delegate in the Follow-up Committee of the Greentree Agreement and the Chairman of the Follow-up Committee of that Agreement, Sir Kieran Prendergast.[94] After the speech-making; the leaders of the Nigerian and Cameroonian delegations, Anodoakan and Kamto respectively appended their signatures on the transfer documents. Following the signing, the flags of the two countries were exchanged between the two delegation leaders. Meanwhile, soldiers were also disengaging in the field in Bakassi. Equally, Nigeria's flag was being lowered in the peninsula and that of Cameroon was being hoisted.

This marked the end of the retrocession and transfer of sovereignty on disputed border territories by Cameroon and Nigeria in accordance with the ICJ ruling. Attention was then turned to the demarcation of the Land and Maritime Boundary.

---

23. *Cameroon Tribune*, n° 8662/4861, Wednesday, August 16, 2006.

24._____ , n° 9162/5361, Friday, August 15, 2008.

The Demarcation of the Land and Maritime Boundary, 2002-2011

In its judgement, the ICJ delimited the Cameroon-Nigeria Boundary from Lake Chad through the Land and Maritme Boundary. The Cameroon-Nigeria Mixed Commission had the task of demarcating the entire frontier from Lake Chad to the sea. In order to achieve this, the Commission created a Sub Commission for the demarcation of the Land Boundary between the two countries and a Working Group charged with the demarcation of the Maritime Boundary. The work plan, meetings and reports of these sub units were approved by the ad hoc Mixed Commission whose work was again approved by the Follow-up Committee of the Greentree Accord. The Sub Commission on the Demarcation of the Land Boundary kicked starts its work in 2002 while the Working Group on the Maritime Boundary started its work in 2004.

The demarcation of the Land Boundary, 2002-2011

On December 2, 2002, the Sub Commission for the demarcation of the Land Boundary was established. The Sub Commission was composed of legal experts and cartographers from the two parties and the UN. The Sub Commission met in January 2003 and prepared a small scale map indicating the boundary and also considered the nature and characteristics of the maps that needed to be prepared for the demarcation process. It also prepared a comprehensive report for the demarcation process which was approved by the Mixed Commission. According to the report, the demarcation activities were estimated at 12 million dollars (about FCFA 8.4 billion).[95] In 2003, Cameroon and Nigeria deposited US $1.25million each (about FCFA 875million) to the UN Trust Fund for the initial financing of the demarcation activities. Meanwhile, the Mixed Commission went ahead and prepared a document to seek for sources of funding for the boundary demarcation exercise. The Mixed Commission then examined and adopted this document during its 5th session in Yaounde in August 2003.

---

25. *Cameroon Tribune*, n° 7903/4192, Wednesday, August 6, 2003.

138

With these financial details being sorted out, the Mixed Commission identified the contracts on demarcation and defined the specifications of the process. To do this, a Joint Technical Team (JTT) was formed to make field verification with the contractor for the imagery of the pillar emplacements shown on the Ortho-imagery, and preliminary instructions for the demarcation. A draft programme for the field visit by interested contractors was equally prepared by the Commission's Secretariat. The Sub Commission on demarcation equally prepared the contract procedures for the demarcation during its meeting in Abuja in October 2003. According to this procedure, the call for bids was to be posted on the UN website. Between February and April 2004, the Sub Commission on demarcation caused the posting on the UN website of the invitation for the expression of interest on contracts 2, 3 and 4 pertaining to the satellite imagery for mapping.[96] That is, taking satellite images of the boundary.

As the contract procedures were being sorted out, the Mixed Commission and the UN Secretary General tried to galvanize for financial help for the demarcation process. As a consequence, during the Tripartite Summit of Annan, Biya and Obasanjo on January 31, 2004, the UN Scribe appealed to the international community within the context of preventive diplomacy to provide financial assistance for the demarcation process. The Mixed Commission equally undertook a mission to London, Paris, Washington D.C and New York from March 5-13, 2004 to galvanize for financial help. These efforts continued in earnest as the Mixed Commission during its 13th session in Yaounde in July 2005 invited the British High Commissioner to Cameroon, Syd Madiccot, in his capacity as representing the Presidency of the EU, and requested the support of the government of his country over the joint application of Cameroon and Nigeria for funding by the EU for the demarcation activities.

The request by the UN Scribe and diplomatic offensives by the Mixed Commission for funding, yielded dividends as Britain chipped in 1 million pound sterling into the UN Trust Fund for the

26. *Cameroon Tribune,* n° 8073/4362, Monday, April 12, 2004.

demarcation process; while the EU contributed a supplementary amount of 4 million Euros to add to the 400.000Euros already contributed.[97] Cameroon and Nigeria, pursuant to the decision of the Commission taken on February 8, 2004 chipped in an additional contribution of US $1.75 millions into the UN Trust Fund for demarcation in the first half of May 2004.[98] Canada and Norway equally contributed money and/or technical assistance for the demarcation efforts. During the 3rd session of the Mixed Commission in Yaounde in April 2003, the Chairman announced that the World Bank had pledged US $200.000 (about FCFA 130 million) for the needs of the Mixed Commission.

With the financial means in place, the Sub Commission on demarcation put in place a JTT led by Madam Christa Meindersma, Specialist on frontier demarcation questions at the UN, whose role was to put into practice the decisions of the Commission by demarcating the Land Boundary from Lake Chad to the Bakassi Peninsula. Concerning technical logistics, the UN put at the disposal of the parties, preliminary maps of the frontier produced by the cartographic service at New York. Each party was requested to prepare its reactions concerning these maps and send to the President of the JTT, Mme Christa Meindersma.

Before the demarcation proper, the JTT visited the Land Boundary in order to validate the preliminary maps on which is marked the frontier as decided by the ICJ. This verification was preceded by the execution of a pilot project whose results permitted for the evaluation of the work on the field. The JTT effectively validated the maps and continued with the work of the identification of areas to plant pillars. As these technical details were being sorted out; the UN Secretary General, Kofi Annan held a Tripartite Meeting with Presidents Biya and Obasanjo in Geneva in May 2005 to examine the state of the advancement of the process of demarcation. They noted with satisfaction that the technical visits to the field for demarcation efforts were going on hitch free.

---

27. *Cameroon Tribune*, n° 8618/4817, Tuesday, June 13, 2006.

28. _____ , n° 8113/4402, Wednesday, June 9, 2004.

After the verification mission by the Sub Commission on demarcation and the JTT; members met in Yaounde from July 26-27, 2005 and prepared a report which was submitted to the Mixed Commission for adoption. This report was examined and adopted by the Mixed Commission during its 15th session in Yaounde in September 2006. The Mixed Commission however instructed the JTT to go back to the sector of Mada – Sahle – Zigague and map the area in conformity with the ICJ ruling.

Following these precisions, phase I of the demarcation activities kicked start in 2006. It concerned the Lake Chad region and covered a distance of 401km. Phase II with a distance of 460km downwards from Lake Chad and along rivers and watersheds started in February 2007. This second phase was however interrupted by the rainy season. Therefore, in order to expedite the process, the JTT charged with the demarcation was split up into two teams which worked simultaneously. In the same vein, the Mixed Commission decided that contract V concerning the emplacement of boundary pillars was subdivided into three separate contracts which should involve local contractors of Cameroon and Nigeria. Phase III of the demarcation exercise; split into two groups, was launched in November 2007. One group had to demarcate the Mount Alantika zone and the region of Kotcha (Kontcha) in the then North and Adamawa Provinces of Cameroon covering a distance of 300km. Another group was to continue from this region southwards for a distance of 245km. The JTT equally had the task of establishing a geodetic datum network on either side of the entire boundary. That is, it had to install a series of antennas which could permit the capture of satellite signals in order to know with exactitude where the pillars should be planted.

By March 2008, more than 830km of the Land Boundary had been demarcated.[99] At this juncture, the Mixed Commission urged the JTT to complete the demarcation exercise by the end of 2009. But this calendar was not respected as the demarcation of 270km was programmed for 2010.[100] Meanwhile, in July 2011, some 350km of

---

29. *Cameroon Tribune,* n° 9058/5257, Friday, March 14, 2008.

30. *The Post* (Cameroon), n° 01093, Friday October 16, 2009.

the 1950km boundary remained to be demarcated. Before the completion of the demarcation process; the emplacement of boundary pillars kicked start on the already demarcated areas.

The placement of boundary identification pillars on the Cameroon – Nigeria border

In order to achieve this, the Mixed Commission through the UN Office for West Africa (UNOWA) entered into an agreement with the United Nations Office for Project Services (UNOPS) to support the first phase of the placement of the boundary identification pillars. UNOPS had the task of implementing contract 5A relating to demarcation and pillar emplacement. The technical supervision was on the shoulders of the JTT. Originally planned to commence within the first week of 2009, the exercise only took off on December 14, 2009.

The main pillars were placed after every 5 kilometers and the secondary pillars after every 500metres. Therefore, over 400 major pillars and 4000 secondary pillars were to be constructed and laid down in some 1950km of border line between Cameroon and Nigeria. According to the call for the expression of interest launched by UNOPS, the pillars had the following specifications. Each boundary pillar was to be offset with two permanent witness marks and constructed to meet the minimum required concrete strength that conforms to international standard engineering practice. They were also to be constructed within 250mm of the pre-evaluated position indicated by coordinates on signed templates.[101]

The first pillar on the Cameroon-Nigeria border was implanted in the localities of Banki (Nigeria) and Amchide (Cameroon) in the Lake Chad region on December 14, 2009. The pillars were placed two meters into the soil and 1m70 on the surface with the flags of the two countries on them. The ceremony marking the pillar emplacement activities started at 1p.m. local time with the arrival of delegations.

---

31. *Cameroon Tribune*, n° 9460/5661, Thursday, October 22, 2009.

142

Amadou Ali led the Cameroon delegation while Marafa Diggi led that of Nigeria. Said Djinnit represented the UN. The Ambassadors of the Witness states of the Greentree Accord—USA, France, Germany and UK—represented their respective countries.[102] During the 27th session of the Mixed Commission in Yaounde in March 2011, it was revealed that 378km of the boundary was already demarcated with pillars.During this meeting too, the Commission agreed to set up a sensitization mission within the Sub-Commission on Demarcation, comprising representatives of Cameroon, Nigeria and the UN in collaboration with local Authorities and security services to sensitise the frontier populations on the demarcation activities.

The Demarcation of the Maritime Boundary, 2004-2008

The demarcation of the Maritime Boundary was bestowed on a Working Group created by the Mixed Commission in February 2004 to realize such a task. This Working Group was composed of five experts each from Nigeria and Cameroon and other experts from the UN. During the 9th session of the Mixed Commission in Yaounde in April 2004, the list of the Cameroonian and Nigerian representatives in the Working Group was received. The Group held its first meeting on May 28, 2004 in Abuja and elaborated a work plan which was adopted by the Mixed Commission during its 10th session in Abuja in June 2004. According to the work plan, the Working Group was to present a map in December 2004 featuring a delineation of the Maritime Boundary as delimited by the ICJ in its decision of October 10, 2002, and make recommendations pertaining to the demarcation of the Maritime Boundary.

In order to expedite the process, the Chairman of the Mixed Commission, Ould-Abdallah, wrote a letter to the UN expert dated November 29, 2004, calling on him to propose a map delineating the Maritime Boundary as delimited by the Court in conformity with the agreement between the two parties; Cameroon and Nigeria. This

---

32. *Cameroon Tribune*, n° 9497/5698, Tuesday, December 15, 2009.

proposed map was presented in the next meeting of the Working Group and during the 14th session of the Mixed Commission in Abuja in October 2005. This map was later examined and adopted by the Mixed Commission in its 15th session in Yaounde in September 2006. Meanwhile, the Working Group met in Yaounde in October 2006 and planned a field mission at sea in November 2006. This field mission was intended to survey and see the flexibility of instituting the 4-points option proposed by the Cameroonian party and the 14-points option presented by the UN experts; and to consider any other option from the surveyed points that will realistically respect the terms of reference.

The Commission equally exhorted the Joint Team to finalize the conversion of the British Admiralty Chart 3433 (1994 edition) containing the Maritime Boundary line approved by the parties and adopted by the Mixed Commission into the World Geodetic System 84 (WGS84) Datum (see table 2).

Table 2. Geo-Referencing Coordinates for the Demarcation of theCameroon-Nigeria Maritime Boundary (10 points option)

POINT	UTM CO-ORDINATES		GEOGRAPHICAL	
	X	Y	LATITUDE	LONGITUDE
1	446007.7	516514.3	4⁰40'22.06"	8⁰30'47.46
2	4444647.5	515666.3	4⁰39'54.41"	8⁰30'03.33"
3	442480.7	513844.7	4⁰38'55.04"	8⁰28'53.04"
4	440686.7	512018.4	4⁰37'55.51"	8⁰27'54.86"
5	439349.8	510185.6	4⁰36'55.80"	8⁰27'11.51"
6	438323.6	508356.1	4⁰35'56.19"	8⁰26'38.26"

144

7	437299.1	506525.0	4°34'56.53"	8°26'05.05"
8	436645.2	505241.1	4°34'14.70"	8°25'43.87"
9	436425.7	504690.7	4°33'56.77"	8°25'36.76"
10	435584.1	502857.9	4°32'57.06"	8°25'09.49"
11	434927.1	501020.4	4°31'57.20"	8°24'48.22"
12	434645.5	499980.0	4°31'23.31"	8°24'39.11"
A	434212.7	500108.8	4°31'27.50"	8°24'25.06"
A₁	434212.7	499800.2	4°31'17.44"	8°24'25.07"
B	433735.5	490967.5	4°26'29.78"	8°24'09.81"
C	432843.0	485330.9	4°23'26.19"	8°23'41.00"
D	430932.3	478965.7	4°19'58.85"	8°22'39.18"
E	430184.6	478113.0	4°19'31.06"	8°22'14.95"
F	430241.8	476700.2	4°18'45.05"	8°22'16.84"
G	430224.3	473448.4	4°16'59.15"	8°22'16.36"
X	428404.3	473465.9	4°16'59.67"	8°21'17.32"

Source: *Cameroon Tribune,* no. 8850/5049, Wednesday, May 16, 2007.

Note: The coordinates are based on the geo-referencing of the British Admiralty chart 3433, 1994 edition.

The WGS84 is an International Agreement that was signed in 1984 harmonising the method for the calculation of distances and areas so that anybody anywhere in the world using the system could have the same results. Coordinate points of reference using the system are referred to as Universal Traverse Mercator (UTM), measured in metres across 60 bands North and South of the Equator.

The Working Group on the Maritime Boundary held its 9th meeting alternatively in Yaounde and Abuja in May 2007 and compiled its report following the field mission at sea in November 2006. During the extraordinary meeting of the Mixed Commission in Abuja on May 11, 2007, the 10-point option presented by the Working Group as well as the map relating thereto, together with the corresponding coordinates were approved. Since the map provided by the UN experts did not have geodetic references, it required many missions at sea in order to have these topographic points identified on the map. Therefore, the list of coordinates for all points on the Maritime Frontier was converted into the WGS84.

After agreeing on the geo-referencing coordinates, the Working Group on the Maritime Boundary met and evaluated the consequences of tracing the Maritime Boundary notably with regard to the exploitation of natural resources especially oil and gas fields straddling or along the Maritime Boundary. The Working Group equally took steps to finalize the loxodrome which extends beyond point X (fixed by the ICJ in 2002) seawards. Meeting in Yaounde in 2008, the parties agreed on the delineation of this loxodrome. Here, the British Admiralty Chart 1387, 'Calabar to Bata, including Isla de Bioko' 2007 edition, and including the transposition of the loxodrome line was formally approved and signed by the Heads of Delegation; Ajibola for Nigeria, Ahmadou Ali for Cameroon and Ould-Abdallah, UN Secretary General's Special Representative.This therefore ended the implementation of the ICJ verdict in respect of the Maritime Boundary.

Following this agreement, Cameroon and Nigeria then agreed that Nigeria will hand over to Cameroon, information on the Nigerian offshore installations in Cameroonian territorial waters in keeping with the Minutes of the meeting held at Greentree on June 12, 2006. The two countries equally agreed to provide information to the UN on areas immediately adjacent to the Maritime Boundary where concessions, licenses or contracts have been awarded or concluded. All this was intended to establish an acceptable formula for the harmonious exploitation of resources straddling or along the Maritime Boundary.

Generally, the implementation of the ICJ judgement on the Cameroon-Nigeria border dispute case was given the maximum ceremonial attention in consonance with the prescriptions of experts on conflict resolution. In this line, Zartman writes;

> If secrecy is useful during the diplomatic discussion, publicity is necessary during the implementation to enhance commitment and keep the process honest. Public statements, monitoring and witnessing are all helpful instruments to ensure implementation.... [in order] to assist their future observance.[103]

This publicity was very much present during the process of the retrocession and establishment of sovereignty on disputed territories between 2002 and 2008; and during the process of the demarcation of the Land and Maritime Boundary.

By July 2011, Cameroon and Nigeria had reached consensus on the demarcation of some 1600km of the 1950km common Boundary. That notwithstanding, certain challenges still remain to be overcomed. First, the demarcation of the remaining 350km including areas of disagreement that were skipped, and inaccessible ones, is quite challenging for the ad hoc Mixed Commission. There was disagreement in the localities of Kerawa River, Mada-Gourgourou, Mada-Sahle-Zigague, and in kotcha (Kontcha). Meanwhile, inaccessible areas like those across streams, thick forests in the Equatorial Zone and in the swamps and mangrove forests in the Bakassi-Akwayafe Zone remained to be demarcated. Second, the

---

33. Zartman, *Ripe for Resolution*, p. 244.

emplacement of identification pillars begun in December 2009 has been progressing at a snail pace. Indeed, if it took more than 16 months to place pillars in 378km between December 2009 and July 2011; the deadline for the completion of the demarcation process set for the end of 2012, may not be respected if the process is not expedited. In order to expedite the process, the numbers of teams for the pillar emplacement exercise needs to be increased. This will however depend on the availability of the financial means. Third, the demarcation of the Land Boundary divided settlements, families and even houses. Meanwhile, the socio-economic needs of the affected populations like the provision of education and health infrastructures, potable water and environmental protection remain unresolved. Therefore, the manner of addressing these problems has to be sorted out. Finally, another daunting task for the two countries is to fix the tripoint of their Maritime Boundary with Equatorial Guinea. Unlike Nigeria which concluded a Treaty with Equatorial Guinea on September 23, 2000 delimiting their Maritime Frontier, Cameroon and Equatorial Guinea have not yet concluded such an agreement. As a result, Cameroon and Equatorial Guinea will have to finalize negotiations for the delimitation of their Maritime Border before the tripoint—Cameroon, Nigeria, Equatorial Guinea—can be fixed.

The resolution of the dispute was not limited to the re-establishment of sovereignty by Cameroon and Nigeria on disputed border territories and the fixing and accepting of frontier lines. It equally involved concerted effort to resolve the causes of the dispute, as well as reconciliation and restoration of cooperation between the two countries. In its ruling, the ICJ set the pace for this reconciliation and cooperation by considering the commitment of Cameroon to protect Nigerian citizens living in Bakassi and the Lake Chad area and refusing to pronounce the international liability of Nigeria as demanded by Cameroon.

Chapter 6

Confidence Building Measures between Cameroon and Nigeria, 2002-2011

Confidence building became the fulcrum of the resolution of the Cameroon-Nigeria border problem as the two countries found formulas that would satisfy them. These formulas were on two distinct levels: first, resolving the issues that sparked off the dispute and second, improving bilateral and sub regional integration. As a consequence, the two countries addressed the security and strategic concerns as well as the socio-economic concerns that sparked off the conflict. They also carried out measures to revamp diplomatic relations and sub regional integration. In this process, Cameroonian and Nigerian authorities with the help of the international community instituted a formidable machinery of conciliation and provided an exceptional mechanism by skirting out knotty issues like the juridical regime of Nigerians in the Bakassi Peninsula right up to 2013.

Measures to Address the Socio-Economic Concerns of the Two Countries

Boosting the social and economic needs of Nigeria and Cameroon was part and parcel of the resolution of their border dispute. This was necessary as these social and economic imperatives partly contributed to the outbreak of the border skirmishes. These socio-economic concerns involved the building of trans-frontier road infrastructures, electricity exportation, research partnership, and the boosting of formal trade. These projects were discussed and adopted at the level of the Joint Commission, ad hoc Mixed Commission and at various bilateral meetings between the two countries.

Boosting trans-frontier road infrastructures

The maintenance and construction of trans-frontier road infrastructures became the pivot of confidence building between Cameroon and Nigeria. Two main corridors were identified. They included; the Mutengene-Kumba-Mamfe-Eyumujock-Ekok-Mfum-Ikom-Abakaliki road and the Bamenda-Mamfe-Ekok-Abakaliki-Enugu road and its various arteries. These road projects are part of the proposed Lagos-Mombassa African Highway infrastructure Development. There was also the construction of cross-border bridges.

The Mutengene-Abakaliki road project

During the first session of the Cameroon–Nigeria ad hoc Mixed Commission in Yaounde in December 2002, it was agreed that the two governments should proceed with the construction of the Mamfe-Eyumojock-Ekok-Mfum-Ikom-Abakaliki stretch which had been identified and adopted by the two governments. As a consequence, a joint team was dispatched to the project site to assess the state of the road. The joint team assessed the state of the road and recommended that it should be graded. During the fourth session of the Mixed Commission in Abuja in June 2003, the parties agreed that the project to grade the Mamfe-Abakaliki road be extended to Kumba and Mutengene on the Cameroon side.

The Mixed Commission equally indicated its commitment to the African Development Bank (ADB) to finance the construction of the road. As a result, the Mixed Commission undertook a tripartite visit to Tunis which was temporarily hosting the headquarters of the ADB following social unrest in the host country, Ivory Coast in 2002. The Commission Members met with the President and Staff of the bank and reviewed the status of the trans-border Abakaliki-Mutengene road development project. The bank informed the mission of its readiness to support the project. The bank equally indicated its preparedness to consider other projects in the area of the environment especially for which Cameroon and Nigeria would submit appropriate proposals. Meanwhile, the UN Secretary General,

Kofi Annan, enjoined the Mixed Commission and appealed to the international community to provide support within the context of preventive diplomacy for the rehabilitation of this road and other cross-border environmental projects.

During its 44th annual meeting in Dakar, Senegal on May 14, 2009, the ADB accorded a loan of 155.29million dollars to Cameroon and Nigeria for the construction of trans-frontier roads. Nigeria was represented at the signing ceremony by its Permanent Secretary at the Ministry of Finance, Stephen Orosanye and Cameroon by its Minister of the Economy and Regional Development, Louis Paul Motaze.[1] Before the acquisition of this loan, the Cameroon government had rehabilitated the 12km Mutengene-Muea stretch of the road on the Cameroon side with its own funds. Cameroon equally kicked starts the construction of the 63km Muea-Kumba stretch in March 2007 with 50 percent assistance from the EU. This FCFA 31 billion road project was completed and inaugurated by Cameroon's Prime Minister; Philemon Yang on September 25, 2009 in the locality of Bombe Bakundu, Mbonge Sub Division, Meme Division in the South West Region of Cameroon.The project also involved the construction of 18 classrooms and drilled water points.[2]

The Bamenda-Enugu road project

The 443km Bamenda-Enugu corridor and its various arteries was another confidence building road identified by Nigerian and Cameroonian authorities. On the Cameroon side, the road runs from Bamenda-Batibo (42km), Batibo-Numba (20km), Numba-Bachuo Akagbe (50km), Bachuo Akagbe-Mamfe (21km) and Mamfe-Ekok (70km). On the Nigerian side, the road runs for a distance of 240km from the Cameroon-Nigeria frontier on the Cross River, then to

---

1. *EDEV* (Cameroon), no.00002, Tuesday, May 19, 2009.

2. *Cameroon Tribune ,no.* 9442/5643, Monday, September 28, 2009;*The Post* (Cameroon) no. 01088, Monday, September 28, 2009.

Mfum- Ikom-Mbok-Abakaliki-Enugu.[3] The project will also include the building of the 100m long bridge over the Munaya River in Cameroon and the 280m long bridge over the Cross River at the border. By 2009, the Bamenda-Batibo stretch was already completed. Programmed equally too is the rehabilitation of feeder roads in order to disenclave the border settlements and ease the evacuation of agricultural products. There will also be the rehabilitation and construction of social infrastructures such as schools, health centres, markets, potable boreholes and women empowerment centres.

The FCFA 188.79 billion project will be executed thanks to contributions from the two countries and donor agencies. The giant in the contribution chain is the ADB which was to disburse FCFA 128.69 billion, the Japan International Cooperation Agency (JICA) which was to give FCFA 18.67 billion and the World Bank, FCFA 12.8 billion. Other contributions were to come from the governments of Nigeria (FCFA 9.69 billion) and Cameroon (FCFA 7.4 billion) among others.[4]

The cross border road code-named Bamenda-Enugu Multinational Highway and Transport Facilitation programme was officially launched on June 17, 2010 by the Ministers of Public Works of Cameroon and Nigeria. The Cameroon Minister of Public Works, Bernard Messengue Avom unveiled the commemorative plaque in Mfum, Cross River state, Nigeria while the Minister of Works for Nigeria, Senator Mohammed Sanusi Daggash, did same in Ekok, Manyu Division, South West Region of Cameroon.

Upon the completion of the road, trade will increase and cooperation between Cameroon and Nigeria in particular and the Countries of the Economic Community for Central African States (ECCAS) and ECOWAS in general will be strengthened. The road will have many socio-economic fallouts for the people of Cameroon and Nigeria. It will facilitate the flow of goods and services between

---

3. *Cameroon Tribune* ,no. 9382/5583, Thursday, July 2, 2009 and no.9623/5824, Monday, June 21, 2010.

4._____ ,no. 9623/5824, Monday, June 21, 2010.

the two countries; thereby boosting customs revenue. The road will also facilitate the evacuation of harvested crops given that the project involves the construction of feeder roads. It will also enhance social interaction between the populations of the two countries. Indeed, in terms of cost and distance, it is the most ambitious road project undertaken by the Cameroon government concomitantly with a neighbouring state.The road is programmed to be completed in December 2013.

Nigerian and Cameroonian authorities equally identified and approved the construction of a bridge on the Mayo Tiel between the localities of Demsa in the North Region of Cameroon and Balel in the Adamawa State of Nigeria. Work on this bridge kicked start by 2009.

Exportation of electricity

The foundation of cooperation between Cameroon and Nigeria in the electricity sector is laid in Article 22 of the Economic, Scientific and Technical Cooperation Agreement signed by the two countries on April 21, 1983. It also falls under the spirit of the Tripartite Summit of Biya, Annan and Obasanjo on September 5, 2002 in the Parisian outskirts of Saint Cloud wherein they discussed the possibility of cooperation in the economic domain especially partnership in water and electricity sectors. In the aftermath of the ICJ verdict on the Cameroon–Nigeria border dispute case, the ad hoc Mixed Commission decided to develop bilateral projects along the Cameroon–Nigeria border as one of the confidence building measures in the resolution of the border dispute. The project equally falls within the framework of the Niger Basin Development Programme which is aimed at exploring and exploiting the potentials of the Basin.[5]

---

5. The Niger Basin Authority (NBA) in 2008 earmarked 639 projects worth over FCFA 3.645 trillion for realization in member states (Benin, Burkina Faso, Cameroon, Chad, Guinea, Ivory Coast, Mali, Niger, and Nigeria) between 2008 and 2027. See *Cameroon Tribune*, no. 9415/5616, Tuesday, August 18, 2009.

It was against this backdrop that authorities of Cameroon's Ministry of Energy and Water Resources on February 9, 2009, had the first ever working session with the delegation of experts from the Adamawa State of Nigeria on possibilities of rehabilitating the Lagdo Dam in the North Region of Cameroon; reinforcing its capacity to enable the exportation of energy to Nigeria. This became very necessary because the electricity production in Nigeria was some 3.000 megawatts (3.000MW), largely inadequate for the country's estimated population of 150 million inhabitants and for the sustenance of serious industrial initiatives. It also came at the time that the Nigerian President elect, Umaru Musa Yar'Adua (May 29,2007-May 5,2010) announced an ambitious programme to increase electricity production ten-fold by taking it up to 25.000MW by 2011.[6]

The meeting was presided over by Cameroon's Minister of Energy and Water, Jean Bernard Sindeu. The 15-member Nigerian delegation was headed by Ali Dandiyya Sardaunan Kebbi, Principal Staff Officer to the Governor of the Adamawa state of Nigeria. The delegation comprised representatives from the High Commission of Nigeria to Cameroon, senior staff from three sectors namely; the Adamawa state Governor's Office, the Power Holding Company of Nigeria (PHCN) and power consultants from the Zungero Power Limited. The Cameroonian side consisted of close collaborators to the Ministry of Energy and Water Resources such as the Permanent Secretary, the Inspector General, Technical Advisers and Directors. Others included representatives of MINREX and the management staff from the Electricity Sector Regulatory Agency (ARSEL), the Electricity Development Corporation (EDC) and the Rural Electricity Agency (AER).

In his opening presentation, Sindeu made a run down of Cameroon's hydropower potentials and her readiness to embrace such a project. He enumerated other hydro potentials including the Menchum River hydroelectricity power project in the North West Region of Cameroon and Central African Sub Regional Inga Project which Cameroon is part and where Nigeria has expressed readiness to sign an agreement to that effect. Sindeu equally set out to pave the

6. *Cameroon Tribune, no.* 8857/5056, Tuesday, May 29, 2007.

way for laying down legal, technical and financial groundwork to foster the execution of the project. Kebbi on his part declared that Nigeria will appreciate if Cameroon can offer her up to 30MW of electricity.[7]

The meeting concluded on three key notes: the establishment of formal Inter-Country Agreement or Treaty as precedent condition to power export and/or grid interconnection between Cameroon and Nigeria and the implementation of mechanisms such as Memorandum of Understanding (MOU) and other legal instruments to be concluded at the level of the Joint Commission between the two countries; both sides could designate technical experts to exchange technical information available on the public domain in view of preparing feasible export or interconnection projects which could serve as guidance to the governments of Cameroon and Nigeria in the conclusion of an Electricity Export Treaty ; finally ,the mission made a technical visit to the Lagdo Hydro-electricity Power Plant on February 11 and 12, 2009.

Partnership between Cameroon and Nigeria in the electricity sector was again revisited during the fifth session of the Joint Commission in Abuja in November 2010 where an agreement was initiated to that effect. Then, on February 18, 2011 in Yaounde, a Framework Agreement on Electricity Interconnection focused at laying down the institutional framework for the planning, coordination, financing and realization of electricity supply between Cameroon and Nigeria was signed. Cameroon's Minister of External Relations Henri Eyebe Ayissi signed for Cameroon while his counterpart, Nigeria's Minister of Foreign Affairs, Henry Odein Ajumogobia signed for his country.[8]

---

7. *Cameroon Tribune, no.* 9285/5484, Tuesday, February 10, 2009.

8. _____ ,no.9790/5991, Monday, February 21, 2011.

Research partnership

Cooperation on research between Cameroon and Nigeria falls under the spirit of the Protocol Agreement on Cultural, Social and Technical Relations signed between the two countries on March 27, 1974.This agreement envisaged bilateral cooperation in the areas of education, technical assistance, exchange of theatrical groups, and organization of sporting events in both countries among others.[9] It also falls within the realm of the recommendations of the third, fourth and fifth sessions of the Cameroon-Nigeria Joint Commission which met in Abuja in 2002, in Yaounde in 2008 and in Abuja in 2010.Meeting in 2002, the Joint Commission agreed on joint scientific research and cooperation in sporting, cultural and youth activities. This was again reiterated during the Joint Commission's meeting in Yaounde in 2008 and in Abuja in 2010.

It was against this backdrop that experts and administrators of the Institute of Agricultural Research for Development (IRAD) Ekona, Cameroon and those of Pamol Nigeria Limited met on April 26, 2007 at the IRAD premises in Ekona to chart a way forward for a research partnership. Pamol Nigeria was represented at the meeting by its Managing Director, Chief Emmanuel Bassey, while Cameroon was represented by the Chief of Centre of IRAD Ekona, Dr Mafeni Joseph Base and Dr Ehabe Eugene Ejolle, Head of Latex Plants Programme. The meeting took place in the presence of the General Manager of Pamol Plantations Cameroon, Obi-Okpun Wanobi Osang. The partnership agreement involved research in rubber cultivation, production, processing and management. It also involved capacity building and the establishing of a rubber research programme with Pamol Nigeria having 15.000 hectares of rubber with barely 5.500 doing well.[10]

Other areas of partnership were formally discussed by the Nigerian Foreign Minister, Ojo Maduekwe and Cameroon's Prime

---

9. Pondi and Zang, "The Cameroon-Nigeria Border Cooperation," p.179.

10. *Cameroon Tribune, no.* 8840/5039, Wednesday, May 2, 2007.

Minister, Ephraim Inoni on October 9, 2008, on the sidelines of the fourth session of the Cameroon–Nigeria Joint Commission that was meeting in Yaounde from September 9-11, 2009. Meanwhile, a framework agreement in matters of sports and physical education initiated during the Cameroon–Nigeria Joint Commission session in Abuja in November 2010 was signed between the two countries in Yaounde on February 18, 2011.Cameroon's Minister of External Relations, Henri Eyebe Ayissi signed on behalf of Cameroon while his counterpart, Nigerian Foreign Minister, Henry Odein Ajumogobia, signed for his country.[11]

The agreement aims at strengthening collaboration in the development of research in matters of sports between the two countries on the basis of reciprocity and as a vector of peace. The agreement stipulates that the two countries would promote relations between their civil sporting federations, universities and schools and the organization of sporting events between the national teams of the two countries in diverse disciplines.The agreement also envisages the facilitation of exchange of scholarships in professional training and the training of trainers in matters of sports and physical education.Therefore, Cameroon and Nigeria could prepare great competitions like the African and Commonwealth games together and benefit from infrastructures in the two countries.The agreement also spells out that the two countries would work towards a system of equivalency of university certificates,academic grades and school certificates obtained in either Cameroon or Nigeria.[12]

Meanwhile, on June 22, 2011, the Cameroon Minister of Forestry and Wildlife, Elvis Ngolle Ngolle; in the presence of the Nigerian High Commissioner to Cameroon, Philip A. Dauda; launched in Yaounde, a regional plan for the conservation of the Nigeria–Cameroon chimpanzee. The plan code-named Pan Troglodytes Ellioti (sub species of the chimpanzees in the two countries) is the fruit of two long term research projects on the conservation of the Nigeria–Cameroon chimpanzee undertaken in the Gashaka Gumti Park in Nigeria since 2000 and in the forest of

---

11. *Cameroon Tribune*, no.9790/5991, Monday, February 21, 2011.

12. Ibid.

the proposed Ebo National Park in the Littoral Region of Cameroon in 2002. The plan is aimed at determining priority sites for the conservation of some 3.500 chimpanzees in Nigeria and Cameroon. The Cameroon–Nigeria region harbours 24 primate species with eight of them said to be unique in the world.[13]

Boosting formal trade

A bilateral trade agreement was signed by Cameroon and Nigeria in 1963 intended especially to increase the volume of formal trade between the two countries .This agreement was revised in 1982 with a more determined vigour especially to improve trade between the two countries. As a consequence, the agreement envisaged the granting of freedom of transit to commercial goods originating from a third country and destined for the other contracting party ; all payments to be made between the contracting parties freely through normal banking channels and the comparison of trade statistics on a yearly basis in order to detect trade imbalances.[14] In spite of this optimism, formal trade between Cameroon and Nigeria remained very low following persistent border skirmishes and the non application of these agreements.

It was as a result of this realization that members of the Cameroon–Nigeria Joint Commission meeting in Abuja in 2002 agreed to improve this low level of formal trade through the speedy re-negotiation of these existing bilateral trade agreements. As a consequence, various initiatives were undertaken by Cameroon and Nigeria to boost trade. The two countries reached consensus on the principle of the construction of a unique frontier control post in the Bamenda-Enugu corridor in order to make traffic more fluid.[15] This was intended to facilitate the transportation of trade items between

---

13. *Cameroon Tribune*, no. 9872/6073, Thursday, June 23, 2011.

14. Pondi and Zang, "The Cameroon-Nigeria Border Cooperation," pp.174 and 180.

15. *Cameroon Tribune, no.* 9058/5257, Wednesday, Friday March 14, 2008.

the two countries .The rehabilitation of feeder roads along this corridor will equally facilitate the evacuation of agricultural products which would be sold in the envisaged border markets as decided by the Joint Commission in 2002 and even beyond.

Measures to Address the Security and Strategic Concerns of the Two Countries

Security and geostrategic issues like the non respect of the laws of the resident country by the settler population, perceived violation of the rights of the settler population by law enforcement officers in the course of enforcing immigration laws, poor administration of frontiers, neglect of frontier settlements and the equitable exploitation of resources straddling or along the common frontier which were at the root cause of the border dispute were not addressed by the ICJ ruling. Therefore, these issues had to be resolved by Nigerian and Cameroonian authorities in concert with the international community to bring about a definite end to the border dispute.

Boosting frontier security

The germ of an agreement on trans-frontier security was laid in the Protocol Agreement of March 27, 1972 pertaining to periodic courtesy visits between high level security officers in civilian clothes between the police force of the two countries; and the sharing of new technical information on criminal activities.[16]

Before and after the ICJ verdict on the border dispute case, the Heads of State of Cameroon and Nigeria in various tripartite summits with the UN Secretary General discussed measures on how to solve these security concerns. In November 2002 at Geneva, Presidents Biya and Obasanjo expressed the need to reconvene a summit of the two parties to examine the question of defence and security. Meeting

---

16. Pondi and Zang, "The Cameroon-Nigeria Border Cooperation," pp.182-183.

again in Geneva in January 2004, the two Heads of State agreed to open consulates along their common border and also to introduce joint patrols by security forces and to conclude a Treaty of Friendship and Non Aggression between the two countries. They also agreed to take appropriate measures for the preservation of security and property of the concerned populations in the two countries. Meeting in Yaounde in October 2008, the fourth session of the Cameroon–Nigeria Joint Commission proposed that there should be the establishment of joint patrols along border areas to check trans-border criminality such as human trafficking, smuggling and the activities of pirates around the maritime area.

These proposals were made at the time that there was an upsurge of insecurity around the maritime area. On the Nigerian side, the Movement for the Emancipation of the Niger Delta (Mend), the Front for Ijaw Survival and Hope, Niger Delta Vigilantes, Martyrs Brigade Coma and Icelanders continued with its kidnapping activities while unidentified assailants continued with kidnapping and looting on the Cameroonian side, especially in the Bakassi Peninsula. Such instances abound. On November 12, 2007, a contingent of Cameroonian soldiers was attacked in the Bakassi Peninsula between Rio del Rey and Isangele creek by unidentified assailants killing 21 soldiers and wounding 10.[17] On June 9, 2008, the DO of Kombo Abedimo, Fonya Felix Morfan was kidnapped by unidentified assailants.[18] Meanwhile, on the morning of July 24, 2008, the locality of Kombo a Janea, situated in the Bakassi Peninsula was attacked by an armed band, without any military attributes, on three power boats. Ten assailants were killed, 8 taken prisoners, an important stock of weapons and ammunition seized, one power boat and its contents sank and one other boat equipped with two outboard engines seized. Two Cameroonian soldiers were killed and 4 wounded.[19]

---

17. *Cameroon Tribune, no.* 8976/5175, Wednesday, November 14, 2007.

18. *Mutations,* no.2170, 10 Juin 2008 ; *Le Messanger*, no. 2629, Mardi, 10 Juin 2008.

19. *Cameroon Tribune*, no. 9148/5347, Friday, July 25, 2008.

It was as a result of these security concerns that Cameroon's President, Paul Biya on August 11, 2008 created 12 police units in the littoral area of Ndian Division in the South West Region of Cameroon. Public Police Security Posts were created at Ngosso and Akwa while Special Police Security Posts were created at Akwa, Isangele, Idabato and Barrack's. Frontier Police Security Posts were also created at Akwa, Barrack's, Idabato, Bongo and Djangassa.[20] As the personnel appointed to these posts get to work, the activities of pirates continued in earnest.

On the night of Saturday, September 27, 2008, a group of about 30 armed men, who came in three power boats stormed banks in Limbe, Cameroon, killing one worker with Cosy hotel. They also attacked the Société Générale de Banques au Cameroun (SGBC) and Amity Bank and carted away with the safe of Amity Bank and an undisclosed amount of money.[21] Pirates again attacked a Cameroonian army unit at Jabane on October 18, 2008 and the army reacted by sinking their boat.[22] On the night of Thursday, October 30 to Friday, October 31, 2008, pirates again struck in the peninsula and attacked a vessel belonging to the Bourbon enterprise owned by Eric Verrière and operating under the platform of the Total Oil Group and kidnapped 10 persons.[23] The 10 persons included 6 Frenchmen, 1 Senegalese, 1 Tunisian and 2 Cameroonians. The 10 hostages were only released after more than a week in captivity and were received by Cameroon's President, Paul Biya on November 11, 2008.[24]

Although there was no official declaration on the circumstances leading to the freeing of the hostages, independent reports indicated that the hostages were captured by the Bakassi Freedom Fighters and liberated in exchanged for 13 members of their group captured by

---

20. *Cameroon Tribune*, no. 9159/5358, Tuesday, August 12, 2008.

21. _____ ,no. 9193/5392, Monday, September 29, 2008.

22._____ ,no. 9207/5406, Monday, October 20, 2008.

23._____ ,no. 9218/5417, Tuesday, November 4, 2008.

24._____ ,no. 9224/5423, Wednesday, November 12, 2008.

Cameroonian soldiers. The leader of the Group, Ebi Dari declared that what took place was the exchanged of prisoners.[25] On October 10 and 11, 2009, pirates in power boats fired on Cameroonian army units and the army reacted killing 4 pirates, wounding 3 and destroying their boat and also seizing ammunition. Two of the pirates escaped.

This upsurge of insecurity and state intervention is an indication that Non State Actors (NSAs) are increasingly imposing themselves in international relations. This notion has been theorized by Neo-liberalists who postulate the fact that although states are the main actors in international relations, NSAs like Non Governmental Organizations (NGOs), International Governmental Organizations (IGOs), Multinational Corporations(MNCs) and more recently terrorist groups equally matter.

With this upsurge of insecurity in the Bakassi Peninsula, the Cameroon government and friendly nations took steps to enforce security in the peninsula. In March 2009, Cameroon sent her elite force; the Rapid Intervention Brigade (BIR) to Bakassi to reinforce the former service there code-named Operation Delta. Meanwhile, the US government donated boats, equipment and trained the Cameroonian army and planned security strategies involving Cameroon and Nigeria. This initiative was captured vividly by the American Ambassador to Cameroon, Janet E. Garvey:

> We will continue to seek other ways to assist, including promoting dialogue and exploring the possibility of joint exercises between the Cameroonian and Nigerian security forces. Another element of our support of security in the Gulf of Guinea is our Africa Partnership Station Initiative, which includes significant training for Cameroonian naval forces with those of other African nations.[26]

---

25. *Le Jour* (Cameroon), no. 0310, Mercredi 12 Novembre 2008.

26. Interview with Janet E. Garvey, American Ambassador to Cameroon, interview, Raphael Mvogo, *Cameroon Tribune*, no. 9194/5393, Wednesday, October 1, 2008. The translation is mine.

Meanwhile, the US government continued to train the Cameroonian elite force, BIR on maritime security. By March 21, 2011 the US government had installed an active radar system which could permit Cameroonian authorities to identify unauthorized ships and boats at high speed particularly in Bakassi.[27]

In spite of these security reinforcements, pirates continued to operate in the Bakassi Peninsula and in the territorial waters of Cameroon and Nigeria. On November 16, 2010, unidentified pirates on board two fast boats attacked the Muddy Tanker ship used by Pecten-Perenco oil companies to transport petroleum products. The Cameroon elite force, BIR and those of the unit code-named Operation Delta who was on security patrol on board the Moungo 7 boat chartered by Pecten-Perenco companies attempted to intercept the pirates' boat leading to the exchange of gun fire. This resulted in the death of three soldiers, the pilot of the boat and a civilian mechanic. Again, on February 6, 2011 the DO of Akwa, Edward Ayuk was kidnapped alongside ten other people in his delegation.

Meanwhile, on the night of February 6 to 7, 2011, the Mbonjo Maritime Gendarmerie Brigade was attacked by an armed band on board two boats killing two gendarmes and wounding one. The eleven hostages were only released on February 16, 2011 after the intervention of the Cameroonian Forces of Defence and Security.[28] The hostages' were received by Cameroon's Prime Minister, Philemon Yang on February 17, 2011. Meanwhile, on the night of Friday March 18 breaking 19, 2011, pirates in two speed boats traverse the Cameroonian coastal waters, infiltrated Douala and break into the branch of ECO-Bank Bonaberi and carted away with some FCFA 201 million. Two of the bandits were arrested while one was shot. Meanwhile, the 18 assaillants that escaped were later intercepted and killed by the Cameroon elite force, BIR on Cameroon coastal waters[29]

---

27. *Cameroon Tribune*, no.9811/6012, Tuesday, March 22, 2011.

28. _____ , no.9784/5985, Thursday, February 10, 2011; and no.9789/5990, Friday, February 18, 2011.

29. *Mutations*, no. 2871, Mardi, 22 Mars 2011.

This upsurge of insecurity in the Cameroon territorial waters spurred Nigerian and Cameroonian authorities to express the readiness of the two countries to implement the Cross-Border Security Committee agreed during the third, fourth and fifth sessions of the Cameroon-Nigeria Joint Commission respectively in Abuja in 2002, in Yaounde in 2008, and in Abuja in 2010. This concern was expressed by Cameroon's Minister of External Relations, Henri Eyebe Ayissi and his Nigerian counterpart, Henry Odein Ajumogobia in Yaounde on February 18, 2011 during the signing of two framework agreements on electricity interconnection and on sports and physical education between the two countriues. Meanwhile, Cameroonian and Nigerian officials met in Yaounde from April 6-7, 2011 and prepared a draft agreement setting up a Cross-Border Security Committee between the two countries. During this meeting also, the experts equally identified the causes and manifestations of insecurity along their common frontier and committed themselves to eradicate the problem. The Cameroon delegation was led by Ferdinand Ngoh Ngoh, Secretary General in the Ministry of External Relations and that of Nigeria by Ambassador M.K. Ibrahim, Director of African Affairs (bilateral) in the Ministry of Foreign Affairs. The agreement will permit the two countries to fight criminal activities along their common border through joint border patrols by security forces. Its implementation will also secure trade and promote the socio-economic development of the two countries.

By and large, Cameroon and Nigeria continued to work with friendly nations and the international community to check insecurity in the Gulf of Guinea in particular and Africa in general. On August 26, 2004, the Committee of Intelligence and Security Services of Africa (CISSA) was established in Abuja, Nigeria to provide intelligence to the policy making organs of the AU. During its eighth ordinary session in Khartoum, Sudan from June 5-8, 2011, CISSA decided to hold a mini-conference in Ebolowa, Cameroon from July 6-9, 2011 to brainstorm on the AU Draft Policy Framework on the Security Sector Reform in Africa. These security issues relate to the actors in the area of security, type of security and the method of rendering it in the continent.

Meanwhile, on March 21, 2011, a multinational initiative code-named Obangame Express 2011 was launched at the Douala Naval

Base intended to beef up security in Zone D countries of the CEMAC Zone comprising Cameroon, Congo and Chad. This was a follow-up to the May 6, 2009 Technical Accord signed by Cameroon, Sao Tome and Principe, Gabon and Equatorial Guinea for the security of the Gulf of Guinea. Furthermore, on April 22, 2011, a training session on anti-terrorism techniques was jointly organised by the governments of Cameroon, the USA, and Nigeria, in Douala, Cameroon to train military and security personnel of Zone D countries of the CEMAC Zone which was witnessing a rise in terrorist activities, insurgency, trafficking in arms, drugs and human beings; thereby posing a threat to the security of the Gulf of Guinea in particular and the rest of the world at large.The training was facilitated by a delegation of the US Joint Special Operations University, comprising the US and Canadian military officers.[30]

The decision by the AU in 2005 to create a Continental Logistics Base (CLB) of the African Standing Force (ASF) in a city generally accepted to be either at a deep-sea port and/or co-located at an international air base, was another laudable initiative to curb insecurity and conflict in Africa. Following an official study mission in April 2009, Douala in Cameroon was chosen to host the CLB of the ASF.[31] The purpose of the standing force is to provide the AU with capabilities to respond to conflicts through a multiplicity of peace support operations notably preventive deployment, peacekeeping, peace building, post-conflict disarmament, demobilization, re-integration, and humanitarian assistance. Therefore, its location in Douala will certainly boost the security needs of the Gulf of Guinea in particular and those of Africa in general.

_____

30. *Cameroon Tribune*, no. 9833/6034, Monday, April 26, 2011.

31. Following the choosing of Douala to host the CLB of the AU, a Prime Ministerial decision no. 44/CAB/PM of February 28, 2011 by the Cameroon government defined the practical modalities for the effective setting of this structure in Douala. The Douala population was informed of the decision on March 16, 2011. The CLB is expected to become functional by 2013.

Reconciling the dual geostrategy in the Bakassi Peninsula and the Maritime Frontier

The capstone of reconciliation and the promotion of conviviality between Cameroon and Nigeria lie in the guarantee of some of their geostrategic considerations in the Bakassi Peninsula and in the maritime zone. The ICJ ruling declared Bakassi Cameroonian implying that Cameroon was to exercise sovereignty over it with more than 90 percent of the population Nigerians. The ICJ equally delimited the Maritime Frontier without fixing the tripoint nor defined the manner through which resources straddling or along the frontier was to be exploited. Therefore, Cameroonian and Nigerian authorities had to iron these issues.

Given that most of the border skirmishes in the Bakassi Peninsula were sparked off by issues related to immigration and violation of human rights; Cameroonian and Nigerian authorities with the help of the international community made guarantees related to such issues in the Greentree Accord of June 12, 2006. Article 4 of Annex I of the Accord specifies that following the transfer of sovereignty over Bakassi to Cameroon—which took place in 2008—she shall apply in the zone a special transitional regime for a non-renewable period of five years (2008-2013). Such special considerations includes: access by Nigerian civil authorities to the Nigerian population living in Bakassi; non application of Cameroonian customs and immigration laws to Nigerian nationals living in the zone on their direct return from Nigeria; access of Nigerian police to the zone in cooperation with Cameroonian police and finally innocent passage in the territorial waters of the zone to civilian ships sailing under the Nigerian flag. A multilateral Follow-up Committee made up of 10 representatives from Cameroon, Nigeria, UN, UK, France and Germany was formed to monitor the implementation of the agreement and to settle any dispute regarding the interpretation and its implementation.

Within this five years transitional period, stakeholders will be able to sensitize the population and local administrators of the area respectively on the need of the respect of the law and its judicious application. The pacesetter to this preoccupation took place from

August 30 through September 2, 2009 at Mundemba, Ndian Division of the South West Region of Cameroon when South West Governor, Louis Eyeya Zanga organized a capacity building workshop for administrative officers on the management of the Bakassi Peninsula.[32]

Concerning the manner of exploiting resources straddling or along the frontier, a framework agreement was reached by the two countries during the 23rd session of the ad hoc Mixed Commission in Yaounde in October 2008 pertaining to oil and gas production from fields straddling or along the Maritime Frontier. According to the agreement, the two countries will review national legislations on oil and gas resources to take into account the requirements of cross-border cooperation which will involve national institutions in charge of matters concerning oil and gas, as well as oil and gas companies operating in the maritime area. Another daunting task will be for the two countries to fix the tripoint of their Maritime Boundary with Equatorial Guinea. Unlike Nigeria which concluded a Treaty with Equatorial Guinea on September 23, 2000 delimiting their Maritime Frontier, Cameroon and Equatorial Guinea have not yet concluded such an agreement.Therefore, Cameroon and Equatorial Guinea will have to first finalize negotiations for the delimitation of their Maritime Border. The Cameroon-Equato-Guinean ad hoc Commission on the delimitation of their Maritime Frontier met in its sixth session in Yaounde from September 8-9, 2009 to iron out such issues. Meanwhile, the second session of the Cameroon-Equatorial Guinea ad hoc Commission on Consular and trans-Border issues met from February 21-22, 2011 in Yaounde to prepare a framework agreement expected to be signed at the level of the Cameroon-Equatorial Guinea Mixed Commission.

Development of border settlements

In the aftermath of the ICJ verdict on the border dispute case, Cameroon and Nigeria took commitments to develop their frontier settlements. The commitment made by Cameroon at the Greentree

---

32. *Cameroon Tribune*, no. 9421/5622, Wednesday, August 26, 2009 and no. 9430/5632,Wednesday, September 9, 2009.

Tripartite Summit of June 12, 2006 to guarantee the fundamental rights and freedoms of Nigerian nationals living in the Bakassi Peninsula was a precursor to frontier development. This is so because the respect of human rights entails the provision of social amenities, protection and assurance of cultural heritage. The avowal by Cameroon to uphold these principles was enforceable given that a multilateral Follow-up Committee was formed to monitor its implementation. The mandate of this Committee was to span for five years following Nigerian withdrawal from Bakassi; which took place in 2008. Although these commitments were limited to the Bakassi Peninsula, subsequent policies by Nigeria and Cameroon showed some verve and vitality to develop border settlements from Lake Chad to the sea in partnership with donor nations and organizations.

With this spirit, Nigeria constructed hundreds of housing units at Ikang to host families that opted to leave Bakassi.[33] Concerning the development of Bakassi, Cameroon's Prime Minister, Ephraim Inoni on August 7, 2007, created the Committee for Coordination and Follow-up for the Putting into Place Priority Projects in the zone.[34] Then on August 27, 2007, the Cameroon government created a Coordination Committee for this goal headed by Jacob Lekunze Ketuma, Special Adviser of the Prime Minister. The Committee went to work and prepared a 280 page bilingual document outlining these priority projects to be realized in the Bakassi Peninsula. The document was made public on September 19, 2008. The multidimensional projects were slated to be realized in the short, mid and long term. They involved all the five Sub Divisions in Bakassi—Idabato, Kombo Abedimo, Kombo Itindi, Bamusso and Isangele.

The projects range from the construction and furnishing of government offices, health centres, schools, residences of workers, markets, social centres, sports and leisure infrastructures, women empowerment centres, smoke houses, cold stores, fuel stations, roads, air strips and seaport. Other projects include the supply of power boats, vehicles and bikes for administrative authorities,

---

33. *The Post* (Cameroon), no.0994, Monday, October 13, 2008.

34. Decree no. 2007/1132/PM of August 27, 2007 establishes this Committee.

168

generators for energy supply, water supply, support to farmers' organizations, mobile telephone relay antennas, *Cameroon Radio Television* (CRTV) signal relay tower, broadcast centre, equipping of security and defence forces and the acquisition of land for state use.

The Cameroon government is undertaking these projects in partnership with friendly countries and organizations, notably France and the EU. Before the retrocession of Bakassi to Cameroon on August 14, 2008, France had made available FCFA 250 million for frontier projects.[35] Meanwhile, on May 30, 2008, Javier Puyol, Head of the EU Commission Delegation to Cameroon inaugurated a primary school and a health centre financed by the EU in Bakassi to the tune of FCFA 100 million. On June 3, 2008, Javier Puyol announced that the EU was to make available the sum of FCFA 2.7 billion to enable the Cameroon government provide health, education, potable water and other social amenities to the population of Bakassi, Darack and other territories Nigeria retroceded to Cameroon.[36] Cameroon and the EU through the European Development Fund (EDF) and the French Development Agency (AFD) from 2007-2009 spent over FCFA 12 billion to execute some priority projects in the Bakassi Peninsula. More than FCFA 2.3 billion from the public investment budget was earmarked for development projects in the Bakassi Peninsula in 2008, close to FCFA 6 billion in 2009, over FCFA 5 billion in 2010, and FCFA 1billion in 2011. The reports of the evaluation missions of December 27-30, 2010 and January 5-9, 2011 indicate that the rate of project implementation in the zone was 70 percent.[37]

The construction of the 75km Mundemba-Isangele-Akwa road will greatly facilitate the transportation of material and equipment for the realization of these projects. The FCFA 1 billion earth road

---

35. Interview with Georges Serre, French Ambassador to Cameroon, interview, Raphael Mvogo, *Cameroon Tribune*, no. 9194/5393, Wednesday, October 1, 2008.

36. *Cameroon Tribune*, no.9111/5310, Wednesday, June 4, 2008.The EU is not involved in road projects in these border settlements because its road programme is focused on international axis especially to promote trade between countries.

37. *Cameroon Tribune*, no. 9842/6043, Monday, May 9, 2011.

project, financed by the Cameroon government and constructed by the Military Engineering Pool was inaugurated on March 23, 2010 by the Minister Delegate for Defence, Rene Claude Meka.Two million FCFA was budgeted in 2011for the rehabilitation of this road.

The Cameroon government equally marked its presence in areas retroceded to Cameroon by Nigeria in the Lake Chad region notably Naga'a, Tchika, Toro Liman, Darack and their environs through the construction of administrative buildings, schools, security posts, telecentres, post office services, CRTV relay stations and extension of electricity to the area.[38] Meanwhile, on August 12, 2008, the Cameroon government launched an ambitious project to provide free electricity in 26 frontier villages. The first phase of the three–phase programme was launched at Idenau, Fako Division, South West Region by the Minister of Energy and Water Resources, Jean-Bernard Sindeu. The programme stipulates that all the villages along the border with Nigeria will be electrified in partnership with the Spanish government which has already disbursed FCFA 3 billion for the project.[39] The Spanish government promised to provide more assistance depending on how effective the first phase of the project is executed. According to the agreement, Spain will manufacture and supply electricity material like cables and bulbs while Cameroon provides the poles. The project kicked start in 2009 and on November 18, 2010, Cameroon's Minister of Water and Energy, Michael Ngako Tomdio during the launching of a giant project to electrify 420 localities by 2014 announced that this first phase was realized hitch free.[40]

---

38. Interview with Abba Sadou, President of the Coordination and Follow-up Committee of Priority Projects in the Lake Chad region, interview, Alliance Nyobia, *Cameroon Tribune*, no.9273/5472, Friday, January 23, 2009.

39. *Cameroon Tribune*, no. 9159/5358, Tuesday, August 12, 2008.

40. _____ ,no. 9726/5927, Friday, November 19, 2010.

Measures to Revamp Diplomatic Relations and Sub Regional Integration

Diplomatic relations between Cameroon and Nigeria witnessed a nose dive in the nineties as tension rose between the two countries. An examination of instances of this decline in diplomatic relations provides an indication in the direction the enforcement of these relations would take. The outbreak of the boundary dispute along the Bakassi Peninsula in 1993 short-circuited the third Cameroon–Nigeria Joint Commission meeting which was scheduled to hold in Cameroon in 1995. The incidents of 1993 and 1994 equally prompted Yaounde not to appoint a High Commissioner to Nigeria as she chose to operate at the Chargé d'Affairs level. High profile politico-diplomatic exchanges equally remained at low ebb. Efforts to revamp diplomatic relations were therefore oriented towards solving these problems and related issues. Furthermore, the LCBC which commissioned a French firm, IGN-FI to demarcate the border in the Lake Chad region had gone into inactivity at the level of Heads of State summit. Therefore, measures were undertaken to activate it.

Reconvening of the standing Joint Commission

Before and after the ICJ verdict on the border dispute case, the need to reconvene and revamp this Joint Commission was very much held by Presidents Biya and Obasanjo; in their various tripartite summits with the UN Secretary General, Kofi Annan. At their first tripartite summit at Saint Cloud, France on September 5, 2002, the two Presidents agreed to reconvene the meeting of the Joint commission. When this meeting finally held in Abuja in September/October 2002, the two countries agreed to negotiate a Memorandum of Understanding (MOU) on bilateral consultations between the two Foreign Ministries and the exchange of official visits by governors, parliamentarians, federal and state government officials including ministers, commissioners, local dignitaries and traditional rulers at least once in a year.

This new dawn of Cameroon-Nigeria relations was lauded by Presidents Biya and Obasanjo during their second tripartite summit with UN Secretary General, Annan, in Geneva in November 2002. At the third tripartite summit in Geneva in January 2004, the two Presidents agreed that the Joint Commission should meet subsequently at higher level and yearly. This renewed vigour and determination paid dividends as the fourth session of the Joint Commission met in Yaounde in October 2008. This fourth session ended with a wide range of proposals to boost bilateral relations. The two countries reiterated the need for regular consultations with their Ministers of Foreign Affairs and the need for high level government exchange visits. The two countries equally agreed to create a common commission between them. The fifth session of the Joint Commission was held in Abuja in November 2010 where two agreements on electricity interconnection and on sports and physical education were initiated.

Diplomatic representation

Another way to revamp diplomatic relations was by strengthening confidence building at the ambassadorial level. This view was expressed by Presidents Biya and Obasanjo during their tripartite summit with the UN Secretary General, Annan on January 31, 2004 where they agreed to exchange ambassadors.

In 2004, the Nigerian President, Obasanjo appointed a new High Commissioner to Cameroon, Edwin Enosakhare Edobor, who presented his letter of credence to President Biya on July 26, 2004. Edobor was replaced by Philip Ali Dauda who presented his letter of credence to Cameroon's Minister of External Relations on May 19, 2008. In April 2008, Cameroon appointed a new resident High Commissioner to Abuja, Salaheddine Abbas Ibrahima after over 10 years of working at the Chargé d'Affairs level. While receiving the letter of credence from the new Cameroon High Commissioner to Abuja on July 25, 2008, the Nigerian Head of State Yar'Adua reiterated his commitment to hand back Bakassi to Cameroon.[41] Nigeria and Cameroon also reinforced bilateral relations through the creation of consulates and the appointment of consuls. Cameroon

41. *Cameroon Tribune, no.* 9146/5345, Wednesday, July 23, 2008.

created a consulate in Lagos and on April 8, 2009, appointed Ekorong à Dong Paul as Consul General. Atangana Michel Auguste was also appointed Cameroon's consul to Calabar on April 8, 2009 in replacement of Foe Atangana Bienvenu Joseph. Cameroon equally moved her High Commission from Lagos to Abuja, Nigeria's capital. Meanwhile, Nigeria expressed the intention to create new consulates in Garoua, Maroua and Bamenda to add to those of Douala and Buea.

Politico-diplomatic exchanges

Politico-diplomatic exchanges equally witnessed renewed verve and vitality. At the Presidential level, the Cameroon Head of State, Paul Biya accompanied by wife, Chantal, visited Nigeria on May 29, 2003 to participate in the oath taking ceremony of President Olusegun Obasanjo and his Vice, Atiku Abubakar, elected on April 19, 2003. Meanwhile, on July 1, 2003, the Nigerian Vice President, Atiku Abubakar, visited Cameroon to extend gratitude to President Biya and wife and the Cameroonian people for participating in the ceremony for the investiture of Nigerian leaders on May 29, 2003. President Biya and wife equally attended the Commonwealth summit in Abuja from December 5-8, 2003.

These diplomatic exchanges continued in earnest as President Obasanjo paid a two day official visit to Cameroon from July 28-29, 2004. During the visit, President Obasanjo commissioned the new premises of the Nigerian High Commission in Yaounde and praised the contractor, Cameroonian born, Alhaji Baba Danpullo for a job well done. Cameroon therefore became the first country to host President Obasanjo on an official visit after he was re-elected President of the AU during its summit at Addis Ababa on July 6, 2004. [42] Before his investiture, the Nigerian President elect, Yar'Adua visited Yaounde on May 12, 2007. President Biya attended the ceremony for the investiture of President Yar'Adua and Vice, Dr

---

42. *Cameroon Tribune, no.* 8149/4434, Thursday, July 29,2004 and *no.* 8134/4419, Thursday, July 8, 2004.

Goodluck Ebele Jonathan at the Eagle Square in Abuja on May 29, 2007. Presidents Obasanjo, Biya, Yar'Adua and Vice President Goodluck Jonathan—who became President on May 5, 2010 following the death of Yar'adua—through their patience, tenacity, flexibility, and restraint successfully implemented the ICJ verdict (see plate 4).

Politico-diplomatic exchanges were also at the level of the dispatching of special envoys and emissaries by the Presidents of Nigeria and Cameroon. Cameroon's Deputy Secretary General, Ephraim Inoni and Army General, James Tataw led for several times Cameroon's delegation to Nigeria as the two countries look for ways to implement the ICJ verdict on the border dispute case. On the side of Nigeria, her Minister in charge of Petrol, Dr Jackson Gaius Obaseki, was received by President Biya on August 29, 2003; bearer of a message from President Obasanjo. The Nigerian High Commissioner to Cameroon, Edwin Enosakhare Edobor on November 19, 2004 conveyed a sealed message from President Obasanjo to his Cameroonian counterpart. The message was handed to Cameroon's Minister of External Relations, François-Xavier Ngoubeyou.

When a contingent of Cameroonian soldiers was attacked in the Bakassi Peninsula on November 12, 2007 by unidentified assailants, killing 21 soldiers and wounding 10; the Nigerian President, Yar'Adua dispatched his Minister of State in charge of Foreign Affairs, Alhaji Tijjani Yahaya Kaurato to Yaounde on December 3, 2007 to express his condolences to the Cameroonian people. He also re-affirmed his country's attachment to the Greentree Accord. Meanwhile, from July 28-29, 2008, Cameroon's Minister of External Relations, Henri Eyebe Ayissi arrived Abuja, with a sealed message from Cameroon's President, Paul Biya to his Nigerian counterpart.

The presence of the new Nigerian Head of State, Goodluck Jonathan alongside former Presidents, Gowon and Obasanjo at the May 20, 2010 National Day celebrations in Yaounde commemorated under the banner of the fifty years of independence was equally a manifestation of this confidence building initiatives. President Biya and wife, Chantal equally attended the festivities marking the fifty years of independence of Nigeria in Abuja on October 1, 2010.

Plate 4. Cameroonian and Nigerian Leaders whose Ingenuity led to the Successful Implementation of the ICJ Verdict

President O. Obasanjo.

President Paul Biya

President Musa Yar'Adua.

President Goodluck Jonathan.

Source: http://www.google.cm/images.

Reactivation of the Lake Chad Basin Commission

The desirability to reactivate the LCBC was expressed by Nigerian and Cameroonian authorities in the aftermath of the ICJ verdict on their border dispute case. This became very imperative because the Lake Chad which covered a surface area of 250.000 sq km in 1964 when the LCBC was created had reduced to only 25.000 sq km especially because of irrigation which quadrupled between 1983 and 1994.[43] As a consequence, the potentials offered by the lake to member states notably fishing, farming and as environmental regulator were at risk especially at the time that the international community was bent on staving off environmental disaster caused by rising temperatures. Therefore, the Heads of State and Government Summit which had gone into inactivity became very necessary in order to discuss the basin-to-basin water transfer project from the Obangui Basin proposed by experts in order to save the Lake from draught.

In the maiden meeting of the Cameroon-Nigeria ad hoc Mixed Commission in Yaounde in December 2002, members agreed that the LCBC should be re-energized at the earliest possible date. They also agreed that the assistance of the international community be sought to support the work plan of the LCBC. With these commitments, the Mixed Commission dispatched a joint team to N'Djamena, headquarters of the LCBC, on March 13, 2003 to concert with its Executive Secretary. During the meeting, steps to secure financing for the project to transfer water from the Obangui Basin to the Lake Chad were discussed. The Mixed Commission equally took note of the LCBC projects which could have special relevance for its goals. It equally took steps to sensitize the world community and especially stakeholders on the desirability of re-charging the Lake Chad. Meanwhile, the UN Secretary General, Kofi Annan enjoined the Mixed Commission and appealed to the international community to provide financial assistance for the

---

43. *Cameroon Tribune,* no. 9436/5637, Thursday, September 17, 2009.

project. The World Bank demonstrated its commitment in that regard by its grant of 2.9 million US dollars (about FCFA 2 billion).[44]

The Mixed Commission equally reiterated its appeal to member states of the LCBC to organize a summit of Heads of State on the disturbing environmental situation in the Lake Chad Basin, and define appropriate strategies for the mobilization of the required resources to finance the inter-basin water transfer project. To that end, it requested the chairman of the Mixed Commission, to relaunch contact with the LCBC Secretariat in view of the organization of such a summit in the near future. The Heads of State and Government Summit of the LCBC was finally held in N'Djamena, Chad from November 1-2, 2010. Chaired by Dr Goodluck Jonathan, President of Nigeria; the summit equally witnessed the participation of Presidents Idriss Deby Itno of Chad, François Bozize of the Central African Republic, and Mouammar Khadafi of Libya. Cameroon was represented by the Speaker of the National Assembly, Cavaye Yeguie Djibril and Niger by her Minister of Water, Environment and Dissertification Control, Brigadier General Abdokaza. There were Observers from the Sudan Republic,[45] Republic of Congo and the Democratic Republic of Congo.

During this 13th Ordinary Summit of the Heads of State and Government of the LCBC, the resolutions of the 56th Ordinary Session of the Council of Ministers held on October 28, 2010 at the Kempinski hotel in N'Djamena were approved. These resolutions were notably on security in the sub region, measures to bail Lake Chad from draught and on the future organization of summit meetings of the Commission.

---

44. *Cameroon Tribune*, no. 7903/4192, Wednesday, August 6, 2003.

45. Sudan which was Africa's biggest country was on Saturday July 9, 2011 split into two states with the birth of the Republic of South Sudan.This followed an overwhelming 98.8 % vote for secession by South Sudan from the Republic of Sudan in January 2011. The referendum was in line with the 2005 peace deal between President Omar Hassan El Bashir and former South Sudan rebel leader, John Garang, to end the civil war (1983-2005).Southern Sudan became the 54th African country and the 193 member state of the UN.

On security, the Heads of State and Government Summit approved the organization of the official reception of boundary demarcation beacons in the Lake Chad, reactivation of the multinational Security Mechanism in the Lake, and recommended to Cameroon to join Chad, Niger and Nigeria in the setting up of the Security Mechanism around the Lake.On the proposed water transfer project from the Oubangui Basin to Lake Chad, the Summit acknowledged the mid-term report on the feasibility study of the water transfer project.The Summit equally gave firm directives to monitor works in order to comply with deadlines for submitting the final report of the study.In the same vein, the Summit praised the initiative relating to the organization of the World Forum of the Sustainable Development on the Safeguarding of the Lake Chad. The Summit equally decided to strongly support the execution and monitoring of projects and programmes issued by the Forum. On the organization of future summits, the Leaders decided to hold annually the Conference of the Summit of Heads of State and Government every year.[46]

This reconciliation by Cameroom and Nigeria was a logical process in dispute resolution especially as it had to do with the elimination of the causes of the dispute and confidence building. Its resolution through peaceful means has been a model for the African continent in particular and to the world in general.

---

46. Final Communiqué of the 13th Heads of State and Government Summit of the LCBC, http://www.cblt.org, retrieved on 11/01/2011.

Conclusion

The study set out to examine how the protracted border skirmishes between Cameroon and Nigeria from 1981 were managed and eventually resolved by 2011. Through the historical analysis of the Cameroon-Nigeria border dispute, its causes were grasped. This causality was then linked to the settlement and resolution of the dispute thereby giving a total picture of its nature and dynamics. Generally, the findings respected the logic that in international relations, there are no permanent friends or enemies but permanent interests.Cameroon and Nigeria therefore engaged in conflict or disagreed when their interests were threatened. Furthermore, the process of the resolution of the dispute in spite of certain peculiarities, notably the employment of a UN Mixed Commission, was a logical process in dipute resolution especially as it had to do with the elimination of the causes of the dispute and confidence building.

Generally, although various socio-economic, historico-diplomatic, security and strategic considerations was at the root cause of the border dispute; Nigeria's dilatory and diversionary tactics very much caused the border dispute because such behaviour contributed to the non application of bilateral border agreements reached by the two countries after independence. This behavior therefore orchestrated the confusion, consternation and consequently dispute between the two countries. Nigeria's dilatory and diversionary behavior even continued after 2002; during the implementation phase of the ICJ verdict on the border dispute case. For example, the non respect of the September 15, 2004 deadline by Nigeria to withdraw from Bakassi and the eight months break in the meetings of the ad hoc Mixed Commission between the 12th and 13th sessions, while meetings of the Commission were to be held after every two months, was blamed on Nigeria's intransigence.

The Cameroon-Nigeria border dispute was managed through bilateral and multilateral initiatives. Bilaterally, Cameroon and Nigeria managed the dispute through the use of Mixed Boundary Commissions, standing Joint Commission, diplomatic interventions, seminar workshop, and by maintaining bilateral cooperation even at the time of crisis over the Bakassi Peninsula from 1993-2008. These bilateral management initiatives; in spite of their regularity and encompassing decisions did not lead to the implementation of the decisions taken. This was particularly because there was the lack of mutual trust, mutual assurance of goodwill and the absence of a multilateral actor to guarantee and enforce the decisions taken.Thus, inspite of the fact that Nigeria continued to hark on bilateral management initiatives where she could have a greater leverage to manipulate; Cameroon in 1994 because of loss of faith in bilateral negotiations and frustration over Nigeria's claim to her territory of Bakassi, decided to involve multilateral actors notably the UN Security Council, the ICJ and the OAU.

The role of multilateral actors impinged greatly on the border dispute. The mediation of Togo brought to the limelight the will of the disputing parties to peacefully resolve the dispute, especially as it led to the meeting of the Presidents of Nigeria and Cameroon during the OAU summit in Tunis in 1994. In the same vein, French conciliation efforts paid dividends as she was able to couch and coax Nigeria to move away from her intransigent and obstinate position into a pacific posture. This success story in trilateral management and resolution of Africa's conflicts was confirmed two decades ago, in 1991, by Zartman when he opined that; "Despite the precariousness of mediation, trilateral management and resolution of conflicts has a much better record in Africa than does bilateral management."[1] Further, the use of pressure and coordination of good offices by states in the international arena equally diffuse tension and encouraged the conflicting parties to think more creatively about the resolution of the border dispute. Collective effort at the level of regional and international organisations notably the LCBC, OAU, UNO, EU and UDEAC, through the legitimisation of the choice of mediators, issuing of declarations pertaining to their stance in the face of the dispute, the call for normalisation, organisation of

---

1. Zartman, "Conflict Resolution: Prevention, Management and Resolution," p. 313.

conferences for dialogue, and the provision of good offices for negotiation equally helped in various ways to dissipate tension between the disputing parties.Apart from the LCBC which took steps to delimit and demarcate the common boundary in the Lake Chad region—although its efforts were reneged by Nigeria—the role of the OAU, UNO, EU, and UDEAC was limited to declarations and recommendations, notably the call on the conflicting parties to have confidence in the ICJ and to show restraint.Although tension remained high between the disputing parties, this call caused Nigeria to face the ICJ as she saw the world gradually turning against her action.This is an indication that conflict resolution can best be carried out in concert.It is also a pointer to the fact that interstate frontier disputes may be managed bilaterally but can better be resolved multilaterally.

The dispute was settled through adjudication by the ICJ from 1994 when Cameroon seised the Court till 2002 when the Court passed its verdict giving most of the contested border territory, and more significantly, the Bakassi Peninsula to Cameroon. The verdict was passed in consideration of the various conventions, treaties, declarations and decisions concluded by the Colonial masters of Cameroon and Nigeria, Mandatory and Trusteeship powers of Cameroon, as well as agreements concluded by Cameroon and Nigeria and the LCBC after independence. The Court equally took intermediate or neutral decisions to delimit some sectors on the Land Boundary area and the undelimited sector of the Maritime Boundary without however fixing the tripoint—Cameroon, Nigeria, Equatorial Guinea. The passing of the verdict did not however mean that the dispute was brought to rest as the pronouncement was one thing and its implementation another.[2]

---

2. Cases of flouting the ICJ verdict abound. This was the case between Britain and Albania in 1946 pertaining to the drowning of British warships in the Albanian territorial waters in which the Court ruled against Albania; the hostage affair between the USA and Iran in late 1979 in which the Court ruled in 1980 against Iran; the 1971 Court's ruling on the illegal occupation of Namibia by the Republic of South Africa and the 1984 mining imbroglio between Nicaragua and the USA in which the Court ruled infavour of Nicaragua.

The dispute was finally resolved through the implementation of the Court's verdict by the disputing parties, Cameroon and Nigeria under the aegis of the UN system and by addressing the security, strategic and socio-economic issues that sparked off the dispute as well as boosting bilateral and sub regional cooperation.The employment of a Mixed Commission of Cameroon and Nigeria in synergy with the UN in the resolution of the border dispute was an exemplarary model for preventive diplomacy and confidence building. Indeed; it was a new paradigm in conflict resolution in Africa because through it, the conflicting parties were able to address the sources of the conflict. Equally too, the involvement of the UN in the resolution process was an indication that bilateral initiatives in conflict resolution need the help of multilateral actors for the process to be sincere and enforceable. The retrocession and establishment of sovereignty on disputed territories in conformity with the Court's verdict was completed in 2008. The demarcation of the Maritime Boundary was also completed in 2008. Meanwhile, by July 2011, close to 1600km (more than ¾) of the 1950km long boundary had been demarcated; 378km of these with boundary identification pillars.

The implementation of the Court's verdict from 2002 to 2011 under the aegis of the UN system only constituted part of the resolution process. This is so because the resolution of disputes goes beyond the implementation of the verdict of an independent adjudicator like the ICJ. It equally involved mechanisms to eliminate the causes of the dispute as well as machinery for dealing with foreseeable problems and confidence building. Much ground was covered by 2011 to address these concerns. This involved the boosting of trans-frontier road infrastructures, frontier security and formal trade between the two countries; groundwork for electricity exportation treaty and research partnership; development of border settlements and reconciling the geostrategy in the Bakassi Peninsula; and finally, revamping diplomatic relations and sub regional integration by reconvening the standing Joint Commission, and by boosting diplomatic representation, politico-diplomatic exchanges and reactivating the LCBC which offers a wide range of benefits to the two countries.

The pacific settlement by Cameroon and Nigeria of their bilateral territorial dispute marked a further step towards the fulfilment of their international obligations and sets an historic milestone for sustainable relationship and confidence building initiatives between the two brotherly countries. Its resolution through peaceful means has been a model for the African sub region in particular and to the world in general. Long standing historical and socio-cultural relations between the two countries favoured the resolution of the dispute. This metaphor was re-echoed frequently in the aftermath of the Court's verdict on the border dispute case. For example, during a toast at the end of the Cameroon-Nigeria Joint Commission in Yaounde in October 2008; the Nigerian Foreign Minister, Chief Ojo Maduekwe remarked that; "We cannot choose brothers and neighbours, but we can choose friends." Meanwhile, his Cameroonian counterpart, Henri Eyebe Ayissi, opined that; "together, we are condemned to be united by the 'Camnigeria' new spirit,"[3] These long standing relations between Cameroon and Nigeria was reinforced by the notion by the International Society Theoretians, that there is a society of states at the international level. As a consequence, the international community threw its weight on the resolution process, especially as Cameroon and Nigeria were members of regional and international organizations like the LCBC, NBA, GGC, OAU, AU, Commonwealth of Nations and the UN.

The process of the resolution of the Cameroon-Nigeria border dispute is on course especially as the ad hoc Mixed Commission committed itself during the 27th session in Yaounde in March 2011 and the 28th session in Abuja in July 2011, to complete the demarcation of the entire boundary by November 2012. That is, before the tenth anniversary of the ad hoc Mixed Commission (November 15, 2002-November 15, 2012). This renewed determination to complete the demarcation process by 2012 augurs well with the process of conflict resolution which needs a sort of artificial deadline.

---

3. *Cameroon Tribune*, no. 9202/5401, Monday, October 13, 2008.

Cameroonian and Nigerian authorities are also committed towards promoting confidence building through the activation of moribund agreements, the revision of outdated ones and also looking into new areas of cooperation. For this confidence building initiative to be improved and sustained; there should be permanent dialogue between the two countries in order to implement bilateral agreements reached since independence and to enforce border regulations to respond to frontier exigencies.

Appendices

Appendix 1. Communiqué on the Ministerial Meeting of Foreign Ministers of Nigeria and Camroon Held in Kara, on Friday 16 February, 1996

On Saturday, February 3, 1996, Skirmishes erupted between the Nigerian forces and the Cameroonian forces, stationed on the Bakassi Peninsula, resulting in several casualties on both sides. This unfortunate incident which occurred after several months of relative peace on the peninsula, led President Gnassingbe Eyadema of the Republic of Togo to appeal to the Heads of State of the two brotherly countries to demonstrate their confidence in his mediatory role in this matter, and to stop hostilities and resort to dialogue and negotiation in resolving the dispute. This appeal for the diffusion of renewed tension which threatened the previously existing peace sustained by the political will of the two countries to seek peaceful resolution of the dispute was conveyed by President Eyadema in separate correspondences, to his brothers and colleagues.

In response to the invitation of President Eyadema, the ministers of Foreign Affairs of Nigeria, Cameroon and Togo met at Kara, Togo on 16 and 17 February 1996. The Foreign Ministers of the two countries in conflict were received separately and then jointly by President Eyadema. Recalling the Tunis communiqué of 13 June 1994 and the Kara meeting of 4 to 6 July 1994, which allowed the maintenance of peace until the eruption of the last incident, the Togolese President stressed the need to protect the lives of the peaceful population of the Bakassi Peninsula pending a final and lasting solution of the matter. President Eyadema observed that at a time when the African continent is already saddled with tensions which are dangerously threatening the already fragile equilibrium, African states must eschew playing surrogates of some World Powers which are seeking to divide our peoples and nations and distract them from the goals of economic development which can only be achieved in an atmosphere of peace, security, stability and solidarity.

The two Ministers assessed the prevailing situation in the Bakassi peninsula and agreed to stop all hostilities. They recognized that the dispute is pending at the International Court of Justice. They agreed to meet again in the first week of March 1996, to prepare for the summit of the Heads of State of Nigeria and Cameroon under the auspices of President Eyadema. The Foreign Ministers of Nigeria and Cameroon expressed their gratitude to President Eyadema for the efforts he has been making in order to restore peace in the sub-region and appealed to him to continue with the mediation.

Done at Kara, on 17 February, 1996
For the Republic of Nigeria: H.E. CHIEF TOM IKIMI
For the Republic of Cameroon: H.E. FERDINAND LEOPOLD OYONO
For the Republic of Togo: H.E. BARRY MOUSSA BARQUE

Source: *CameroonTribune, no.6040/*2329, Monday, February19, 1996

.Appendix 2. Press Release by the President of the ICJ on the Verdict of the Cameroon-Nigeria Border Dispute Case, October 10, 2002

Land and Maritime Boundary between Cameroon and Nigeria (Cameroon v. Nigeria: Equatorial Guinea intervening) .The Court determines the boundary between Cameroon and Nigeria from Lake Chad to the sea.

It requests each Party to withdraw all administration and military or police forces present on territories falling under the sovereignty of the other Party.

The Hague, 10 October 2002, The International Court of Justice (ICJ), principal judicial organ of the United Nations, has today given Judgement in the case concerning the Land and Maritime Boundary between Cameroon and Nigeria (Cameroon v. Nigeria: Equatorial Guinea intervening).

In its judgment, which is final, without appeal and binding for the Parties, the Court determines as follows the course of the boundary, from north to south, between Cameroon and Nigeria:

In the Lake Chad area, the Court decides that the boundary is delimited by the Thomson-Marchand Declaration of 1929-1930, as incorporated in the Henderson-Fleuriau Exchange of Notes of 1931 (between Great Britain and France); it finds that the boundary starts in the Lake from the Cameroon-Nigeria-Chad tripoint (whose co-ordinates it defines) and following a straight line to the mouth of the River Ebeji as it was in 1931 (whose co-ordinates it also defines) and thence runs in a straight line to the point where the river today divides into two branches.

Between Lake Chad and the Bakassi Peninsula, the Court confirms that the boundary is delimited by the following instruments:

i) From the point where the River Ebeji bifurcates, as far as Tamnyar Peak, by the Thomson-Marchand Declaration of 1929-1930 (paras, 2-60), as incorporated in the Henderson-Fleuriau Exchange of Notes of 1930;

ii) From Tamnyar Peak to pillar 64 referred to in Article XII of the Anglo-German Agreement of 12 April 1913, by the British Order in Council of 2 August 1946;

iii) From pillar 64 to the Bakassi Peninsula, by the Anglo-German Agreements of 11 March and 12 April 1913.

The Court examines point by point 17 sectors of the Land Boundary and specifies for each one how the above-mentioned instruments are to be interpreted (paras, 91, 96, 102, 114, 124, 129, 134, 139, 146, 152, 155, 160, 168, 179, 184 and 189 of the Judgment).

In Bakassi, the Court decides that the boundary is delimited by the Anglo-German Agreement of 11 March 1913 (Arts. XVIII-XX) and that sovereignty over the Bakassi peninsula lies with Cameroon. It decides that in this area the boundary follows the thalweg of the River Akpakorum (Akwayafe), dividing the Mangrove Islands near Ikang in the way shown on map TSGS 2240, as far as a straight line joining Bakassi Point and King Point.

As regards the Maritime Boundary, the Court, having established that it has jurisdiction to address that aspect of the case ¾ which Nigeria had disputed 3/4, fixes the course of the boundary between the two States' maritime areas.

In its Judgment the Court requests Nigeria expeditiously and without condition to withdraw its administration and military or police forces from the area of Lake Chad falling within Cameroonian sovereignty and from the Bakassi Peninsula. It also requests Cameroon expeditiously and without condition to withdraw any administration or military or police forces which may be present along the Land Boundary from Lake Chad to the Bakassi peninsula on territories which pursuant to the Judgement fall within the sovereignty of Nigeria. The latter has the same obligation in regard to territories in that area which fall within the sovereignty of Cameroon.

The Court takes note of Cameroon's undertaking, given at the hearings, to "continue to afford protection to Nigerians living in the Bakassi peninsula and in the Lake Chad area".

Finally, the Court rejects Cameroon's submissions regarding the State responsibility of Nigeria. It likewise rejects Nigeria's counterclaims.

Composition of the Court

The Court was composed as follows: President Guillaume; Vice President Shi; Judges Oda, Ranjeva, Herczegh, Fleischhauer, koroma, Higgins, Parra-Aranguren, Kooijmans, Rezek, Al-Khasawneh, Buergenthal, Elaraby; Judges ad hoc Mbaye, Ajibola; Registrar Couvreur.

Judge Oda appends a declaration to the Judgment of the Court; Judge Ranjeva appends a separate opinion to the Judgment of the Court; Judge Herczegh appends a declaration to the Judgment of the Court; Judge Koroma appends a dissenting opinion to the Judgment of the Court; Judge Parra-Aranguren appends a separate opinion to the Judgment of the Court; Judge Rezek appends a declaration to the Judgment of the Court; Judge Al-Khasawneh and Judge ad hoc Mbaye append separate opinions to the Judgment of the Court; Judge ad hoc Ajibola appends a dissenting opinion to the Judgment of the Court.

SOURCE: *CameroonTribune, no.9161*/5360, Thursday, August14,2008.

Appendix 3. Greentree Accord Between the Republic of Cameroon and the Federal Republic of Nigeria Concerning the Modalities of Withdrawal and Transfer of Authority in the Bakassi Peninsula

The Republic of Cameroon (herein referred to as "Cameroon") and the Federal Republic of Nigeria (hereinafter referred to as "Nigeria),

Reaffirming their willingness to peacefully implement the judgment of the International Court of Justice, Commending the Secretary General of the United Nations for his efforts made in this respect in organizing the tripartite summits and establishing the Cameroon-Nigeria Mixed Commission,

Considering that the question of the withdrawal from and transfer of authority over the Bakassi Peninsula should be treated in a forward-looking spirit of goodwill in order to open new prospects for cooperation between the two countries after decades of difficult bilateral relations,

Determined to encourage the consolidation of confidence and peace between their two countries for the well-being of their peoples and for stability in the sub-region,

Have decided to conclude the present Agreement.

Article 1

Nigeria recognizes the sovereignty of Cameroon over the Bakassi Peninsula in accordance with the judgment of the International Court of Justice of 10 October 2002 in the matter of the Land and Maritime Boundary between Cameroon and Nigeria. Cameroon and Nigeria recognize the land and maritime boundary between the two countries as delineated by the Court and commit themselves to continuing the process of implementation already begun.

Article 2

Nigeria agrees to withdraw all its armed forces from the Bakassi Peninsula within sixty days of the date of the signing of this

190

Agreement. If exceptional circumstances so require, the Secretary General of the United Nations may extend the period, as necessary, for a further period not exceeding a total of thirty days. This withdrawal shall be conducted in accordance with the modalities envisaged in Annex I to this Agreement.

Article 3

1.   Cameroon, after the transfer of authority to it by Nigeria, guarantees to Nigerian nationals living in the Bakassi Peninsula the exercise of the fundamental rights and freedoms enshrined in international human rights law and in other relevant provisions of international law.

2.   In particular, Cameroon shall:

a)   Not force Nigerian nationals living in the Bakassi Peninsula to leave the Zone or to change their nationality;

b)   Respect their culture, language and beliefs;

c)   Respect their right to continue their agricultural and fishing activities

d)   Protect their property and their customary land rights;

e)   Not levy in any discriminatory manner any taxes and other dues on Nigerian nationals living in the Zone; and

f)   Take every necessary measure to protect Nigerian nationals living in the Zone from any harassment or harm.

Article 4

Annex I and the map contained in Annex II to this Agreement shall constitute an integral part thereof. No part of this Agreement shall be interpreted as a renunciation by Cameroon of its sovereignty over any part of its territory.

Article 5

This Agreement shall be implemented in good faith by the Parties, with the good offices of the Secretary General of the United Nations, the Federal Republic of Germany, the French Republic, the

United Kingdom of Great Britain and Northern Ireland and the United States of America.

Article 6

1. A Follow-up Committee to monitor the implementation of this Agreement is hereby established. It shall be composed of representatives of Cameroon, Nigeria, the United Nations and the witness States. The Committee shall monitor the implementation of the Agreement by the Parties with the assistance of the United Nations observers of the Mixed Commission

2. The Follow-up Committee shall settle any dispute regarding the interpretation and implementation of this Agreement.

3. The activities of the Follow-up Committee shall cease at the end of the period of the special transitional regime provided for in paragraph 4 of Annex I to this Agreement.

Article 7

This Agreement shall in no way be construed as an interpretation or modification of the judgment of the International Court of Justice of 10 October 2002, for which the Agreement only sets out the modalities of implementation.

Article 8

This Agreement is concluded in English and French, both texts being equally authentic. Done at Greentree, New York, on 12 June 2006. For the Republic of Cameroon: (ed) Paul Biya, President.For the Federal Republic of Nigeria: (ed) Olusegun Obasanjo, President

Witnesses

For the United Nations: Kofi Ata Annan, Secretary General

For the Federal Republic of Germany: Gunter Pleuger, Permanent Representative of Germany at the UN

For the United States of America: Ms Fakie Sanders, Ambassador and Head of the US Mission

For the French Republic: Michel Duclos, Deputy Permanent Representative of France at the UN

For the United Kingdom of Great Britain and Northern Ireland: Ms Karen Pierce, Deputy Permanent Representative of the United Kingdom

Annex I

Zone in question of the Bakassi Peninsula

1.   In order to prepare the Nigerian nationals living in the zone in question of the Bakassi Peninsula (hereinafter "the Zone") for the transfer of authority to Cameroon, the Zone shall temporarily be subject to a special status as laid down in this Annex. For the purpose of this Annex, the details of the delimitation of the Zone are set out in the attached map (Annex II).

2.   a) Cameroon shall allow Nigeria to keep its civil administration and a police force necessary for the maintenance of law and order in the Zone for a non-renewable period of two years from the time of the withdrawal of the Nigerian forces. At the end of this period, Nigeria shall withdraw its administration and its police force and Cameroon shall take over the administration of the Zone.

b) The United Nations and the witness States shall be invited to attend the ceremony of the transfer of authority.

3.   For the duration of this period, Nigeria shall:

a)   Not conduct or allow the conduct of any activities in the Zone which would prejudice Cameroon's peace or security;

b)   Take every necessary measure, under the supervision of the United Nations observers of the Cameroon-Nigerian Mixed Commission, to stop any transfer or influx of its nationals into the Zone;

c)   Not engage in any activity in the Zone which would complicate or hinder the transfer of authority to Cameroon;

d)   Equip its police force in the Zone with only the light equipment strictly necessary for the maintenance of law and order and for personal defence;

e)   Guarantee to Cameroonian nationals wishing to return to their village in the Zone the exercise of their rights;

f)   Not conduct or continue the exploitation of natural resources in the sub-soil of the Zone, or to engage in any other activity harmful to the environment;

g) Take every necessary measure to prevent any change in land property rights; and

h) Not position any armed forces in the Zone.

4. Following the transfer of authority over the Zone to Cameroon, the latter shall apply to the Zone a special transitional regime for a non-renewable period of five years. In the application of the special transitional regime, Cameroon shall:

a) Facilitate the exercise of the rights of Nigerian nationals living in the Zone and access by Nigerian civil authorities to the Nigerian population living in the Zone;

b) Not apply its customs or immigration laws to Nigerian nationals living in the Zone on their direct return from Nigeria for the purpose of exercising their activities;

c) Allow officers and uniformed personnel of the Nigerian police access to the Zone, in cooperation with the Cameroonian police, with the minimum of formalities when dealing with inquiries into crimes and offences or other incidents exclusively concerning Nigerian nationals; and

d) Allow innocent passage in the territorial waters of the Zone to civilian ships sailing under the Nigerian flag, consistent with the provisions of this Agreement, to the exclusion of Nigerian warships.

5. At the end of the special transitional regime, Cameroon shall fully exercise its rights of sovereignty over the Zone.

6. In accordance with paragraph 4 of this Annex, any acquisition of land in the Zone by Nigerian nationals not resident in the Zone at the time shall be perfected only in accordance with the laws and regulations of Cameroon.

Source: *Cameroon Tribune,* no.8618/4817, Tuesday, June 13, 2006.

Appendix 4. Press Release Following a Meeting of Cameroonian and Nigerian Authorities to Prepare the Groundwork for an Electricity Export Treaty

The Minister of Energy and Water Resources, His Excellency Jean-Bernard SINDEU, on Monday, the 9th of February, 2009 received, on request of the Ministry of External Relations (MINREX), an 18-man delegation from the ADAMAWA State of the Federal Republic of Nigeria. This delegation was led by Mr. Ali Dandiyya Sardaunan Kebbi, Principal staff officer to the Governor of the Adamawa State in the Federal Republic of Nigeria. The delegation comprised representatives from the High Commission of Nigeria to Cameroon, senior staff from three sectors namely: The ADAMAWA State Governor's Office; the Power Holding Company of Nigeria (PHCN) and Power Consultants (from the Zungero Power Limited).The Cameroonian side consisted of close collaborators of the Minister of Energy and Water Resources such as the Permanent Secretary, the Inspector General, Technical Advisers and Directors; and representatives of the Ministry of External Relations (MINREX) as well as management staff from electricity sector actors such as the regulator (ARSEL), the electricity sector asset-holding company (EDC), the rural electrification agency (AER).

Minister Sindeu's welcome address provided information on the reforms and organization of the power sector in Cameroon, hydropower potentials and opportunity for export to neighbouring countries; Government's policy to adher to regional integration as exemplified by Cameroon's adherence to the Central African Power Pool (CAPP) of the CEMAC, a similar structure to the West African Power Pool (WAPP) of the ECOWAS. According to the Head of the delegation from Adamawa State of the Federal Republic of Nigeria, the main purpose of their visit was to seek for agreement between Cameroon and the Adamawa State for the supply of Electricity to Adamawa State; with preference from the Lagdo Hydro-Electric Power Plant of the Northern Inter-Connected Network. At this stage, the Adamawa State expressed an urgent need for thirty megawatts or 30MW of firm power delivered to Adamawa State's border town of Yola or Zungeru.

Ensuing discussions focused on such appropriate/conducive climate for power experts or grid interconnection: the institutional/legal framework, the technical feasibility for a specific export project, specifics being:

- The feasibility of project requires prior existence of a formal Inter-Country Agreement (ICA) or Treaty on export of electricity to Nigeria and/or interconnection of electricity grids between Cameroon and Nigeria.

- In absence of a formal ICA or treaty, discussions could be limited to principles and policy issues surrounding power exports i.e. Technical, Financial and Legal aspects.

- Various institutional arrangements in the light of international experiences or best practices to learn from in view of mutually beneficial export/interconnection project(s) such as joint ventures, private investor/independent generation of power from Cameroon's hydro-power potentials and examples of potential generation candidates for export of electricity supply from Cameroon, regulatory regime for export projects (generation, and transmission).

- Constraints associated with providing surplus power from Lagdo for export to neighbouring countries: limitation of available power due to climate change/unfavorable hydrological regime, need for rehabilitation/renovation of some installations of the plant; Cameroon's own growing needs for power. To better understand the technical operation limits of the Lagdo plant, the Nigerian delegation submitted a questionnaire to MINEE which was conveyed to the plant operator for answers.

The meeting concluded on three key notes:

- The establishment of an ICA, as precedent condition to power export and/or grid interconnection, between the Republic of Cameroon and Federal Republic of Nigeria. Thereafter implementation mechanisms such as MOU (memorandum of understanding), or other, could now be signed for business to become effective. These legal documents would be concluded at the established joint commission between Nigeria and Cameroon, whose fifth session is forthcoming.

-       Both sides could designate technical experts to exchange technical information (available on the public domain), this in view to preparing feasible/bankable export/interconnection project(s); which reports will provide guidance to the Governments of Cameroon and Nigeria to make reasoned decisions to conclude export of power to Adamawa State in particular.

-       The mission ended with a Technical visit to the Lagdo Hydro-Electric power plant, on the 11th and 12th of February, 2009, facilitated by MINEE and guidance by AES SONEL.

Yaounde, February 16, 2009
Sindeu Jean Bernard
Minister of Energy and Water Resources
Cameroon

Source: *Cameroon Tribune,* no.9285/5484, Tuesday, February 10, 2009.

Sources Consulted

Published Works

Books

Basic Facts About the United Nations. New York: United Nations Department of Public Information, 1992.

Brownlie, Ian. *African Boundaries: A Legal and Diplomatic Encyclopaedia*. Los Angeles: University of California Press, 1979.

Cooper, Richard N. *Economic Stabilization and Debt in Developing Countries*. London: The Massachusetts Institute of Technology Press,1992.

Crawley, John and Katherine Graham. *Mediation for Managers: Resolving Conflict and Rebuilding Relationships at Work*. London: Nicholas Brealey Publishing, 2002.

Eba'a, Guy Roger. *Affaire Bakassi: Genèse, Evolution et Dénouement de l'Affaire de la Frontière Terrestre et Maritime Cameroun-Nigeria (1993-2002)*. Yaounde : Presse de l'Université Catholique d'Afrique Centrale, 2008.

Frankel, J. *International Relations in a Changing World*. Oxford: Oxford University Press, 1979.

Holti, Kal J. *International Politics: A Framework for Analysis*. 4th ed. Englewood cliffs, New Jersey: Prentice Hall, 1983.

Kahn, James R. *The Economic Approach to Environmental and Natural Resources* 3rd ed. United States: Thomson, South Western, 2005.

Kombi, Narcisse Mouelle. *La Politique Etrangère du Cameroun*. Paris: Harmattan, 1996.

LeVine, Victor T. *The Cameroon Federal Republic*. London: Cornell University Press, 1971.

Morgenthau, Hans. *Politics Among Nations: A Stuggle for Power and Peace*. New York: Alfred A. Knopf, 1973.

Ngniman, Zacharie. *Nigeria-Cameroun, La Guerre Permanente?* Yaoundé : Editions Clé, 1996.

Rosenau, James N. ed. *Linkage Politics: Essays on the Convergence of National and International Systems*. New York: Macmillan, 1969.

Sinjoun, Luc. *Sociologie des Relations Internationales Africaines.* Paris: Editions Karthala, 2002.

The Government of Cameroon. *Document on the Bakassi Peninsula Dispute.* Yaounde, n.d.

The United Nations. *Résumé des Arêtes, Avis Consultatifs et Ordonnances de la Cour International de Justice, 1997-2002.*New York : 2006

Zartman, I.William. *Ripe for Resolution: Conflict and Intervention in Africa.* New York: Oxford University Press, 1985.

Articles

Chem-Langhëë, Bongfen. "The British and the Northern Kamerun Problem, 1919-1961." *ABBIA* 38, 39, 40 (May 1982), pp.309-331.

Ikome, Francis Nguendi. "The Cameroon-Nigeria Maritime Border and Territorial Conflict: Would the Verdict of the ICJ Engender Lasting Peace." *Juridis Periodique:Revue de Droit et de Science Politique,* Numéro 54, Yaoundé, Cameroun (Avril-Mai-Juin 2003), pp. 77-84.

Mengjo, Lukong Keneth. "From the OAU to the AU—What Lessons from African Conflicts?" *Annales des Faculte des Sciences Juridiques et Politiques,* Université de Dschang, (Tome 12, 2008), pp. 279-302.

Pondi, Jean Emmanuel and Laurent Zang. "The Cameroon-Nigeria Border Cooperation: Presentation and Analysis of Bilateral Agreements and Treaties" *Cameroon Review of International Studies* (Volume V, 1998 n°1-2, May 2000) Presses Universitaires de Yaoundé, pp. 168-186.

Weladji, C. "The Cameroon-Nigeria Border (contd)," *ABBIA* 29-30 (1975), pp.163-195.

_____ . "The Cameroon-Nigeria Border 1914 and After", *ABBIA* 38, 39, 40 (May 1982), pp.213-271.

Zartman, I. William. "Conflict Resolution: Prevention, Management and Resolution." Deng, Francis M. and I. William Zartman.In *Conflict Resolution in Africa*. Washington D.C: The Brookings Institution, 1991, pp. 299-319.

Magazines

Africa. No.23. July 1973; No.39. November 1974; No.48. August 1975;No.90. February 1979; No.102. February 1980;.No.107 July 1980.
Africa Construction. No.2. 1981.
*Africa Renewal.*Vol. 24. No.2-3.August 2010.
Afrika. No.5-6. 1988.
Insight Newsmagazine, February 2003.
West Africa. No.3563. December 9, 1985.

Newspapers

*Cameroon Tribune.*No. 2077(French edition) Samedi 16 Mai 1981;No. 2126(French edition). Mercredi 15 Juillet 1981; No. 5441(French edition) 31 Mai-1Juin 1992; No.5143(French edition). Mardi 2 Juin 1992; No. 5144(French edition). Mercredi 3 Juin 1992; No. 5541/1830. Wednesday, February 23, 1994; No. 5550/1839. Wednesday, March 9, 1994; No. 5554/1843. Wednesday, March 16, 1994; No. 5826/2115. Wednesday, April 12, 1995; No. 6033/2322. Wednesday, February 7, 1996; No. 6040/2329. Monday, February 19, 1996; No. 6042/2331. Tuesday, February 22, 1996; No. 6184/2473. Monday, September 16, 1996; No.6897/3186. Monday, July 26, 1999; No.7538/3827. Tuesday, February 19, 2002; No. 7548/3837, Wednesday, March 6, 2002; No. 7553/3842. Wednesday, March 13, 2002; No. 7903/4192. Wednesday August 6, 2003; No. 7990/4279.Tuesday, December 9, 2003; No. 7996/4285. Wednesday, December 17, 2003; No. 7997/4286. Thursday, December 18, 2003; No. 7999/4288. Monday, December 22, 2003; No. 8073/4362. Monday, April 12, 2004; No. 8113/4402. Wednesday, June 9, 2004; No. 8134/4419.

Thursday, July 8, 2004; No. 8136/4421. Monday, July12, 2004; No. 8131/4423. Wednesday, July 14, 2004; No. 8139/4424. Thursday, July15, 2004; No. 8149/4434. Thursday, July 29, 2004; No. 81234/4433. Thursday, November 29, 2004; No.8618/4817. Tuesday, June 13, 2006; No.8613/4812, Tuesday, June 20, 2006; No.88662/4861.Wednesday, August 16, 2006; No.8775/4974. Thursday, January 2, 2007; No.8840/5039. Wednesday, May 2, 2007; No.8850/5049. Wednesday, May 16, 2007; No.8857/5056. Tuesday, May 29, 2007; No.8976/5175. Wednesday, November 14, 2007; No.9058/5257. Friday, March 14, 2008; No.9111/5310. Wednesday, June 4, 2008;No.9146/5345. Wednesday, July 23, 2008; No. 9148/5347. Friday, July 25, 2008; No.9159/5358. Tuesday, August 12, 2008; No.9161/5360, Thursday, August 14, 2008; No.9162/5361. Friday, August 15, 2008;No.9193/5392. Monday, September 29, 2008; No.9194/5393. Wednesday, October 1, 2008; No.9202/5401. Monday, October 13, 2008; No. 9207/5406. Monday, October 20, 2008; No.9218/5417.Tuesday, November 4, 2008; No.9224/5423. Wednesday, November 12, 2008; No. 9273/5472.Friday, January 23, 2009;No.9285/5484.Tuesday, February 10, 2009; No.9382/5583. Thursday, July 2, 2009; No.9415/5616. Tuesday, August 18, 2009;No. 9421/5622. Wednesday, August 26, 2009; No.9430/5632. Wednesday, September 9, 2009;No.9436/5637. Thursday, September 17, 2009; No. 9442/5643. Monday, September 28, 2009;No.9460/5661. Tuesday, October 22, 2009;No.9496/5097. Monday, December 14, 2009; No.9497/5698. Tuesday, December 15, 2009; No.9623/5824. Monday, June 21, 2010; No.9726/5927. Friday, November 19, 2010; No.9784/5985. Thursday, February 10, 2011; No. 9789/5990. Friday, February 18, 2011; No.9790/5991, Monday, February 21, 2011; No. 9811/6012. Tuesday, March 22, 2011; No. 9833/6034, Monday, April 26, 2011; No. 9842/6043, Monday, May 9, 2011and No. 9872/6073, Thursday, June 23, 2011;

EDEV (Cameroon). No.00002.May 19, 2009;

Le Jour (Cameroon). No.0310, Mercredi 12 Novembre 2008;

Le Messager. No. 343, 10 Janvier 1994; No.2629 Mardi 10 Juin 2008;

Mutations. No.2170, 10 Juin 2008; No. 2871, Mardi 22 Mars 2011; *The Post* (Cameroon).No. 0994. Monday, October 13, 2008; No. 01088. Monday, September 28, 2009; No. 01093. Friday, October 16, 2009.

Websites

Final Communiqué of the 13th Heads of State and Government Summit of the LCBC, Available from http://www.cblt.org. Retrieved on 11/01/2011.

ICJ judgement of June 11, 1998 and October 10, 2002 on the Cameroon – Nigeria border dispute case. Retrieved on 23/07/10 and 24/07/10. Available from *http// icj-cij.org.*

Niall Ferguson, what is power? Retrieved on 21/08/10.Available from *http://www.hoover.org.*

The 1973 oil crisis. Retrieved on 10/04/10. Available from *http://en. Wikipedia.org/wiki/1973* oil crises, retrieved on 10/04/10.

http://www. allafrica.com/ nigeria.

http://www.cblt.org.

http://www.google.cm/images.

http://www Cameroonline.org.

http://www.Cameroon-tribune.cm.

http://www.un.org/news.

http://unowa.unmissions.org.

http://www.untreaty.org.

Wikipedia.org.

http://wikipédia.org/wiki/histoire du Cameroun.

Unpublished Works

Archival Material (MINREX Archives, Yaounde)

File no. 5490/4B300, contentieux avec le Nigeria, 1963-70 and 1973.

File no. 5488/4B300, contentieux avec le Nigeria, 1970-72.

File no.191, [on Nigerian organisation of elections in Bakassi].

Theses and Dissertations

Enoh, Besong Samuel. "Conflict Resolution in the Post-Coldwar Era : A Case Study of the Angolan Civil War" Doctorat de 3ème cycle Thesis, University of Yaounde II, IRIC, 1994.

Hamadou, Mgbale Mbgatou. "La politique Camerounaise de Résolution Pacifique de la Crise de Bakassi" Doctorat de 3ème cycle Thesis, University of Yaounde II, IRIC, 2001.

James, Aji, "The Dynamics of Cameroon-Nigeria Relations, 1993-2002", DESS Dissertation, University of Yaounde II, IRIC, 2003.

Nyamndi, Ndifontah Mo. "Cameroon-Nigeria Relations (1958/1978)" MA Dissertation, University of Yaounde, IRIC, 1979.

Sali, Aliyou. "L'Attitudes des Etats de la CEMAC Face au Conflit de Bakassi et ses Effets sur L'Institution," DEA dissertation, University of Dschang, Faculté des Sciences Juridiques et Politiques, Academic year 2006/2007.

Miscellaneous

Aougui, Niandou. "Le Mécanisme de Prevention, de Gestion et de Règlement des Conflits de l'OUA Face aux Conflit en Afrique: Cas du Burundi, Rwanda et de Bakassi." Rapport de Stage Diplomatique, University of Yaounde II, IRIC, 1997.

Chouala, Yves Alexandre, "Le Monde Selon Yaoundé: Lecture Géopolitique de la Distribution Mondiale des Services Exterièurs du Ministère des Relations Exterières du Cameroun. Rapport du Stage Diplomatique, University of Yaounde II, IRIC, 1998.

Perindap, Tindatie John. "The Cameroon-Nigeria Border Crisis: 1961-2005." Paper Presented at the History and Citizenship Teachers Association Annual General Meeting at LCC Mankon, Bamenda, December 3, 2005 (Typewritten Manuscript).

Index

209

212

123-124, 170
telephone contact 52
terror 25
The Hague 17, 37n, 54, 56,
    59, 69, 82, 85, 92, 106
Thomson, Sir Graeme 16, 92
Tiko 29-30, 35
Timeh, Esabe Simon 2
Tindouf 4
Tipsan 9, 11, 50, 90, 93, 110
Togo 54-55, 63, 66,
    69, 74, 76-80
Tomdio, Michel Ngako 171
Toro Liman 9, 16, 116,
    123-124, 170
Tosso, Mount 110
Toure, Sekou 63, 79n
trenchantly 14
trial baloons 82
Tripartite Summit,
    Geneva I 119, 121
Tripartite Summit,
    Geneva II 127, 139
Tripartite Summit,
    Geneva III 132
Tripartite Summit,
    Greentree 132, 135, 167ff
Tripartite Summit,
    Paris 83, 118, 121, 153
tripoint 17, 89-90, 103, 106,
    107, 109, 148, 167, 181
Trusteeship, period of 1n,
    17, 100, 181
Tsikakiri, River 9, 11
Tunis 75, 150, 180
Tunis Peace Initiative 75

Ubenekang 29
UDEAC 61, 73-74, 180-181
Uganda 54
ultimatum 3, 45
UN 1n, 4, 7, 16, 46, 52, 57,
    59-61, 67, 69, 71-72, 78, 83,
    85n, 88, 96, 112, 114, 124,
    126, 129, 133-134, 138, 140,
    143, 147, 166, 177n, 180-183
underpinnings 9, 31
UN General Assembly 59, 68
unique frontier
    control post 158
United Kingdom 121,
    133-134, 143, 166
Universal Traverse
    Mercator 144-146
UN Office for
    Project Services 142
UN Office for
    West Africa 142
UN Security Council 4, 57,
    67-70, 117, 136, 180
    46, 47, 48, 59, 78, 116
UN Trust Fund 138, 140
upsurge of insecurity 162, 164
USA 35, 54, 57, 58n, 80,
    132- 134, 137, 143, 162-163,
    165, 181n
uti possedetis juris, principle of 1,
    9, 98

verdict, ICJ 108-116,
    131, 153, 166
Verrière, Eric 161

217